UNKNOWN WARS

of Asia, Africa and The America's That Changed History

STEVEN M. JOHNSON

Cover illustration is of the Second Battle of the Bach Dang River in 1288 from the Hanoi
Museum of History.

ISBN-10: 0615846203
ISBN-13: 9780615846200

Library of Congress Control Number: 2013912486
CreateSpace Independent Publishing Platform
North Charleston, South Carolina
Steven M. Johnson, Woodruff, SC.

Table of Contents

This book is dedicated to my children Jordan, Taylor, and Angela whom I could not love or be more proud of.

Also, I would like to dedicate this book to my parents Forrest William and Joan Johnson who have always supported and encouraged me in my teaching, research, and writing.

Acknowledgments

I want to acknowledge my grandparents Dwight and Jean Johnson who gave me a love for history as a boy through our many hours of discussions that often went late into the night.

I want to acknowledge my father Forrest William Johnson for taking me to some fascinating battlefields when I was a boy even though I was disappointed that there weren't any bones and weapons still lying around.

I want to also acknowledge San Sophanara who took me to many places in Cambodia and Southeast Asia on the back of his poor old motorbike that he somehow kept operating to do research for this book.

Lastly, I want to acknowledge Dr. Jim Leavell who greatly influenced me in a graduate course and a travel and research seminar to East Asia in 2005. Dr. Leavell served as a catalyst in my life that opened Asia up to me which started me writing this book and numerous published articles as well.

Introduction

This is a book mostly about wars that few have heard of or have read anything about. In fact, articles on few of these topics can easily be found and yet the events discussed in this book changed the world we live in today. The stories of the unknown wars are bloody tales with deaths often in the millions. Most books that discuss wars that had a great impact on history are centered on events that happened in Europe and often give little attention to events in Asia and Africa. Much of this book concentrates on obscure Asian, African and American wars which are too often ignored or given very brief consideration as to their importance in history, yet they have influenced the course of history to this day.

There were many epic wars that involved China against the warlike nomadic steppe people north of the Great Wall of China. These wars were fought for more than 1,800 years that the wall was used as the main line of defense for the Chinese emperors. Many Chinese that left to perform their duty for the emperor at the Great Wall were never seen again. Millions died building, maintaining, and defending these walls against a very determined enemy that was motivated to go around or through the Great Wall to get at the riches of China.

Had France and the United States studied how the Vietnamese had fought for over a thousand years for independence from China without regard for how many casualties or how much time it would take to win, perhaps these nations would have paused before getting involved in any wars in Indo-China. One chapter in this book discusses the 1,049 year Vietnamese War of Independence against China that lasted from 111 B.C. to 938 A.D. Westerners consider Vietnam's struggle against China as several separate wars fought for more than a thousand years, but the Vietnamese consider it one continuous struggle, which would make this rebellion the longest war in history. Another later chapter deals with the French conquest of Indo-China in the 19th century that later would eventually result in France's defeat in 1954 and the United States involvement in the Vietnam War from 1965 until 1973.

When one studies history, it often can be found that many of the poorest nations of today were at one time wealthy world powers. In fact, almost every nation has had its turn as one of the top powers in the world. One such nation was Cambodia's Khmer Empire that existed from 800 to 1431 A.D. The Khmer Empire at its height actually covered a larger area than the Roman Empire did after the Khmer subjugated what is today the Southern half of Vietnam, Cambodia, Laos, Thailand, and parts of Burma and Malaysia. The Khmer built the largest temple complex and city in the world at this time with a population of over a million people at its capital of Angkor. Today, fifty square miles of ruins in Cambodia testify to the past greatness of this empire. I devote a chapter to an unlikely hero that emerged out of relative obscurity to save the Khmer Empire at a time of crises in the late 11th century. King Jayavarman VII ruled the empire at it's height from 1178 to 1219.

The Mongol conquest of China took a grueling and bloody 74 years to accomplish in which captured and drafted Chinese soldiers had to conduct sieges and to serve in river fleets to complete their conquest. The Mongol Empire was the largest in history, but the armies of Mongol horse archers found that when they tried to conquer areas outside of flat steppe country that was perfect for their cavalry, they more often than not met defeat. Kublai Khan was frustrated by his attempts to spread the Mongol Empire into the deserts of Syria, the islands of Japan, and into the jungles of Southeast Asia. The Mongols didn't make good sailors and couldn't use their horse archer tactics in the jungles of Vietnam and their horses tended to wilt in the deserts of the Middle East. It was after the bankrupting of the Mongol and Chinese treasuries during these failed conquests and the death of Kublai Khan that the Mongol Empire split up into four parts.

Another important topic the book covers are the wars surrounding the African slave trade that raged in Africa and in the Americas for more than 350 years. Only a few articles are available covering these wars that led to the deaths of close to 15 million Africans during the period of the Trans-Atlantic slave trade and to the enslavement of another 12 million Africans that were brought to the Americas. Africans who came to the Americas did not come willingly and had a number of bloody uprisings on the slave ships and in the colonies of the Americas which culminated in the Haitian Revolution from 1791 to 1804.

There are also two chapters devoted to Spain's efforts to conquer the Southeastern and Southwestern portions of what today is the United States that destroyed whole American Indian civilizations through violence and disease in a search for gold. Another chapter is devoted to England's Pirate Wars that were fought to gain control of Spanish gold which was being harvested from Spain's colonies in Mexico and South America. These wars often involved thousands of pirates that boldly attacked Spain's colonies around the Caribbean islands and on the northern coast of South America.

Another chapter is devoted to one of the great powers of the American Southeast. The Cherokee nation nearly wiped out the British colony of South Carolina in the Yamasee War of 1715 – 1717. Cherokee war parties devastated the frontiers of North and South Carolina, Virginia, Kentucky, Tennessee and Georgia in the first and second Cherokee Wars which started in 1759 and continued during and after the American Revolution until 1794. Cherokee warriors also supported Andrew Jackson in his war with the Creek and Seminole Indians only to be rewarded with losing their lands and being forced to live on an Indian reservation in Oklahoma territory after the sorrows of the Trail of Tears. Despite this, Cherokee warriors fought for both sides in the American Civil War. Sadly, the Cherokee Wars are given virtually no coverage in American History textbooks other than a brief mention of the Trail of Tears.

A chapter is included on a little known European topic about an attempted genocide against Protestants in Germany between 1618 and 1648. Catholics in the states of southern Germany killed over 2 million German Protestants for leaving the Catholic faith in the early phases of the war. This led the north German Protestant nations along with Denmark, and Sweden to enter the Thirty Years War to stop the violence of the Catholic League which also included Spain and the Austrian Holy Roman Empire. Massacres committed by both sides' depopulated large areas of Bohemia and Germany. It took the entrance in the war of Catholic France who surprisingly entered on the Protestant side to bring about an end to the war. France feared that Spain and the Austrian Holy Roman Empire would come to dominate Europe if they did not enter the war on the Protestant side. It is estimated that as many as eight million people died in the Thirty Years War which is an event that is mostly unknown and over looked by most of the world.

One of the bloodiest wars in history after World War II can be traced to a poorly translated gospel tract that led a poor Confucian scholar named Hong Xuiquan to start a quasi-Christian cult that led to the Taiping Rebellion. The war lasted from 1851 to 1871 with over

30 million Chinese dying in a rebellion that nearly toppled the Qing Dynasty. The war led to a weakened system in China that ultimately would cause the complete collapse of the Qing Dynasty in 1911 and a time of internal wars that ultimately would result in the triumph of communism in China in 1948.

Events in the Middle East have been important for more than three thousand years. Two chapters are included that discuss the three Jewish wars against Rome between 66 AD and 136 AD. These Jewish revolts resulted in the first holocaust that killed more than a 1.8 million Jews at the hands of the Romans. The Jewish rebels put up bitter resistance and caused an unusually high 180,000 to 200,000 Roman deaths in the three revolts before Rome could reclaim control of Palestine (Judea). The most difficult Jewish rebellion for the Romans to quell was the little known Bar Kokhba Revolt from 132 to 136. The Diaspora that scattered many of the surviving Jews around the Roman Empire was the direct consequence of these wars.

European nations had a very realistic preview of what the carnage of the trench warfare of World War I would be like when they sent observers to see what lessons could be learned from the very bloody Russo-Japanese War of 1904-1905. The war gave a preview of trench warfare and how tens of thousands of men could be mowed down in minutes by Maxim machine gun fire as waves of attackers attempted to climb over barbed wire to get at enemy trenches. The European observers all criticized the Japanese and the Russians for having gotten so many of their men killed in trench assaults, yet learned nothing from this war because they used the same tactics on a much larger and bloodier scale during World War I. The war also established Japan as a world power and set the stage for their establishing an Asian empire that caused World War II to become a much wider and bloodier war.

The final chapter concerns wars that haven't happened yet, but are anticipated by more than half of the world's population in the near future. Jews, Christians, and Muslims are anticipating an Armageddon war or wars that are very similar in what each believes will take place. The main difference in the monotheistic views of the wars to come is that each religion has their own messiah figure that they believe will be ruling when the fighting is brought to an end. Apocalyptic scriptures describe in detail the campaigns that are believed by many to come in the near future. One thing that all three religions agree on from their scriptures is that the body count will be in the billions not millions. The scriptures mention the ancient names of nations that will participate in the end time's wars that also happen to be major players by different names in world affairs today. The events discussed in the Bible are quite plausible given the political climate of today's world.

CHAPTER 1

The Wars of the Great Wall of China: 1,000 B.C. – 1644

The Great Wall of China is a defensive wall that was built across the northern borders of China's frontier with Mongolia and Manchuria. Its purpose was to keep out Mongol and Manchurian tribes that went by various names from 1,000 B.C. to 1644. The Mongol and Manchu tribes fought almost entirely as horse archers for most of this period and were very difficult to defeat on open ground. They often raided into China to capture goods and women to supplement the needs of the tribes. These barbarians, as the Chinese referred to them, would leave a number of cities in northern China sacked, with tens of thousands dead and taken as captives. The Chinese response to these attacks was expensive and labor intensive wall construction to form a barrier to halt the barbarian horsemen.

The Chinese eventually built between six and seven thousand miles (the Chinese aren't sure themselves) of walls at a huge cost in lives and taxes to block the barbarians from their northern frontier. At least 5 million Chinese died just garrisoning the Great Wall from

215 B.C. to 1644. In the 1400s, the Ming Dynasty built the part of the Great Wall that is best known today. As we have learned from the Roman Empire's many walls, the Maginot Line of World War II, and the Iron Curtain and Berlin Wall of the Cold War era, walls afford only temporary protection.

The Great Wall extended for more than 6,000 miles by the late 1500's. More than a million men were needed to properly man and to maintain the largest manmade fortification in history.

Before 1,000 B.C., China was dominated by infantry armies that had a strong chariot arm to protect their flanks or to overtake the flanks of an enemy. Around 1,000 B.C., various tribes in what is today Mongolia and Manchuria developed all cavalry armies dominated by horse archers. These horse archers easily defeated infantry armies supported by chariots and made the chariot obsolete against them. The barbarian horse archers raided deep into many of the 170 nations that made up China at that time and killed thousands while stealing wealth and disrupting families by taking the most beautiful of China's wives and daughters back to Mongolia. The Chinese states of Qin, Wei, Zhao, Yan, Chu, and Qi responded by building walls separately to block and disrupt the barbarian cavalry hordes. These first early walls were built by hundreds of thousands of laborers who stamped earth tightly between logs and then used the wall as a platform with a wooden stockade wall to their front to fight from. Some of these Chinese nations such as Zhao didn't man their walls or put stockade fortifications on them, but used them as a funnel to force barbarian horse armies to fight on ground of their own choosing that couldn't be flanked.

During the Warring States Period from 475 - 221 B.C., seven nations emerged to fight over control of China. The northern Chinese states had to fight a two front war as they continued to defend their northern walls while remaining in a constant state of war against each other. It was during the Warring States Period that the Xiongnu came to unite and dominate the tribes of Mongolia and became a much bigger threat to China and later the Roman Empire in the 400s A.D. The Xiongnu are known to the West as the Huns who nearly destroyed the Roman Empire under their famous leader Attila. These Xiongnu horse archers were difficult to defeat and required larger forces to be committed to check them. This fit into the plans of Emperor Shi Huangdi of Qin who first attacked and defeated nations that had this dilemma as he began his unifying conquest of China.

Shi Huangdi was able to build an army in Qin of over a million men to defend his own northern borders with and to conquer the other nations of China. By the time Shi Huangdi completed his unification of China in 221 B.C., over a million Chinese had died in his conquests of the other six nations that made up China at this time. After his victory, the emperor proved to be very paranoid of being overthrown by the barbarian Xiongnu or by death itself. He ordered 3 million Chinese laborers to connect the northern walls of the previous nations into a continuous

3,000 mile long wall made of earth and stockade fortifications. Of these, fully one third or one million laborers died in the construction of the Qin Great Wall. Some walls were built north of the previous frontier walls as a way of keeping workers far away from Chinese society doing hard manual labor so that they would not be a problem for their totalitarian emperor.

One Qin laborer wrote, "If you have a son, don't raise him. Can't you see? The long wall is propped up on skeletons." Another 750,000 Chinese laborers were ordered to build Shi Huangdi's mausoleum complete with thousands of life size terra cotta warriors. Thousands of miles of roads were also ordered to be built by a million more workers to connect China as one nation. Shi Huangdi began slowly poisoning himself and going insane by taking mercury which he believed would give him eternal life. In 210 B.C., Shi Huangdi died at age 49 and civil war broke out in China in protest over the human cost of China's public works projects.

In 209 B.C., the Xiongnu simply rode around the end of the Great Wall which sat at the edge of the Taklimakan desert in northwest China and began laying waste to northern China. They then occupied much of the land just south of the Qin Great Wall which invalidated all the sacrifice that had gone into building it. By 202 B.C., the Han Dynasty was established by Liu Bang who had defeated all of the other factions left from the death of Shi Huangdi. In 201 B.C., Emperor Liu Bang then led over 200,000 troops against the Xiongnu after they began attacking the city of Mayi after a defection of a previously loyal Han general. The Xiongnu leader, Maodun, pretended to retreat before the Chinese army and drew them into the open Mongol steppes where they were surrounded by a larger army of Xiongnu horse archers. The Xiongnu held the Chinese in an unbreakable siege on the steppes and Liu Bang then offered to negotiate with Maodun. The Xiongnu offered peace in return for brides and bribes. Liu Bang agreed to offer yearly gifts of thousands of the most beautiful Chinese women (the Xiongnu considered their own women very plain looking) along with silk and grain in return for peace, but no return of land. This would become the normal practice of regaining peace for the Chinese with the people of the Mongol steppes if the Great Wall failed them. History would show that the Great Wall failed China for over 800 years of its 1,859 year existence to 1644.

In 141 B.C., the Han Emperor Wu refused to send the normal Chinese tribute to the Xiongnu and stated that it was the Xiongnu who needed to send tribute to him. Emperor Wu began trading silks and spices for the much larger war horses of Ferghana, east of Bactria (Afghanistan) that Alexander the Great had prized for his own cavalry and that the Mughals later used to conquer India within the 1500s. These horses made a superior cavalry for the Han armies. The Chinese then started sending cavalry dominated armies to push back the Xiongnu out of land that they occupied south of the Great Wall and deeper and deeper into the steppes.

In 127 B.C., Emperor Wei retreated before the Xiongnu to draw them into an ambush of over 30,000 Chinese crossbowmen hiding in grass covered pits in a wide arc on two sides of the steppe. The Chinese crossbowmen killed and wounded tens of thousands of Xiongnu and their horses followed by three Han cavalry forces attacking from the front and both flanks. The Xiongnu were driven to over 400 miles north of Beijing. The Han Dynasty then reacted by rebuilding and lengthening the Great Wall so that it went for 6,237 miles from what is today North Korea to deep into the Taklimakan Desert. There were also walls to back up walls in areas that were considered the most vulnerable.

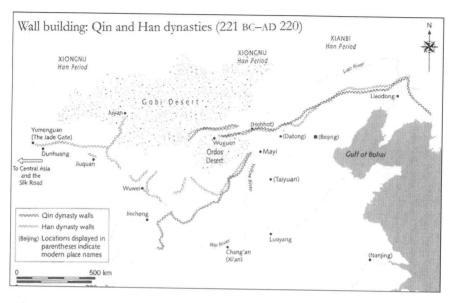

The Han Empire extended and lengthened the Great Wall between 221 B.C. and 220 AD.

The Han Great Wall consisted of stamped earth with a stone front facing with embankments, beacon stations and with over 6,000 forts to station garrisons. The repair and lengthening of the Great Wall took 20 years to complete and cost another one million lives lost while working on the wall. At least a million Han soldiers were required to garrison the Great Wall in 5 year tours of duty at any given time at a huge cost in taxes from the Chinese people. When Han soldiers received word that they were being assigned to a 5 year tour of duty on the Great Wall, they often viewed it like they had just received a prison or even a death sentence because many men didn't return from their duty at the wall. The hard labor of constantly repairing and improving the wall, as well as the extreme cold winter and hot summer temperatures in northern China combined with disease killed far more men than fighting with the Xiongnu ever did.

In 120 B.C., the Han sent over 300,000 cavalry dominated troops to chase a raiding force of 40,000 Xiongnu into the Taklimakan desert in northwestern China. The name 'Taklimakan' that the desert was accurately named after means in Chinese, "desert that you will enter, but will never leave." The Xiongnu were eventually hunted down and killed over a two year period, but over 100,000 Han troops and horses died in the Taklimakan desert mostly from getting lost in the constantly blowing sands where it is quite easy to lose one's orientation and sense of direction. Columns of cavalry of a few hundred to over 10,000 men and horses would leave the Great Wall in the desert to go on patrol or to search for the enemy to never be seen again because they got lost and died as they were covered over by the blowing shifting Taklimakan sands. In one battle, both the Han and Xiongnu forces were engulfed in a sand storm. When the sand storm passed, the Han force had disappeared never to be seen again. The Xiongnu abandoned the battle and left the Han cavalry to their fate. The elements in the Taklimakan or the adjacent Gobi Deserts were more dangerous than the enemy. The Han cavalry also died from the extreme temperatures in the desert which reach minus 10 to 75 degrees below 0 in the winter and temperatures up to around 130 degrees in the summer. In fact, the Han often sent convicts and undesirables to garrison the Great Wall in the Taklimakan or Gobi Deserts because the mortality rate was so high at these parts of the wall.

Many Chinese patrols into the Taklimakan Desert at the western end of the Great Wall often became disoriented by the constantly shifting sands and winds that they never returned. Taklimakan translates from Chinese to say, "You will go in, but you will not return."

A poem was written by a Han soldier that described life at the Great Wall in northwestern China, "We fight south of the wall, we die north of the wall; If we die, unburied, in the wilds, our corpses will feed the crows." The Chinese were often unnerved by the sight of crows and vultures following them overhead when they ventured north of the wall just waiting for men to drop and die so that the birds can consume their dead bodies. In 104 B.C., over 80% of another force of 200,000 Han troops and another 100,000 horses died in an expedition north of the wall in similar conditions in the Gobi Desert against the Xiongnu. The Xiongnu just retreated deeper into the desert until most of the Han force had died in the inhospitable desert and then counter attacked and massacred most of what was left of this once mighty army that had foolishly left the Great Wall to attack them.

In 33 B.C., the Han went back to the old brides and bribes method to buy off Xiongnu aggression against the Great Wall. That same year, a stunningly beautiful concubine refused to give money or a sex bribe to the court painter, so he painted her as unattractive for Emperor Yuandi's concubine catalog. The concubine was chosen by her unattractive picture to be given to the Xiongnu king as a bride for him to buy peace along the wall. The emperor became enraged and had the court painter put to death when the most beautiful Chinese woman he had ever seen had been given to the Xiongnu king to be his bride. The Xiongnu king was so happy that he promised peace with the Chinese for 1,000 years (as long as the bribes continued to be paid of course). The Han were able to mostly keep the peace by providing brides and bribes to the Xiongnu until the Han collapse in 220 A.D. In the end, the Han Dynasty was not destroyed by the greatly feared Xiongnu, but by peasant rebellions inside of China to protest the sacrifices of providing so much in taxes, labor and soldiers for the Great Wall. The Great Wall didn't save the Han Dynasty, but in fact caused its' downfall from within.

After the collapse of the Han Dynasty, China had separated into 6 warring nations and dynasties. The Great Wall had gone into disrepair and some sections had collapsed by 300 A.D. from no one manning or constantly repairing them. The Xiongnu invaded and raided northern China often during this time. The Xiongnu sacked the capital of the northern Wei (Luoyang) in 311 A.D. and often raided all the way into central China until 386. After 386, the Xiongnu (Huns) migrated west toward the Roman Empire in which they invaded in the 400's under Attila the Hun. The Xiongnu disappeared from Chinese history after this time. It is believed that the wars with the Romans and a plague wiped out the Xiongnu or Huns in the mid to late 400s.

In 386, the northern Wei, followed by the northern Qi rebuilt up to a thousand miles of the Great Wall and fought with the various Mongol tribes until 581A.D. The fragmented Mongol tribes were not the threat to China that they had been when they were unified as the Xiongnu. Some Mongol tribes were hired by the Chinese as mercenaries to defend areas near the Great Wall which proved more effective than the wall actually had been. Only sections of the Great Wall were rebuilt opposite of the most threatening Mongol tribes and territory along the wall. Most tribes were still bought off by the old brides and bribes method of buying peace.

Nevertheless, the Great Wall was breached in 424 and 538 until several years later the Mongol tribes could be forced back north of the wall. In 607, the unified Sui Dynasty (581-618) sent a million men to rebuild sections of the Great Wall followed by another 200,000 men in 608. The Sui Dynasty was only able to rebuild around a thousand miles of the Great Wall before the project faltered under the weight of a half million dead workers. Even the Chinese commanders in charge of the rebuilding project had little enthusiasm to build more of the wall.

In 618, a Chinese general named Li Yuan overthrew the Sui Dynasty and with his brother Taizong formed the Tang Dynasty which lasted until 907. The Tang Dynasty fought against Turkish tribes that had migrated into western Mongolia and with a unified coalition of Mongol and Manchu tribes called the Rouran. The Tang was aided by the fact that the Rouran and the Turks were always at war with each other. The Tang put less emphasis on wall building and more emphasis on maintaining large mobile cavalry based armies that would intercept the Turkish and Rouran horse armies. The existing walls that consisted of what was left of the Great Wall were still manned and used as barriers to the barbarians. The Tang cavalry armies were stationed where the Great Wall was either none existent or was in a dilapidated condition. The wall supplemented by trenches with militia crossbowmen then proved most effective in funneling the barbarian hordes into areas where the Chinese cavalry armies were waiting for them.

The Tang did not for the most part place large armies in the Gobi or Taklimakan Deserts where in the past so many had died. Instead, they placed a large cavalry army outside of the deserts that waited to pounce on any Turkish or Rouran armies that would try to come through the deserts and into China. The Tang also often launched pre-emptive attacks deep into Mongol territories when their well paid spies warned them of renewed plans for attacks into China. The Tang still kept a million men near the Great Wall, but more as mobile strike forces rather than as static wall garrisons. The Tang started having difficulties in the late 700s until 907 when they began depending more and more on militia infantry forces instead of the far more expensive professional cavalry armies while the emperors, bureaucrats, and army commanders skimmed away defense money to be spent on lavish personal lifestyles. The Mongol tribes renewed raids deep into China before often returning to the steppes heavy laden with wealth and women.

In 907, the Tang Dynasty collapsed under pressure from the Jurchen (Jin), Khitan and Liao tribes in Manchuria and from peasant rebellions all over China. The Manchurian tribes easily broke through the porous Great Wall and rode down and massacred the Tang militia forces that were supposed to defend the northern Chinese frontier. The result was that China split up into three nations: Xi Xia in the mostly desert part of northwestern China, the Jin Dynasty (later known as Manchus in the 1600s) in northern China, and the Song Dynasty in southern China. The Xi Xia was able to resist the Mongol tribes until 1205 by hiring another Mongol tribe called the Tangut to fight them to a stand still on their frontier. Neither the Xi Xia nor the Song maintained any walls themselves except for fortifying cities. In 1126, a Jin cavalry army of over 500,000 defeated an invading Liao horse army of 700,000 in the biggest cavalry battle in history and sent them back north of the Great Wall into Manchuria. The battle was a confusing affair that got out of control with many attacks and counter attacks and masses of horse archers firing at each other. The Liao army retreated after both sides had lost over 100,000 casualties in a running battle that was fought over several days.

Toward the late 1100s, the Jin started giving up the nomad life and adopted Chinese culture and customs. They began seeing themselves as civilized Chinese that needed to be protected from the other barbarian Manchu and Mongol tribes. Their answer to the barbarian problem was to rebuild the dilapidated Great Wall. They sent groups of 750,000 to 1 million Chinese workers to rebuild the Great Wall in 1188, 1193, 1196, and in 1201. The Jin maintained and rebuilt 700 miles of walls north and northeast of Beijing to defend against incursions from Manchuria. They also built two sections that were 1,000 miles and 300 miles to the northwest of Beijing because they felt the Mongols were becoming a very real threat also. Again hundreds of thousands of workers died in the back breaking labor that went into building the Great Wall. The Jin Great Wall was an improvement on all previous wall constructions. It had a 50 yard wide dry moat backed by a 10 yard tall outer stockade and stone wall with another 50 yard dry moat followed by the main 20 yard tall earth, stockade and stone wall.

Between 1205 and 1210, the unified Mongols under Genghis Khan defeated Xi Xia (northwest China) and then looked toward conquering Chin (Jin) China. The Great Wall's greatest failure was in 1211, when Genghis Khan's Mongol hordes used a diversionary force under his great general Subotai and bribes to force their way into China which is recounted in detail in a later chapter. By 1274, the Mongols had conquered China after massacring multiple millions of Chinese. After all the sacrifice and expense to rebuild and restore the Great Wall had not saved China from the very people that the Chinese had feared so greatly.

After the conquest of China had been completed, the Mongols had grown fat and lived a life of ease at the expense of the Chinese until 1368. Most had given up the hard riding life of the steppe warrior. The Mongols had grown almost completely dependent on Chinese soldiers to keep them in power. Between 1356 and 1368, these Chinese soldiers killed their Mongol masters in several battles and defeated other rebel groups in China to found the Ming Dynasty. The Ming were traumatized by what the Chinese people had endured from the Mongols and decided that their answer to the barbarian hordes was the longest, most impressive and expensive fortification in history. The Ming started by repairing and reconnecting the Jin Wall which was in pretty bad condition because it hadn't been worked on since 1213. The Ming kept a million workers at the Great Wall constantly repairing it. Again many died in the back breaking work. Several mobile armies numbering another million men were also stationed at the Great Wall which often made preemptive raids deep into Mongolia to keep the barbarians in check. This strategy proved effective until the mid 1400s in keeping the Mongols out of China.

Millions of Chinese died in the harsh winter and summer conditions at the Great Wall in maintaining and defending it over its' 1,865 year use as a defensive barrier. Many Chinese considered an assignment to work or garrison the wall as a death sentence.

In 1421, the Ming moved their capital from Nanjing in the south of China back to Beijing which had never been rebuilt after the Mongol sacking of 1215. Beijing was less than 20 miles from the Great Wall and this move was meant to send a message to the barbarians north of the Great Wall that Ming China does not fear them any longer. It wasn't long however, before the Ming became lax in their military spending and preparations at the Great Wall.

In the 1440s, the Ming started to become alarmed when they learned that the Mongols had unified again under a tribal leader named Esen Tayisi Khan. By this time, the Ming military was becoming more dependent on militia garrisons rather than the expensive but effective professional cavalry armies that had checked the Mongols since 1368. In 1442, Esen Khan with 30,000 Mongols poured through the Great Wall when a small group of warriors captured a gateway from some sleeping Chinese militia. Esen Khan's men then rampaged through northern China killing 200,000 Chinese and stealing 100,000 horses and livestock animals before retiring back into Mongolia. The Chinese response to this was to increase the number of militia that was defending the wall.

In 1449, the Mongols again successfully captured a section of the Great Wall defended by militia and again 30,000 Mongols rode into northern China. The Mongols under Esen Khan then destroyed a number of towns before withdrawing back into the Mongol steppes with his army heavy laden with wealth and women. On August 4, 1449, the 22 year old Ming Emperor Zhengtong rashly ordered that an overwhelming Chinese army be readied to march into the steppes north of the wall to punish and destroy the Mongols once and for all. Ming advisors told the emperor that his militia forces weren't up to this kind of incursion into the Mongol steppes. Emperor Zhengtong dismissed this advice and gathered his army together in just two days. The emperor then advanced with his 500,000 man militia army with 20,000 cavalry into Mongolia. Essen Khan's scouts reported to him that except for the cavalry, the emperor's army had dissolved into a huge slow moving armed mob after they had traveled no more than ten miles north of the Great Wall. The Ming army headed through torrential rains for a fortification they maintained three hundred miles northwest of the wall near the Gobi Desert in a town called Datong. Upon discovering that its garrison of ten thousand had been massacred, the young emperor lost his nerve and ordered a retreat back to the Chinese frontier.

On August 30, Essen Khan's 30,000 Mongols defeated the Chinese cavalry in a hard fought rear guard action near the Tumu watering station that destroyed the entire Chinese cavalry force of 20,000 at a cost of 5,000 of their own force. On Sept. 1, 1449, the Mongols then attacked the 500,000-man Ming militia army. Esen Khan's horse archers could not miss killing and wounding multitudes of militiamen from the showers of arrows that they fired into the masses of terrified Chinese. The Chinese tried to surrender, but Esen Khan ordered that all of them were to be killed because he didn't have the food or manpower to feed and guard such a multitude of men. Tens of thousands of Chinese militia that were attempting to surrender were cut down by arrows. The Chinese army turned into a panic stricken mob as the Mongols expended all of their arrows into them before finishing the militia off with swords and maces.

The second day of the Battle of Tumu was the bloodiest single day of battle in history with few of the half million Chinese escaping. Emperor Zhengtong was captured and held as prisoner by Esen Khan. Esen Khan then appeared before Beijing with his 25,000 Mongols and demanded the surrender of Beijing and the Ming Empire to him. Zhengtong's younger brother refused to submit and Esen Khan returned to Mongolia after raiding and destroying several more towns in China because he didn't have the forces to conduct a siege at Beijing. Emperor Zhengtong was then returned to the Ming and continued to reign as emperor. Esen Khan was assassinated by Altan Khan in 1455 for not exploiting his overwhelming victory over Ming China.

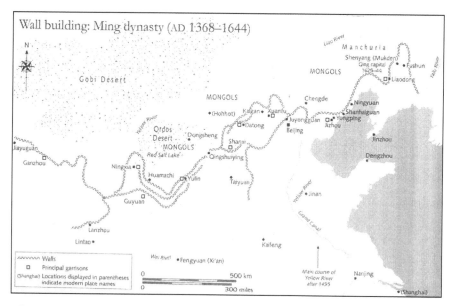

The Ming Dynasty built the Great Wall to it's greatest size and length from the mid 1500's until 1644 when the Manchu's or Qing swarmed through the wall to conquer China.

The direct result of this crushing defeat was to rebuild the Great Wall as the greatest masonry fortification ever constructed. The Ming started the rebuilding of the Great Wall with100,000 workers who had rebuilt over 1,200 miles of wall by 1471. The Mongols continued to raid northern China as this was going on and a more determined effort was proposed to close off the northern frontier. Between 1471 and 1572, over 4,000 more miles of masonry walls with towers every 100 yards were built at a huge expense in money and another million lives lost in the project. In addition, there was another thousand miles of walls to back up walls that made the Great Wall one of the most formidable defensive structures ever built. Over a million soldiers manned the walls with several cavalry armies to pursue barbarian forces north of the wall or to destroy forces trapped by the second or third walls. The Ming felt that the wall had been worth the huge cost in building it when on several occasions Mongol and Manchu (Jin) forces broke through the first wall only to be trapped and destroyed by the second wall and the Chinese cavalry armies.

In 1616, the Jin Dynasty was reestablished by a Manchu leader named Nurhachi after he had unified all of the Manchurian tribes. In 1618, the Manchu declared war on the Ming Dynasty and captured all Chinese territory north of the Great Wall by 1621. The Great Wall seemed to prove its worth when several attempts to assault the wall were defeated by Ming forces backed by artillery. In 1630, a former Chinese soldier named Li Zicheng led a rebellion against the Ming Dynasty that grew in size and in violence. Over a million Chinese would eventually die in the rebellion. In 1644, Emperor Chongzhen, the last Ming or truly Chinese emperor, committed suicide by hanging himself in the imperial gardens as Li Zicheng's rebel army took control of Beijing. As this was occurring, Ming General Wu Sangui with 40,000 troops was desperately holding off 100,000 Manchu troops under Dorgan as they were assaulting the Great Wall. When Wu Sangui heard that over 60,000 rebel troops were marching on him from Beijing he asked for a truce and an alliance with Dorgan and the Manchu army to help him defeat the rebels. As the Manchus waited quietly outside of the Great Wall to be allowed in to attack the rebels, Wu Sangui decided to see if his army could defeat the rebels alone before actually letting the Manchus through the wall. General Wu knew that the Manchus would aide him, but would then take over Ming China. On May 27, 1644, the Battle of Shanhai Pass started with a cannonade and musket volleys by both Ming and rebel forces followed by a general melee with pikes and swords. Li Zicheng's 60,000 rebels started getting the upper hand after several hours of hand to hand fighting. Wu's Ming troops were flanked and started to break as they were being pushed back toward the Great Wall. Wu then gave the order to open the gates and to let the Manchu troops in. Over 100,000 Manchu cavalry poured through the Great Wall and routed and massacred the rebels. In June of 1644, Shunzhi was crowned the first Qing (Manchu) emperor of China. Wu Sangui was given his own province to rule until he rebelled and was defeated and killed by the Manchus. It took Manchu forces until 1662 to defeat loyal Ming forces in the south of China. No more work on the Great Wall as a defensive structure was ever undertaken after this.

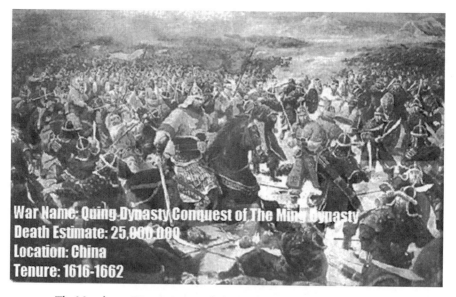

War Name: Quing Dynasty Conquest of The Ming Dynasty
Death Estimate: 25,000,000
Location: China
Tenure: 1616-1662

The Manchu or Qing conquest of China took from 1616 until 1662. The Qing were the last dynasty to rule China from 1644 until 1911.

The Manchu's would rule China until 1912 when warlords and then the Nationalists, the Communists, and the Japanese would fight for control of China until the Communists won in 1949. There were several battles during this period that used the Great Wall as a defensive barrier held with machine guns before modern artillery breached its masonry walls.

The Great Wall of China was only temporarily successful in holding out the feared northern barbarians. The Mongols and Manchu's still ruled all or parts of China during much of the period of the Great Wall's existence as a defensive structure. The Great Wall was only successful if the Chinese maintained large professional cavalry armies to conduct offensive operations from the wall. Today, the Great Wall stands as a memorial to a structure that only a great people and nation could have built and maintained despite the huge cost in manpower and money.

BIBLIOGRAPHY

Cummins, Joseph. *The War Chronicles Vol.1.* Fair Winds Press, Beverly, Massachusetts, 2008.Pp. 296-311.

Davis, Paul. *100 Decisive Battles.* Oxford Press, 1999. Pp.213-216.

Graff, David. *Medieval Chinese Warfare 300-900.* Routledge Press, New York, 2002.

Graff, David and Higham, Robin. *A Military history of China.*Westview Press, Kansas State University, 2002.

Man, John. *Genghis Khan.* Da Capo Press, Cambridge, Ma. 2006.

Man, John. *The Great Wall.* Da Capo Press, Cambridge, Ma. 2008.

Lindsey, William and Michael Yamashita. *The Great Wall.* Sterling Press, NY. 2007.

Lovell, Julia. *The Great Wall.* Grove Press, NY. 2006.

Wintle, John. *The Timeline History of China.* Barnes & Noble Press, NY. 2002.

CHAPTER 2

The Longest War:
Vietnam's War of Independence
from 111 B.C. – 938 A.D. and
The Struggle to Stay Independent to 1428

Most Westerners considers the many wars that Vietnam fought with China from 111 B.C. to 938 A.D. for independence as many separate wars, but the Vietnamese consider these conflicts as one war, a war that lasted 1,049 years. This would make the Vietnamese War of Independence the longest war in history. The fact that Vietnam resisted China for over a thousand years before winning independence speaks of the fortitude, determination, and longsuffering that the Vietnamese people showed when confronted with an enemy. Vietnam has often been more committed in terms of casualties and time that it took to win its wars than its enemies were willing to accept themselves.

Vietnam first became a nation in 258 B.C., when the new kingdom of Au Lac emerged as the union of the kingdoms of Au Viet and Lac Viet. Au Lac had excellent archers and crossbowmen that often ambushed

Chinese troops when they would cross into Vietnam on raiding missions, but these troops never reached the capital or any other large population centers at this time. The Vietnamese maintained a number of earthworks and stockade forts along the border with China to block Chinese raids into Au Lac (North Vietnam). According to Chinese records, the first Chinese invasion into Vietnam took place in 207 B.C. when a turncoat Chinese general named Trieu Da took his army into Vietnam to escape the Ch'in (Qin) Empire and its insane Emperor Shi Huangdi. General Trieu Da arranged a marriage of his son Trong Thuy to the daughter of Au Lac's King Duong Vuong so that he could spy for him. Trong Thuy betrayed his father-in-law, King Duong Vuong by arranging to have Au Lac's army go into what is today South Vietnam on raids as his father's Chinese army assaulted and captured Au Lac's capital at Co Loa. Trong Thuy committed suicide after he found out that his wife whom he genuinely loved died along with her father in the assault. Trieu Da then proclaimed himself emperor of the new nation of Nam Viet. Most Vietnamese didn't consider this a Chinese invasion because Emperor Trieu Da assimilated himself into all things Vietnamese and still defended the border near Guangxi, China from Ch'in and later Han Chinese attacks into Nam Viet. In 185 B.C., a massive Han army was sent against Nam Viet, but was destroyed by a cholera epidemic.

In 111 B.C., huge Han Dynasty armies overwhelmed the Nam Viet army and fortifications and assaulted its capital at Co Loc. The Han armies forced Vietnamese prisoners to fill in the ditches in front of the earthwork and stockade fortifications and to pull forward their siege engines to assault the Nam Viet capital. The Vietnamese archers and crossbowmen were reluctant to fire on their own people given that many were women and children as well as captured soldiers that were filling in the ditches and waited for the final assault. The Vietnamese fired thousands of arrows and bolts and poured boiling oil onto the enemy to kill thousands of the Han troops, but the huge Han army continued the assault for days until the exhausted Vietnamese were eventually overwhelmed. The Han called Vietnam the province of Giao Chi or Annam which means "pacified south" and then forced the Vietnamese to pay them heavy tribute and taxes. The Chinese language, writing system, and cultural practices were forced upon the Vietnamese people, but they refused to assimilate to the Chinese customs. There were frequent, but unsuccessful peasant rebellions against the Han Chinese. Untrained farmers with farming tools for weapons were no match for the well trained Han Chinese army.

Trung Trac and her twin sister, Trung Nhi had no intentions of becoming great heroines that would lead a revolt against Han China. Both sisters were very beautiful and simply wanted to marry and raise their children in the Vietnamese way. The Trung sisters were born in 12 A.D. in a rural village in northern Vietnam. The sisters grew up being taught martial arts and the art of warfare from their father, Me Linh, who didn't have a son to teach these things to. Their father was also a prefect for the Han Chinese, but was often disturbed by the cruel treatment by the Chinese against the Vietnamese for even the most trivial offenses. The Trung sisters would have to witness Vietnamese being tortured publicly as an example by the favorite Han Chinese torture of "death by a thousand cuts." This torture involved stripping a man or woman of their clothes and tying them up in a public location to be slowly sliced with over a thousand cuts over a one to two day period to die a very slow and agonizing death. The tortured individual was unrecognizable by the time they actually died from this torture. The tortures often had the opposite effect than the Han intended because it caused the Vietnamese to hate and plot against their overlords even more.

When the Trung sisters were 18, a neighboring prefect brought his son, Thi Sach to meet the infamously beautiful Trung sisters. Thi Sach and Trung Trac fell deeply in love and were soon married. The couple had close to 10 happy years together before their lives became disrupted from Han Chinese tyranny. Thi Sach was a government official who protested the torture and abuse of Vietnamese for breaking of the most minor Han laws.

One day, Thi Sach started an anti-Han riot by rescuing some friends of his family who had been sentenced to death by a thousand cuts. The Han officials had Thi Sach arrested and sentenced him to be put to death by this same torture. Trung Trac and her sister wept and pleaded for the Han soldiers to release Thi Sach as they watched him suffer and die. Afterward, the Han soldiers raped the Trung sisters to add to their pain and humiliation. When Trung Trac gathered the mutilated and shredded remains of her husband she had decided to become a revolutionary. Trung Trac and Trung Nhi led a large group of farmers armed with farming tools to attack the local stockade fort held by the Han officials and soldiers who had killed Thi Sach. An elephant was brought to the fort and battered down the gate. The Vietnamese farmers led by the Trung sisters charged through the gates and viciously massacred the entire garrison. The Trung sisters wanted to keep this massacre a secret so that they could gather larger support for the rebellion and then plan something far larger in scale to destroy all sixty-five of the Han fortifications and garrisons in Vietnam. A number of farmers dressed in the Han uniforms from the dead garrison and went about the routines that the soldiers and officials normally did to give the impression that everything was normal at the fort.

The Trung sisters and their supporters recruited tens of thousands of Vietnamese to the rebellion of which around 1/3rd were women, one of the first women's movements in history. The Vietnamese had learned to hate the Han for their heavy taxation and their cruel practices if a family couldn't pay the taxes. Each evening Han soldiers forced the daughters and wives of poor Vietnamese who could not pay their taxes to come to the garrison fortifications and serve as prostitutes to pay off their family's tax debts to the Han. If the women didn't show up then the entire family would be put to death. The Trung sisters decided to recruit all of these women who had to endure this humiliation to use their knowledge of the inside of these forts to massacre the garrisons. The plan was that the women would enter the forts as they normally did each evening except that they would be concealing knives to kill the Han soldiers with once they had taken the women into a room for sex. The women would then open the gates for the peasant forces to enter and massacre the garrisons.

In 39 A.D., during the Tet Chinese New Year celebration when the Han troops would be drinking a lot of alcohol, the plan was put into place. All sixty-five Han fortresses and garrisons were targeted on the same night. In some fortresses, the women succeeded in killing the Han soldiers as they were undressing and were able to open the gates to the enraged Vietnamese peasants who massacred the entire garrisons. In other fortifications, the women were able to stab the Han soldiers, but could not reach the gates to open them. This caused a lot of chaos as wounded and angry Han soldiers chased the women inside of the forts which caused a diversion for the peasants to scale the walls or to break down the gates with the help of elephants and to then massacre all the Han soldiers.

All sixty-five Han fortifications were captured in one night. The daring scheme succeeded in killing all Han soldiers and Chinese officials in Vietnam. In 1968, during the Vietnam War, the North Vietnamese and Viet Cong used a very similar strategy of attacking all U.S. army positions at one time during the Tet Offensive, which was inspired by the Trung sisters 1,929 years earlier.

In 40 A.D., the Trung sisters were crowned as the queens of Vietnam which ended what came to be known as the first Chinese domination of Vietnam (111 B.C.-39 A.D.). The Vietnamese were able to resist all Chinese efforts to reconquer Vietnam and to remain independent for four years until 43 A.D. The Vietnamese though were not prepared to face the might of the Han Empire that was sure to come. Fighting garrison and provincial troops was one thing, but fighting the Han regular army that had been stationed in the north was another. Only half of the Vietnamese army was armed with captured Han armor and weapons and the other half was armed with farming tools. Most Vietnamese soldiers were mostly untrained in warfare.

In 43 A.D., the top Han General Ma Yuan was sent with a huge army of over 100,000 elite Han troops to put down the revolt by the upstart Trung sisters. The Han army and a slightly smaller Vietnamese army faced each other on a plain with rice patties outside of what is today Hanoi. General Ma Yuan had ordered all of the Han soldiers to come out to fight the battle completely naked except for their shields, spears and swords. The Han soldiers were ordered to kill the men and to gang rape the women right on the battlefield. Any women that would survive the rapes would then be chained and forced to work in brothels. The Han soldiers laughed and yelled at the Vietnamese women as they called them whores. This completely unnerved the Vietnamese women. The men told the women to flee and they would hold off the Han army so that they could get away. Over a third of the Vietnamese army, which was made up of women including the Trung sisters, fled the battlefield.

The battle was vicious with the unclothed Han being at a disadvantage to the Vietnamese who wore captured armor. Numbers eventually caused most of the Vietnamese soldiers to be killed. One of the great heroines of the battle was Phung Thih Chinh who was not able to flee because she was in labor and bore a baby in the front line. After the baby was born, Phung Thih Chinh fought as a bear defending its cubs with a sword in one hand and her baby in the other. Finally, she fled the battle while the other Vietnamese held off the Han soldiers long enough for her to get away with her baby.

The Trung sisters and the remainder of the Vietnamese army fled to Tay Son. The Han army followed and this time remained clothed to fight. The night before the battle some Vietnamese women came screaming like demons into the Han camp killing a number of soldiers before being killed or committing suicide. The battle the next day was desperate, but the untrained Vietnamese couldn't defeat the better trained and more numerous Han. Most of the women fought savagely until the Han killed them. The last remnant of fighters held off the Han while the Trung sisters jumped into the Hat River and drowned themselves. Phung Thi Chinh also jumped into the river with her newborn baby and died as well. Today, the Trung sisters are reverenced in Vietnam as genuine heroines and have a number of temples dedicated to them where the Vietnamese offer incense and prayers.

The second Chinese domination of Vietnam was from 43 A.D. to 544 A.D. The Vietnamese rebelled against the Han Empire in 137, 156, and 178 with early victories against garrison troops, but then they would be defeated by overwhelming Chinese invasion forces. In 204, the Han Empire collapsed under the weight of peasant rebellions protesting excessive taxes as well as barbarian invasions from Mongolia. Vietnam came under the control of the Wu who ruled southern China after 204 A.D.

In 248 A.D., another female warrior named Trieu Au led a rebellion against the Wu Chinese. Trieu Au was raised by her brother, Trieu Quoc Dat, after her parents were killed, possibly by Wu soldiers, when she was a child. When Trieu was twenty, she killed her sister-in-law and fled to the mountains where she raised a band of a thousand discontented male and female Vietnamese warriors. Trieu Au and her warriors made guerrilla raids on Wu garrisons and then would lead the pursuing Chinese into ambushes in the jungles. In one battle, Trieu Au's warriors faced an equal size Wu force in open battle. The Wu forces tried the same strategy that had been used against the Trung sisters by removing their clothes before the battle with the intention of gang raping the women warriors on the battlefield. Trieu Au and her warriors didn't flinch and attacked the Wu soldiers and killed them all. The dead Wu soldiers then had their penises and testicles cut off and stuffed in their mouths by the defiant female warriors.

Trieu Au followed this up by leading her band to join her brother's thirty thousand men who had also risen in rebellion against the Wu. Trieu Au fought on an elephant from the front line and was elected leader of the rebellion because of her bravery and leadership qualities. This Vietnamese army held off the Wu armies for over six months, when Trieu Au and her army became trapped in the mountains with their backs to some cliffs and no way of escape. When the Wu commander asked Trieu Au to surrender, she said, "I only want to ride the wind and walk on the waves, slay the big whales of the Eastern Sea, clean up frontiers, and save the people from drowning. Why should I imitate others, bow my head, stoop over and be a slave?" All the Vietnamese rebels and Trieu Au fought to the death beneath the mountain cliffs in a bloody and desperate battle. Today, Trieu Au is also worshipped at a number of temples in Vietnam as well. During the Vietnam Wars (1946-1975), many Viet Minh, North Vietnamese and Viet Cong women looked at the Trung sisters and Trieu Au as examples of what great women could do serving their country as warriors. Because of these women warrior's examples, several hundred thousand Viet Minh, North Vietnamese and Viet Cong women served in the Vietnam Wars against the French, Americans, and the South Vietnamese.

The Chinese called southern Vietnam the province of Linyi, but the Vietnamese people of this area called their country Champa. In 192, the Chinese began having problems with separate revolts and a separate identity from Champa (southern Vietnam). In 431, Fan Hu-ta, the newly pronounced king of Champa, led a successful revolt against the Jin (Chin) Dynasty. King Fan Hu-ta then led an attack into Annam and was killed when his army was ambushed as they traveled through the jungle with the help of troops from Nam Viet (northern Vietnam) in the service of the Jin Chinese. The Cham were able to maintain their independence until 446, when they were brutally defeated and reoccupied by Chinese and Nam Viet troops.

The second Chinese domination of Vietnam ended in 544 when Ly Nam De led a revolt against the Sui Dynasty in China. Because of so much Chinese corruption, Ly Nam De was able to get a large portion of the Chinese Imperial army to join his forces to overthrow the Chinese in Nam Viet. The Ly Dynasty ruled Nam Viet until 602, when the Sui Dynasty sent 120,000 Chinese troops to overwhelm the Vietnamese army of 30,000. In 605, both Nam Viet (northern Vietnam) and Champa (southern Vietnam) rose in revolt against the Sui Dynasty. Nam Viet was crushed and was forced to provide troops to help defeat the Cham as well. King Sambhuvarman led a large army of Cham warriors with hundreds of war elephants against the Sui and Nam Viet army in Annam (another name for northern Vietnam). The Cham elephants charged the Sui and Nam Viet troops in a large jungle clearing followed by the Cham army. The Sui and Nam Viet troops retreated into the jungle on pre-planned paths. The Cham elephants then fell into hundreds of concealed pits that impaled the beasts on giant sharpened bamboo stakes. The Cham warriors also were falling into the pits and then were massacred by a Sui and Nam Viet counterattack.

The Sui army then occupied Champa, while King Sambhuvarman led an insurgency from the Central Highland Mountains in Vietnam. The Chinese troops were ambushed and massacred whenever they entered the Cham jungle sanctuaries in the Central Highlands. The only times that the Chinese won battles was when the Nam Viet troops helped them. In 618, the Nam Viet agreed to stop helping the Chinese troops. King Sambhuvarman was then able to re-establish the nation of Champa in 618 partially because he agreed to pay the Chinese Emperor Yang Kuang tribute after apologizing for his rebellions. Later in 618, the Sui Dynasty was overthrown and replaced by the Tang Dynasty in

China. King Sambhuvarman then had to continue to pay tribute to the Tang emperor and had to allow Chinese occupation troops in Champa in order to retain some limited autonomy.

The third domination of China over Vietnam lasted from 602 to 905. The Tang Chinese were very brutal towards Vietnam in maintaining order. The Chinese soldiers often skinned Vietnamese alive and used the "death by a thousand cuts" torture again for even minor offenses against Tang laws. In 722, Mai Thuc Loan led a massive rebellion that included both Da Viet and Champa. Vietnamese peasants rose up all over Vietnam and massacred Chinese garrisons and occupation troops. Mai Thuc Loan was then named emperor of Vietnam and retreated before several invading Chinese armies before ambushing and destroying them in the Central Highland Mountains. The Vietnamese used thousands of pits of various sizes with sharpened stakes with dung on them to impale Chinese feet and bodies and to kill by infection. Disease killed thousands of horses and tens of thousands of Chinese soldiers who were not used to the tropical heat in Vietnam. Vietnam had become a bottomless pit to consume men and money to subdue the nation. The same problems that France and the United States got into in the Vietnam Wars in the 20th century had been going on for over two thousand years before. The Tang emperor was determined to not lose control of Vietnam and sent a trusted Chinese eunuch general to lead 100,000 Tang troops and to use brutal tactics to regain control. The Chinese troops skinned, scalped, and decapitated over 80,000 Vietnamese in a reign of terror to crush the revolt by 728. Similar Vietnamese rebellions followed from 791 to 802, 803, and from 819 to 820. Even after almost 1,000 years of Chinese occupation, the Vietnamese would not accept anything less than independence.

By 905, the Tang Dynasty had greatly weakened and had little money and few troops to maintain Vietnam as a Chinese province. A wealthy Vietnamese Tang government official, Khuc Thua Du took control of

Vietnam as governor and forced all of the Tang troops and officials out of the country. Khuc Thua Du then gave the pretense of cooperation with the Chinese government, but had actually established an independent Vietnam without a war. The new Chinese Emperor Aidi overthrew the Tang Dynasty in 905 and founded the later Liang Dynasty. In 907, a Chinese general named Taizu took over as emperor of the Liang Dynasty, but was too busy fighting the Khitans in the north and dealing with a number of natural disasters to demand complete submission from Vietnam. The Chinese sent a number of weak armies to try to force Vietnam's submission between 907 and 931, but these forces were all ambushed and defeated in the mountains and jungles of Vietnam. In 931, after the Chinese had been defeated again, Duong Dinh Nghe proclaimed the independent nation of Da Viet in northern Vietnam. Champa also declared independence in the south as well.

In 936, a Chinese general named Gaozu (936-944) usurped the Chinese throne as emperor and formed the later Jin Dynasty. Gaozu wanted to find a way to return Vietnam as a province of China. In 937, an opportunity presented itself to Emperor Gaozu when Duong Dinh Nghe asked for assistance from China to put down a revolt. The Emperor Gaozu ordered for an overwhelming force of 200,000 Chinese troops to invade Da Viet through the Bach Dang River aboard a large fleet of ships under his son, Liu Hung-tsao. Before the Chinese force could arrive, Duong Dinh Nghe was assassinated and Ngo Quyen took over Da Viet and began getting his forces ready for a battle on the Bach Dang River. Ngo Quyen knew the tides of Halong Bay and the Bach Dang River well from his childhood days and decided to use this knowledge against the Chinese. Ngo Quyen could only muster an army of 50,000 troops to fight China's 200,000. Vietnam had been defeated by overwhelming Chinese armies on many occasions over the previous thousand years and Ngo Quyen knew that he must defeat the Chinese before they could disembark their army.

In 938, a massive force of over 1,000 ships and boats passed through Halong Bay at high tide to beating drums and great fanfare to intimidate the Vietnamese. As the Chinese fleet passed through the bay, over a thousand Vietnamese soldiers hid in a cave near Halong Bay waiting for the entire Chinese fleet to pass by and move up the Bach Dang River. A short while after the Chinese fleet passed, the low tide had exposed much of the sand in the bay with very shallow water in areas not exposed. The Vietnamese began placing thousands of 6 to 12 foot tall and one foot thick iron tipped stakes all over Halong Bay and at the mouth of the Bach Dang River so that at high tide the stakes were just below the surface of the water. The Vietnamese river fleet, which consisted of mostly twenty-yard long boats that had paddlers on the sides and room for two ranks of fighting men and archers in the middle, hid silently with their boats in the jungle as the Chinese fleet passed by on the Bach Dang River. After the Chinese fleet passed, the Vietnamese carried their boats into the water and headed up river to attack the Chinese fleet from behind. After some skirmishing, the Vietnamese river fleet pretended to retreat and lured the Chinese fleet back toward Halong Bay.

The Chinese commander Liu Hung-tsao, took the bait and chased the Vietnamese boats to Halong Bay where a battle commenced. The Vietnamese plan was to keep the Chinese fleet fighting until the high tide receded. As the high tide rolled out of Halong Bay, the Chinese ships were impaled on the iron tipped stakes as the Vietnamese boats began attacking and burning ships with fire rafts and fire arrows until the tide had mostly receded. Then fifty thousand Vietnamese warriors with some war elephants attacked into the exposed bay. The elephants knocked over ships, which were then set on fire and the soldiers were killed as they jumped out of the burning vessels. After recovering from his initial shock, Chinese General Liu Hung-tsao then realized that his 200,000 man Chinese army far outnumbered the 50,000 Vietnamese troops that were attacking his forces. He ordered his soldiers to disembark from their ships and to counter-attack the enemy on the sands and shallow water of the bay.

The epic First Battle of Bach Dang ended Vietnam's 1,049 year war for freedom from China. Over 100,000 Chinese were swept away and drowned by the fast moving currents from the high tide at the mouth of the Bach Dang River.

The Vietnamese fought desperately for several hours to hold off the Chinese until the high tide returned. Finally, late in the day their elephants abandoned the battle and headed for the shore and jungles of Halong Bay. The Vietnamese warriors knew that the high tide was going to come in swiftly and they retreated to the shoreline and jungle along the bay. The Chinese at first were jubilant and started celebrating a victory as the tide started rapidly filling Halong Bay. The tide and current was moving so rapidly into the bay that tens of thousands of Chinese were swept away. There was a panic and a mad rush to get back on the remaining ships. Over a hundred thousand Chinese soldiers and ship crews were carried away by the tide currents and drowned. A number of the Chinese ships had their hulls torn open by the iron tipped stakes and sank with all aboard as well. The victory cost 4,500 Vietnamese lives. The remaining Chinese ships returned to Canton, China in humiliation and defeat, and China finally accepted Da Viet and Champa as independent nations.

Ngo Quyen was named as emperor of Da Viet and ruled until his death in 944. Da Viet was then gripped by civil wars and turmoil for much of the rest of the tenth century. The First Battle of Bach Dang is celebrated today in Vietnam as the beginning of Vietnamese independence from China.

From 1057 to 1061, the Chinese recruited the Cham (South Vietnam) and the Khmer Empire (Cambodia, Laos, and Thailand) to invade and crush Da Viet from all sides. The Da Viet was able to defeat each nation's army separately before any of the armies could unite. The Vietnamese won victories with their river fleet on the Red River against separate Khmer and Chinese fleets as well. In 1075, the Da Viet army of a hundred thousand soldiers launched a preemptive strike against Chinese forces who were gathering in staging areas for an invasion in Guangdong and Guangxi, China and then defeated invasions by the allied Khmer and Cham armies before they could unite. The Vietnamese also defeated the

Mongol's Yuan Dynasty after they had conquered China between 1257 to 1288 which is detailed in a later chapter.

Da Viet remained a strong independent country for almost 500 years until the 4th Chinese domination of Vietnam from 1405 to 1428 took place from the powerful Ming Dynasty. In 1405, Ho Qui Ly usurped the throne of Da Viet from the Tran family who then appealed to the Ming Chinese for help restoring their authority. Between 1405 and 1407, the Ming responded by sending a large naval force and army to conquer Champa plus 200,000 more troops to invade Da Viet in the north to force Vietnam to become the Chinese southern province of Annam. Heavy taxation along with having to learn the Chinese language, customs, and beliefs were forced on the Vietnamese people once again.

In 1416, a Vietnamese landowner named, Le Loi, raised a guerrilla army in the interior jungles and mountains of Vietnam to resist the much stronger Ming army. The Vietnamese guerillas only attacked and overran isolated Ming outposts and forts, but never confronted the Ming in open battle. The Ming sent armies into the Central Highlands to try to find and defeat the Vietnamese strongholds, but found they had been lured into ambushes that killed tens of thousands of Chinese troops. Many Ming became casualties from the pits of bamboo stakes that impaled feet and bodies. Thousands of Ming soldiers and horses died from disease. Captured Ming soldiers were tied to trees in the jungle and tortured. The Ming responded by building fortresses in the jungles and mountains close to the Vietnamese sanctuaries as a way of trying to hem in the guerrillas. Instead, the Ming soldiers found themselves isolated and unable to support each other as the fortifications were taken and overrun by Vietnamese guerillas and their war elephants. The war in Vietnam was sucking the Chinese treasury dry with no end in sight. In 1424, Emperor Yung Lo died and the power of the Ming started to decline.

Vietnam was an empire destroyer and had always made nations that invaded it to decline in power. In 1426, the Vietnamese army was ready to confront the Ming in an open battle. Over a hundred thousand Vietnamese soldiers with perhaps a thousand war elephants met over a hundred thousand Ming troops in Nghe An province near the Red River delta in mostly jungle terrain mixed with some rice patties. The Ming cavalry was hindered by the jungle and their horses were terrified of the Vietnamese elephants and wouldn't charge them. This gave the momentum of attack to the Vietnamese whose elephants drove back and eventually routed the Ming army. The Vietnamese infantry then hunted down and killed most of the Ming army for several days as the Ming troops had lost all discipline and was trying to flee back to China. Le Loi's army then besieged the last Ming forces at Hanoi for over a year from 1427 to 1428 where another hundred thousand Chinese troops were either killed or captured.

Finally Vietnam remained independent until 1857 when the French would make Vietnam a colony until 1954. Vietnam did retain a large amount of Chinese religious ideas and customs. Though the Vietnamese have a separate New Year than the Chinese and a slightly different zodiac, considerable similarities exist between the two nations today.

BIBLIOGRAPHY

Complete Annals of Great Viet. Hanoi: Educational Publishing House, 1998.

Dictionary of Wars. Editor, George Childs Kohn, New York; Checkmark Books, 2007.

Gaff, David A. *Medieval Chinese Warfare 300-900.* London: Routledge Publishing, 2002.

Gascoigne, Bamber; Gascoigne, Christina. *The Dynasties of China*. New York, Carrol and Graff Publishing. 2003.

Karnow, Stanley. *Vietnam: a History*. New York, Penguin Books, 1983.

National Bureau for Historical Record. Hanoi: Educational Publishing House, 1998.

Nguyen Khac Vien. *Vietnam-a Long History*. Hanoi, Gioi Publishers, 1999.

Taylor, Keith Weller. *The Birth of Vietnam*. Sacramento, University of California, 1991.

CHAPTER 3

Blood in the Water: The Khmer Empire, The Unlikely King, and The Crises of 1178

The greatest empire of Southeast Asia from A.D. 802 to 1431 was the Khmer Empire which covered what is today much of Cambodia (Khmer), Thailand (Ayutthaya and Siam), South Vietnam (Champa), Laos (many tribes), and Burma. The Khmer Empire at its' height was larger than the Roman Empire. The Khmer capital at Angkor had a population of 1 million people from around 1120 to 1220 and spread out over a 60 mile radius. The greatest of the Khmer kings and the hero of Cambodia to this day was King Jayavarman VII (1128-1219) who ruled from 1178 to 1219 and extended the Khmer Empire to its greatest extent and size. King Jayavarman VII had to retake and re-establish the Khmer Empire between 1178 and 1191 after a disastrous Cham invasion that sacked the Khmer capital at Angkor in 1178. King Jayavarman VII was a devout Buddhist and established Buddhism as the state religion with tolerance for Hinduism in the Khmer Empire which is still practiced in Southeast Asia to this day.

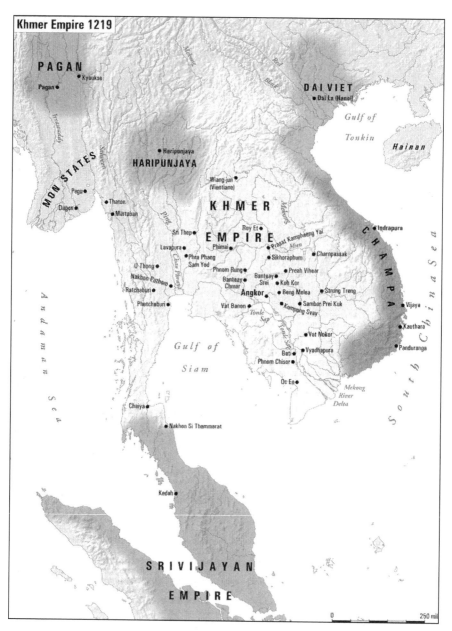

Khmer Empire 1219

PAGAN

Kyaukse

Pagan

DAI VIET

Dai La (Hanoi)

Gulf of

Tonkin

Hainan

MON STATES

Haripunjaya

HARIPUNJAYA

Wiang-jun
(Vientiane)

Pegu

Thaton

Dagon

Martaban

KHMER

Roy Et

Indrapura

Sri Thep

EMPIRE

Prabat Kamphaeng Yai

Lavapura

Phimai

Mun

CHAMPA

Phra Phang
Sam Yod

Sikhoraphum

Charnpassak

U-Thong

Phnom Rung

Banteay
Srei

Preah Vihear

Nakhon Pathom

Bantaay
Chmar

Koh Kor

Ratchaburi

Angkor

Beng Melea

Strung Treng

Phetchaburi

Vat Banon

Sambor Prei Kuk

Vijaya

Tonle
Sap

Kompong Svay

Kauthara

Vat Nokor

Bati

Vyadhapura

Panduranga

Phnom Chisor

Gulf of

Siam

Oc Eo

Mekong
River
Delta

Andaman

Sea

South China Sea

Chaiya

Nakhon Si Thammarat

Kedah

SRIVIJAYAN

EMPIRE

0   250 mil

The Khmer Empire was larger than the Roman Empire was at it's height in 1219.

The pre-Khmer Empire years in what is today Cambodia, Thailand, Laos, and Burma were violent with many small tribal kingdoms that were often at war with one another. It was not unusual for the borders of these small kingdoms to often fluctuate and change in constant warfare and raiding. It was unusual for families to stay together and to not have members killed or taken as captives in the constant tribal raiding. Women were often forced to be the wives or slaves of a number of different warriors from different tribes in the raiding that took place. Houses were built on stilts as they still are today in much of Southeast Asia for protection because of the dangers at night of tigers that would hunt and eat a man just as easily as another animal. Herds of elephants would sometimes stampede and destroy a village if they were being stalked or hunted by tigers at night as well or in a territorial fight. In addition, disease, cobras, and rivers infested with huge crocodiles made life in Southeast Asia very hazardous at this time.

It was normal for most families to lose a number of members due to the many dangers of daily life in the years before the Khmer Empire. Because the forests were such a frightening place, especially at night, the people worshipped ancestral spirits and made human sacrifices to a ferocious demon forest god named P'o-to-li. Life was suffering to the people of Southeast Asia. In the 7th and 8th centuries, Hindu monks from India had success spreading Hinduism into Southeast Asia as the main religion. Later, Buddhism also made an inroad into this area as well especially during and after the rule of King Jayavarman VII.

In 802 A.D., King Jayavarman II established the Khmer Empire in Cambodia when he defeated and expelled invaders from Java of the Srivijayan Empire (Indonesia). Jayavarman II had been held as a prisoner/hostage in Java as a guarantee of good behavior by the Khmer people in Cambodia. A rebellion against the Srivijayan Empire broke out in Cambodia and Jayavarman II offered to put it down for the Javanese. The King of Java allowed him to return to Cambodia to stop the rebellion. Instead, Jayavarman II escaped into the Cambodian jungles and built a fierce army after the Indian model. He defeated the Javanese with a large force of Khmer warriors and several hundred war elephants. He then was made the first king of the Khmer Empire. King Jayavarman II expanded his empire by conquering territory in Laos and Ayutthaya (Thailand). He also established Hinduism as the state religion of the expanding empire and built many Hindu temples called wats. Stability came to the areas controlled by the Khmer Empire after 802 in Southeast Asia.

King Suryavarman II, who ruled the Khmer Empire from 1113 to 1150, is considered the second greatest king of the empire. He became king by killing his uncle King Dharanindravarman I in a bloody battle that is described in a temple inscription that states: "Leaving on the field of combat the oceans of his armies, he delivered a great battle." The inscription goes on to describe an elephant to elephant encounter in the battle between Suryavarman II and his uncle: "Bounding on the head of the elephant of the enemy king, he killed him, as Garuda (Hindu god) on the edge of a mountain would kill a serpent." Suryavarman went on to conquer Champa, Thailand, and Burma, but was frustrated by a series of defeats in three attempts to conquer Da Viet in North Vietnam. In 1128, Suryavarman II lost most of his army of 20,000 in a failed invasion of Dai Viet and in 1129 a seaborne invasion of 700 vessels failed as well.

Most importantly for the Khmer Empire, Suryavarman built a massive Hindu temple at Angkor called Angkor Wat, built as the earthly representation and replica of Mount Meru the home of the Hindu gods in heaven. The temple was covered in gold and magnificent with idols of the Hindu deity Vishnu and other minor Hindu gods. The Khmer and the other nations of the Khmer Empire believed that whoever controlled the earthly Angkor Wat would have access to the heavenly Mount Meru and its power, riches, and glory to maintain an empire. It was for this reason that the Thai, Cham, Laotians, and the Burmese coveted and fought for control of Angkor Wat over hundreds of years, especially after the Khmer Empire went into decline after 1219.

Angkor Wat was believed to be the earthly representation and access point to the heavenly Mount Meru in Hindu beliefs of the Khmer Empire and of Southeast Asia.

In 1076, China had enlisted both the Khmer and the Cham in an unsuccessful effort to re- conquer Da Viet. In 1150, King Suryavarman II wanted the favor returned and sent ambassadors to China to request an alliance to completely subjugate Vietnam and to help keep the Cham under control. China did not enter into the alliance and in fact informed the Cham of the Khmer intentions and sent advisors to aid Champa instead. Nothing came of King Suryavarman's plans for another attempt to conquer the Da Viet and the Cham of Vietnam because he died that same year in 1150.

Suryavarman II was succeeded as king by his cousin Dharanindravarman II from 1150 to 1160, who was Jayavarman VII's father. King Dharanindravarman II had a mostly peaceful and uneventful reign. After King Dharanindravarman's death in 1160, a relative named Yashovarman II succeeded as king and ruled from 1160 to 1167.

King Yashovarman II created a succession problem in 1167 when he sent all of his sons with the Khmer army to reassert control over Champa. The bravest son in battle would be named King Yashovarman's successor. All of King Yashovarman's sons, wanting the honor as successor, died in the same battle with the Cham. A Khmer general named Tribhuvanadityavarman of non royal blood took control of the Khmer army. He returned to Angkor, killed King Yashovarman II in a battle, and proclaimed himself king of the Khmer Empire. Rebellions and instability started tearing apart the Khmer Empire. The Cham saw their chance to spread their own empire into Cambodia and fought with the Khmer Empire from 1167 to 1190.

Jayavarman VII (1128-1219) grew up as one of a thousand princes who lived at the Khmer capital at Angkor. Jayavarman, as a child and young man, mastered the art of archery. He especially liked to stand on the back of a war elephant to hunt or target practice with his bow. Khmer princes generally fought as archers on elephants because it was the most honored and the expected position for a prince to fight in battle. Jayavarman VII was not in line to be king and never thought he would be king of the Khmer Empire.

King Jayavarman VII initially forsook any princely favors or his rightful place as king to seek enlightenment like the Buddha had done, but fate had other plans for this humble man. The only images of King Jayavarman VII are busts of him in peaceful meditation.

A devout Buddhist, Jayavarman rejected the state religion of Hinduism which caused him to go out of favor at Angkor even when his father was king from 1150 to 1160. He wanted to follow the example of the Buddha who rejected the idea of being a prince or king to pursue enlightenment. All the busts, statues, and pictures from that time to now show King Jayavarman VII in peaceful Buddhist meditation. He was scolded many times for rejecting the caste system and befriending servants. He seemed to prefer the company of lower caste people to the other princes and royalty at Angkor.

Jayavarman's bold embracing of Buddhism rather than Hinduism caused his father, King Dharanindravarman II, to choose his cousin as successor instead of his son. Jayavarman married two deeply devout Buddhist sisters, the second after the first died who encouraged his devotion to the teachings of the Buddha. In 1165, Champa wanted a prince hostage from the Khmer as a guarantee of their peaceful intentions. King Yashovarman II sent Jayavarman as that hostage because of his bold embracing of Buddhism. Also, King Yashovarman may have wanted to get rid of Jayavarman despite his lack of interest in the throne, because he was the son of the previous king and this made him a potential threat.

After Tribhuvanadityavarman killed King Yashovarman II in 1167 and made himself king, the Burmese, the Laotians, and the Cham broke free from Khmer control in 1178. The Khmer Empire appeared ready to fall apart, and the Cham saw their chance to take the earthly Mount Meru at Angkor Wat.

That, however, had to wait for ten years because Champa broke out in Civil War as Jaya Indravarman fought against and killed the Cham King Heridiva. Finally, in 1177, King Jaya Indravarman was ready to invade the Khmer Empire and to take the sacred city of Angkor. King Indravarman mounted a land attack of the Khmer capital. Perhaps as many as thirty thousand Cham warriors with hundreds of war elephants headed for Angkor.

King Tribhuvanadityavarman gathered about the same amount of Khmer warriors and war elephants to meet the Cham threat before they could get to Angkor. A desperate and bloody battle took place in jungle and swampy terrain. Both the Cham and the Khmer lost a majority of their elephants, and thousands of dead and wounded. The Cham tried, but could not out flank the Khmer army. The battle ended with both armies exhausted with many dead and wounded. The Cham withdrew and the Khmer army was too beat up to pursue them with about equal losses.

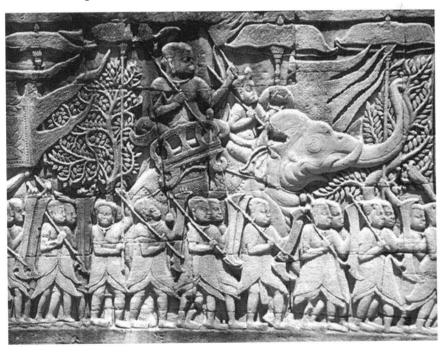

This relief is of the Khmer army marching to war. Elephants were essential to Southeast Asian warfare. No Southeast Asian king usually even considered a land campaign without war elephants.

Battles between the Khmer (Cambodia) and the Cham (southern Vietnam) in bitter hand to hand fighting are depicted in the Bayon Temple at Angkor.

We know about this failed land attempt to take Angkor in 1177 from the Cham and Chinese sources that tell about two Chinese men who had shipwrecked off the coast of Champa at this time. They became military advisors to King Jaya Indravarman once it was discovered that these men were military officers from the Chinese army. One of the Chinese advisors encouraged the Cham to try another land attempt to take Angkor, but they needed cavalry armed with crossbows that would allow the Cham to outflank and to defeat the Khmer who had few cavalry forces themselves. King Indravarman liked this idea and sent the Cham fleet to raid the Chinese mainland and the island of Hainan to capture horses. However, too few horses were found to mount an adequate cavalry force.

With his elephant corps decimated and few horses available for cavalry, King Indravarman knew that another land attempt to take Angkor was out of the question. As it turned out, he found a Chinese navigator who could lead the Cham fleet up the Mekong and Tonle Sap Rivers, across the large Tonle Sap Lake and up the Siem Reap River to surprise the Khmer and attack Angkor. The Khmer army was outside of Angkor waiting for another land attack and would not have many forces to confront an attack from the Siem Reap River.

In 1178, King Jaya Indravarman sent the Cham fleet on the river route to attack Angkor. Early morning fog concealed the Cham fleet. The inhabitants were completely surprised and Angkor was sacked. Panic and chaos reigned as tens of thousands of Khmer were killed in their streets and homes. Everything was taken or destroyed. Thousands not killed were raped and enslaved. Many more hundreds of thousands of residents of Angkor fled into the jungle and wandered with no real certainty of what to do. King Tribhuvanadityavarman and most of the thousand Khmer princes were hunted down and killed as well. Most humiliating of all was the loss of Angkor Wat, the taking of the Ark of Sacred Fire, and the capture and violation in the temple of the thousand beautiful Apsara dancers, who were representations of Hindu angelic beings that served the Hindu gods. Even the Khmer princes did not seek out relations with the Apsara dancers since it would be such a sacrilege because the Apsara dancers were holy unto the gods. The Cham built a large stockade fort at Angkor with log walls over 40 feet tall and kept the Ark of Sacred Fire, the captured Apsara dancers, and the most important captured treasures inside this fortification. All seemed lost and hopeless to the defeated Khmer people who now had no one to lead them. King Jaya Indravarman felt satisfied that he had taken the earthly Mount Meru at Angkor Wat and that he killed off the Khmer succession of princes who could possibly claim the Khmer throne. But then he remembered about his hostage back in Champa. Jayavaraman VII could be dangerous and King Indravarman knew he needed to be killed too.

Jayavarman VII had spent thirteen years in Champa as a hostage from 1165 to 1178 meditating, studying Buddhism, and seeking enlightenment.

In 1178, when he received word about the sacking of Angkor, with the help of some Cham rebels, he escaped from Champa before King Indravarman's assassin could return to kill him. Jayavarman headed up the Mekong River into what is today Cambodia until he found a group of dejected Khmer warriors. Jayavarman enquired about the king and the other princes at Angkor and was informed that they were all dead. The warriors asked the Khmer stranger who he was and he told them that he was Jayavarman VII, son of King Dharanindravarman II (1150-1160). The warriors bowed down and declared Jayavarman VII as their king.

King Jayavarman VII sent runners throughout the Khmer Empire to the scattered remnants of the Khmer army to meet him on the Mekong River and to bring every warrior, baroque war galley, war elephant, and horse that could be found. Khmer and Thai warriors from all over the Khmer Empire answered their king's call. The Thai (Ayutthaya and Siam) were the only people who remained loyal to the Khmer at this time. The Thai brought much needed horses with them, enough for a small cavalry force as well as thousands of warriors.

Depictions of this event can be seen in the Bayon temple at Angkor. Hundreds of war baroque galleys, and a decent size elephant corps were gathered to help make the Khmer army a very formidable one. As it turned out, not all of the Khmer princes were dead and they came to answer King Jayavarman's call as well. No one questioned if Jayavarman VII should be the king, because he had the charisma, the take charge leadership ability, and the royal presence that made everyone follow him as king. He was the warrior king that the Khmer Empire needed for such a time as this.

King Jayavarman VII decided on a two pronged attack to retake Angkor. A land force with the war elephants, cavalry, and a combined Khmer/Thai army would leave first and head overland toward Angkor. King Jayavarman would lead the Khmer river fleet to confront the Cham fleet at the Tonle Sap Lake and then meet up with the ground army at Angkor.

The Battle of Tonle Sap Lake in late 1178 is the most documented battle of the Angkor period. It is depicted in detail in the large temple complex of Bayon at Angkor. King Jayavarman and the Khmer warriors let out a blood curdling war cry as the Khmer fleet and the Cham fleet clashed in a fierce battle on the lake. The Khmer were in a rage at the humiliation and loss of face that they endured at the desecration and sack of their capital and holy places. The Khmer fleet was stronger and faster than the Cham vessels. Their warriors threw themselves onto the Cham vessels killing and knocking Cham warriors into the lake. Even the paddlers used their paddles to strike enemy rowers and tripped up the standing Cham warriors in the center of the boats so that the other Khmer warriors could have an easy kill.

The Khmer also used poles and ropes with hooks to overturn Cham vessels. King Jayavarman was at the front of the battle firing his bow and calling out orders and encouragement to his warriors. The blood in the water along with the thrashing screaming men who had fallen into the lake attracted hundreds of crocodiles that lived on the Tonle Sap Lake at that time. Then, the feast of the crocodiles began as hundreds of warriors were dismembered and eaten alive in the lake. The lake turned into a pool of blood with torn apart bodies everywhere in the water. King Jaya Indravarman and the surviving Cham were unnerved by this and retreated up the Siem Reap River to the stockade fortification that they had built at Angkor.

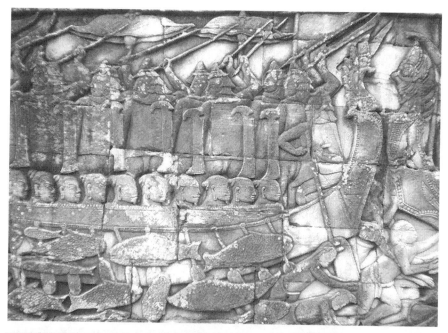

The Battle of Tonle Sap Lake in 1178 that pitted the Cham in their lotus helmets against the helmetless Khmer victors is depicted at the Angkor Thom Temple. Hundreds were devoured during the feast of the crocodiles as warriors from both sides fell into the blood drenched water. This was a morbid feature of warfare for the control of key rivers and lakes in Southeast Asian warfare.

In the meantime, the Khmer and Thai land force met the Cham army in the rain forest outside of Angkor in a bloody battle. The Cham set the forest on fire since it was the dry season and created a wall of flames several miles long to try to turn back the Khmer and Thai forces. Warriors on both sides were burned alive in the massive fire. The Khmer and Thai war elephants brought up logs that had been soaked in streams to throw on the fires in places so that warriors could cross through the fire to get at the Cham. The battle was a seesaw affair until sufficient numbers of the fires were brought under control to allow the Khmer and Thai war elephants through. The elephants turned the tide of battle because the Cham had few of their own.

The Khmer and Thai land force and the warriors from the Khmer fleet joined and pursued the Cham to the stockade fortification. As the Cham army was crowding to get in the gates of their fortification, the Khmer army attacked the Cham still outside. King Jaya Indravarman ordered the gates shut with part of the Cham army trapped outside and desperately fighting for survival. Elephants armed with ballista and Khmer archers led by King Jayavarman swept the walls of the fortification of Cham warriors as other elephants were brought up to push or pull down with ropes the logs of the stockade fort. Other Khmer warriors brought up ladders to scale the walls. The elephants created a breach in the fortification as the Khmer and Thai forces poured in to slaughter the Cham. King Jayavarman spotted King Indravarman surrounded by his body guards and headed straight for him. There must have been quite a bit of anger in King Jayavarman after having been King Indravarman's prisoner for twelve years and then seeing how Angkor had been desecrated and destroyed, because the Khmer sources say that King Jayavarman shot "a million arrows" into King Indravarman. King Jayavarman was in a rage and kept shooting arrows into King Indravarman even after he had obviously died which was an act not characteristic of this gentle Buddhist king.

Angkor was in ruins. The Ark of Sacred Fire and the Apsara dancers had been recovered, but Angkor Wat needed repair. The gold that covered the outside and parts of the inside of the temple had to be replaced. It took three years to repair and rebuild Angkor and Angkor Wat as well as to begin building a new walled city called Angkor Thom where the Bayon temple is located. Angkor Wat briefly became a Buddhist shrine during King Jayavarman's reign. By 1181, all preparations were ready for King Jayavarman VII's coronation. The Ark of Sacred Fire was brought back to Angkor Wat and the Apsara dancers who had been spiritually cleansed in the sacred waters of the Kulen Mountains danced at the king's coronation.

By 1190, King Jayavarman VII had re-established and re-conquered the Khmer Empire including Champa and enlarged the Khmer Empire to its greatest size. King Jayavarman built over eighty Buddhist temples in the Angkor area, but also in Thailand and Laos to show his gratitude to the Buddha for his great fortune in life. He increased the number of Apsara dancers to three thousand to serve adequately all the new temples he had built.

Excessive construction of temples put a great burden on the people who had to provide the labor and taxes. As a result, in the early 1200s insufficient rice fields were planted to meet the needs of the empire. The canals and irrigation systems had also fallen into disrepair and were not providing an adequate water supply to Angkor. Unrest among the people became a problem toward the end of Jayavarman VII's reign. There was anger that Angkor Wat was no longer a Hindu shrine. So the Hindu gods (mainly Vishnu) were brought back and kept with the Buddha as well. Because of King Jayavarman VII's efforts to promote Buddhism with tolerance toward Hinduism, Cambodia, Thailand, Laos, and Burma today practice a type of hybrid Buddhism that mixes in several Hindu gods and beliefs.

King Jayavarman VII died in 1219, at age 91. The Khmer Empire suffered a decline with constant rebellions as well as wars to keep the earthly Mount Meru at Angkor Wat. The capital had to move to Phnom Penh in the 1400s because the canal and irrigation systems completely broke down and could not support the large population. After King Jayavarman's death, the Thai (Ayutthaya) broke free from the Khmer Empire and fought constantly with the Khmer for possession of Angkor Wat. In 1431, the Thai put Angkor under siege. Angkor was too big for the Thai army of a hundred thousand to completely surround. The Khmer army of twenty thousand fought off assaults across the flooded and broken down water systems that surrounded Angkor for seven months. The Khmer warriors fought bravely, but were being worn down. The Thai were finally able to overwhelm the depleted Khmer army until they captured and sacked Angkor. The treasures from Angkor Wat and the Apsara dancers were then brought to Thailand. Except for Angkor Wat, which remained a Buddhist/Hindu shrine, Angkor was abandoned and was virtually forgotten and became overgrown by the surrounding jungle until French archeologists rediscovered it in the nineteenth century.

Apsara dancers were essential to worship at Angkor's many temples
and were considered the property of the Hindu gods.

THE SACRED SENSUAL APSARA DANCERS

Apsara Dancers were representations of Hindu angelic beings that served
and were considered the property of the Hindu gods. Between 1,000 and
3,000 Apsara dancers served the gods in the Hindu and Buddhist wats
(temples) during the Khmer Empire. Apsara dancers were chosen at a
young age (age 5 or 6) for their beauty and grace and most were trained
to live celibate lives to dance sacred dances at the earthly Mount Meru
at Angkor Wat and other wats for the Hindu gods. The Apsara dancers

were stunningly beautiful and very sensual as they danced topless, but could not be touched by men (even royalty) or risk death or some tragic curse because the Apsaras were the sole property of the gods. The Apsaras were fiercely guarded and were never to even be spoken to by men on penalty of death.

A few of the most beautiful and graceful Apsara dancers were considered wives or concubines to the Hindu god Vishnu and had to perform a sexual rite ceremony. A high priest to Vishnu would be present at the ceremony and would go into a trance after being possessed by Vishnu and would then have sexual relations with the Apsara dancer. The high priest was then believed to have had no memory of the sexual encounter since it was supposed to actually be Vishnu making love to one of his wives or concubines.

King Tribhuvanadityavarman after he usurped the throne in 1167 by killing King Yashovarman II was believed to have killed the high priest to Vishnu and performed the ritual himself which was believed to have led to his tragic downfall in 1177 by those who knew about this sacrilege at Angkor Wat. In 1431, after the sack of Angkor, the Thai took all the Apsara dancers to Ayutthaya (Thailand) to serve the Hindu gods there. Both Cambodia and Thailand have a strong tradition for Apsara dancers to this day that dance elaborately clothed and without the sexual ceremony to Vishnu.

SOUTHEAST ASIAN WARFARE: 500 A.D. – 1450 A.D.

The armies of Southeast Asia of Cambodia (Khmer), Thailand (Ayutthaya and Siam), Laos, South Vietnam (Cham), North Vietnam (Da Viet), and Burma looked and fought in a similar way. The main influence for warfare as well as Hinduism came to Southeast Asia from India. The armies consisted of 10,000 to 50,000 foot soldiers, archers, and warriors of the elephant corps. Foot soldiers were armed with spears, swords, daggers, axes, shields and wore only headdresses, sandals and shorts or a loin clothe on their waists. Some warriors wore tunics, but many were bare-chested. The most feared weapon was the battleaxe called a phkeak. Headdresses and shields differentiated the armies so that one could determine friend from foe. The Khmer usually did not wear headdresses, but kept their heads uncovered with the same hair cut style.

The jungle and mountain terrain, the intense tropical heat, and the rainy season made armor unpractical in Southeast Asia though some high status warriors wore a thick weaved twin or a breast plate for some protection on the torso. Archers were important and fought in foot units and in the baskets on the sides of war elephants. A king, prince, or prominent warrior took the honored top archer spot on the back of an elephant and often fought standing.

All the Southeast Asian armies used war elephants as the most important arm of their land armies. No Southeast Asian army would consider an offensive or invasion without a sizeable number of war elephants available. The Bayon temple built by King Jayavarman VII shows war elephants mounted with ballista firing giant arrows that could kill an elephant with one shot. Otherwise, war elephants would take dozens of arrows and spear jabs before the beast would slowly bleed to death. Wounded war elephants often became violent and turned on their own army in which case a mahout would drive a spike into the elephant's skull to kill it and to stop the suffering animal's rampage. Elephants were trained to kill by jabbing with their tusks as well as to step on a warrior and to pull him apart with its trunk. They were often painted and decorated with headdresses. Elephants were also essential in sieges as platforms to ballista and arrows to clear the walls of enemy and were brought up to push and pull down with ropes enemy walls to make a breach for warriors to take the city or fortification.

Cavalry and chariot forces were few and very hard to maintain in Southeast Asia due to the hot tropical climate. Horses had to be imported from India or China at great expense and then had a few months to a few years to live before they died from disease and the tropical weather. Mostly princes and officers rode horses or chariots if available. Only occasionally were enough horses available for any kind of real cavalry force to be available. If cavalry forces were available, they were used to protect the flanks or to out flank the enemy. Cavalry horses were terrified of elephants and would not charge them, so available cavalry were used on the flanks away from the elephants that tended to be in the center of the battlefield. Chinese and Cham sources were clear that the Cham wanted and sought out horses for crossbow cavalry for their 1178 campaign against the Khmer, but could not obtain enough horses to field any real cavalry force and chose an attack from their river battle fleet instead. Also, horses and chariots could not maneuver well in the dense jungles, mountains, and swamps of Southeast Asia. The Bayon in its historical reliefs never show chariots and very few cavalry with the Khmer army on the march or in battle. Chariots are only seen in the mythological Hindu battles depicted at Angkor Wat, but not in the historical reliefs.

Roads were wide dirt trails except at Angkor and the jungle terrain made travel and trade difficult and slow. Control of the rivers was essential to sustaining trade and maintaining any sovereignty over a nation or empire. River war galleys called barques were essential to controlling the rivers, lakes, and delta areas of Southeast Asia. Barques were single decked narrow galleys about fifty feet long that had a row of paddlers or rowers on each side of the boat with a space in the middle for two ranks of warriors from stem to stern for firing arrows, and boarding enemy galleys. They had carvings of Hindu demons and monsters on the front as well as some boats with real elephant tusks used for ramming. Tactics involved ramming, grappling, and boarding for a bloody hand to hand battle or to go by the enemy boats firing arrows while trying to use polls and ropes with hooks to dump the boat over and the enemy into the always crocodile infested waters of Southeast Asia. The blood and thrashing of men in the water always attracted the attention and the swarming of hundreds of crocodiles to the scene of a river or lake battle which added to the death and mayhem in the water.

A Khmer warrior stabs a Cham warrior in the face in vicious fighting in the jungles outside of Angkor.

The Ark of Sacred Fire was carried into battle and was believed to have given the Khmer victory through some mystical power. This belief and practice was similar to the beliefs and practices of the Hebrews concerning the Ark of the Covenant in ancient Israel.

FEROCITY AND SACRED FIRE: THE SECRET TO KHMER DOMINATION

Since all of the Southeast Asian nations fought essentially the same way then what was the secret to the Khmer domination of Southeast Asia from 802 to 1219 A.D.? The secret to the 400 year domination of the Khmer Empire in Southeast Asia was simply the aggressive fierceness and cruelty of the Khmer warriors in battle. This fierceness often unsettled and caused fear in their enemies to give them an edge in battle. The Cham were the enemy that most closely matched the Khmer's own ferocity in battle, but they were still dominated for most of the years of the Khmer Empire.

Interestingly, the Khmer carried an ark into battle that was similar to the Ark of the Covenant in the Bible called the Ark of Sacred Fire. The Ark of Sacred Fire carried a sacred fire that came from Angkor Wat in which the Khmer believed gave them victory in battle. Reliefs of the Ark of Sacred fire are depicted at Angkor Wat and the Bayon. The Ark of Sacred fire was carried into battle for most of the 400 years of the Khmer Empire until the death of Jayavarman VII in 1219 when it mysteriously disappeared just as the Ark of the Covenant disappeared after the death of King Solomon around the 900s B.C. in ancient Israel. The Khmer believed the ark made their warriors ferocious in battle and gave them an edge for victory. King Jayavarman VII had sacred fires maintained at all times in all the Buddhist temples called wats that he had built throughout the Khmer Empire. He believed that these fires and the ark gave him and the Khmer Empire success.

Unfortunately, Pol Pot who ruled Cambodia as a Khmer Rouge communist dictator from 1975 to 1979 stressed the cruelty and ferocity of the Khmer warriors from the Khmer Empire period as an example of how his soldiers should behave in taking over and dealing with the Cambodian population. The result was that the Khmer Rouge's cruelty and ferocity led to the murder and genocide of 2 million out of 8 million Cambodians living in Cambodia at that time.

BIBLIOGRAPHY

Briggs, Lawrence Palmer, *The Ancient Khmer Empire*. Transactions of the American Philosophical Society, Volume 41, Part 1. 1951.

Chandler, P. David, *The History of Cambodia*, Pp.49-68, Westview Press, Oxford, UK. 1992.

Grant, R.G., *Battle*, Pp.100, DK Publishing, NY. 2005.

Higham, Charles, *The Civilization of Angkor*, Pp.117-126, Orion books, UK. 2001.

Jacq-Hergoualc'h, Michel, *Armies of Angkor: Military Structures and Weaponry of the Khmers*, Pp.52 - 53, 82,118 – 121,127, and 173 -174. Orchid Press, UK. 2008.

Jacques, Claude and Lafond, Philipe, *The Khmer Empire*, Pp.201-270, River Books, Bangkok, Thailand, 2007.

Jacobsen, Trudy, *Lost Goddesses*, Pp. 81 – 121, University of Hawaii Press, 2008.

Kohn, George Childs, Editor, *Dictionary of Wars*, Pp.288-289, Checkmark Books, NY. 1986.

National Geographic Magazine, July 2009, Volume 216, No. 1, "Angkor; Why an Ancient Civilization Collapsed."

Preychea, Oknha Sotann, *Gatiloke*, Tuttle Publishing, Tokyo, Japan, 1987. (This is only a small partial English translation. Most of the 10 volume *Gatiloke* is only available at the Cambodian archives and library in Phnom Penh and the few people that own the rare volumes.)

An interview with Buddhist Monk Sov Sarong from Wat Tamov Temple, Cambodia in 2008 was very helpful in filling in some of the holes in the story of King Jayavarman VII from the Cambodian oral tradition. Sov Sarong was one of the few survivors of the Khmer Rouge genocide from 1975 – 1979 that knew the Khmer oral tradition passed down from Buddhist monks for more than 1,000 years in Cambodia. Sov Sarong survived the genocide by hiding in a Buddhist temple in a tiger sanctuary as the Khmer Rouge sought to kill all religious leaders and teachers so that they could teach only communism in Cambodia. The Khmer Rouge came looking for Sov Sarong in 1976 when the tigers attacked and ate two Khmer Rouge soldiers. They never came back. Sov Sarong said that he did not know his age at the time of the interview in 2008, but that he believed that he was 90.

Author Steven Johnson and Buddhist Monk Sav Sarong in 2008.

CHAPTER 4

Blood on the Altar:
Josephus, The Jewish War,
The Roman Conquest of Galilee, and
The Siege of Jerusalem

The seeds of the Jewish War of 66 to 73 A.D. against Rome really started during the Revolt of the Maccabeus in 163 B.C. Judas Maccabeus led the Jews in a revolt against King Antiochus IV of the Seleucid Empire, which came into existence from the carving up of Alexander's conquests after his death. The revolt started when Antiochus placed a statue of Zeus and sacrificed pigs in the Jewish temple at Jerusalem. Antiochus also demanded that the Jews worship Greek gods and adopt Greek cultural practices.

Judas Maccabeus wanted to form an alliance with someone whom Judea could trust and that would come to its defense against the Seleucid Empire if the need arose. Rome was more than happy to enter into a treaty with Judea to guarantee its sovereignty because they saw the Seleucid Empire as a potential enemy. Judea won independence from the Seleucid Empire in 163 B.C. on its own, but felt more secure because of its treaty with Rome.

In 63 B.C., Pompey's legions conquered and annexed the last remaining parts of the Seleucid Empire in Syria. Judea was in the midst of a civil war between brothers, John Hyrcanus and Aristobulus. Both brothers, without the knowledge of the other, rushed to Pompey to seek his support in the war. Because of Rome's alliance with Judea, Pompey decided to support John and defeated Aristobus' forces in an attack on Jerusalem. Pompey caused quite a stir when he curiously entered the Temple and walked right into the Holy of Holies to take a look around. He later apologized for this desecration because he really didn't understand the Jewish beliefs. The Jews then got more than they wanted when Pompey established a Roman occupation army and a tax system to pay for the troops before he left Judea.

In 6 A.D., Caesar Augustus annexed Judea into the Roman Empire. This led to the formation of two terrorist groups in Judea called the Zealots and the Sicarii who would murder Jews that cooperated with the Romans as well as isolated Roman soldiers. For Romans, Jews and Christians were subversive because of their devotion to Yahweh as the only God and their refusal to make the yearly required sacrifices to the emperor. In 40 AD, the Emperor Caligula enraged the Jews when he demanded that his image be set up in the Jewish Temple in Jerusalem which caused an increase in Zealot and Sicarii numbers and attacks. A riot broke out in 49 A.D. at Passover, when one of the Roman soldiers assigned to maintain order at the Temple made a provocative gesture by exposing himself to one of the Jewish women. The crowd became very angry, shouting insults at the Roman soldiers and at the procurator, Pontius Pilate. The Roman troops attacked the crowd, causing panic among the large gathering of pilgrims. Twenty thousand people were reported to have been trampled to death in the panic that took place in the narrow alleyways of Jerusalem.

We know about many of these events in Judea and from the Jewish War in the First century A.D. because of the historian, Flavius Josephus, who lived from 37 to 95 A.D. Josephus was more than a historian, he really was one of the first war correspondents because he reported events that he had witnessed in the Jewish War from 66 – 73 A.D. At age sixteen, Josephus went to live for three years with an Essene ascetic named Banus at Qumran. The Essenes had a prophecy in the now famous Dead Sea Scrolls that a Messiah would rise up to rule the world and destroy all evil and would reestablish the nation of Israel after an apocalyptic war.

The Romans found these ideas very disturbing and destroyed Qumran before moving on to put Jerusalem under siege in the year 70. When the Romans arrived at Qumran, they massacred all the Essenes who remained at the site and destroyed all of their writings except those scrolls hidden in caves near the Dead Sea. One of the items that the Romans found and destroyed was the sacred anointing oil to be used to anoint a king of Israel in the Biblical tradition. The Romans felt that the Essenes helped to bring about the rebellion by their Messianic writings. For the Romans, this Jewish expectation of a Messiah that would overthrow them and rule the world was a constant problem in the occupation of Judea. The Romans had already dealt with a number of people and small rebellions from men claiming to be the Messiah. The Romans tried to destroy the communities of Christians in the Roman Empire for claiming that Jesus of Nazareth (whom they had crucified) had risen from the dead and was the King of Kings to whom they owed devotion.

At age nineteen, Josephus became a Pharisee and respected member of the Sanhedrin in recognition of his scholarship of the scriptures. In 64 AD, when he was twenty-six, Josephus was sent to Rome to obtain the release of certain priests who had been sent by the procurator Felix to be tried in Rome by the Emperor Nero for sedition. The priests had a wall built to prevent the Roman soldiers or King Herod Agrippa in the adjacent Antonia fortress and the palace from being able to view the temple area. When the Romans tried to tear down the wall, a rebellion nearly broke out. The chief priests were sent to Rome to answer for their refusal to let the wall to be torn down. Josephus obtained the release of the priests with the help of Nero's wife, Poppaea, whom he met through a Jewish actor. Poppaea was said to be a "worshipper of God" by Josephus, despite the fact that she had a number of lovers and that she had Nero kill people that she didn't care for. Nero eventually kicked Poppaea to death when she was pregnant in 65 A.D. Josephus returned to his own land determined to work for peace between the Jews and the Romans.

Josephus returned to Rome in 65. He had gained much admiration for his success in returning the high priests to Jerusalem. In the meantime, much tension was developing against the Romans in Jerusalem. Gessius Florus, the procurator of Judea, demanded a cut of the temple treasury money for himself. The people were enraged, and Roman soldiers killed thousands while trying to quell the crowd.

Josephus claims that there was no lack of celestial warnings concerning the ensuing war and disaster that was about to overtake the Jews. He spoke of a sword shaped comet that shone for a year. At Passover, an intense light was seen around the altar for half an hour. A cow was reported to have given birth to a lamb in the temple. The Eastern Gate, which was so heavy that 20 men had difficulty closing or opening it, was reported to have opened by itself in the sixth hour of the night. In May of 66, people all over the country described seeing flaming chariots battling in the skies over Judea. Josephus stated that had it not been for the many eyewitnesses that he himself had spoke with that he would have dismissed all of these claims as imaginary. Even Jesus of Nazareth had predicted in tears the destruction of Jerusalem by the Romans for rejecting him as Messiah a week before he was crucified. Josephus also states that a man named Jesus, son of Ananus, shouted warnings throughout Jerusalem and in the sanctuary of impending doom to come upon Jerusalem. From 62 to 70, this man annoyed the residents with his constant warnings of doom and destruction to come upon Jerusalem. He was beat up many times and finally killed during the siege of Jerusalem.

The rebellion against Rome broke out during the feast of Xylophora in the year 66. The captain of the Temple guard, Eleazar, refused to accept any offerings on behalf of the emperor. The people in the temple cried out unanimously for rebelling against the Romans. Temple guards and Insurgents charged into the fortress Antonia and massacred the Roman garrison and set fire to the archives containing the records of indebtedness. Josephus chose to take refuge in the Temple in an effort to seek asylum. The war party of Zealots was headquartered in the Temple, and they mistook Josephus' presence there as a show of support for the insurgents. The insurgents next besieged the Jaffa Gate fortress. The Roman soldiers, badly outnumbered and cut off from the outside, asked to be allowed to go free if they laid down their weapons. The Zealots agreed and slaughtered the soldiers after they left the fortress.

Upon hearing of the news of the rebellion in Jerusalem, over eighty thousand Jews from around the empire were killed in reprisal. Caesennuis Gallus marched on Jerusalem with the Twelfth Legion. The Jews surprised the Romans by setting up an ambush outside the city. The Jews broke the Roman ranks and killed five hundred at a cost of just twenty men themselves. The Romans counterattacked the Jews outside the city and chased them into Jerusalem. After occupying the outer section of the city, the Romans attacked the Upper City and the Jewish Temple. On the verge of victory, the Romans stopped their attack and retreated from the city, fearing that masses of Jews gathering on their flanks might attack and overwhelm them. The Jews gained renewed courage and ambushed the Romans as they retreated through the pass at Beth-Horon, killing almost six thousand and completely wiping out the Twelfth Legion. In addition, the Jews captured the entire Roman siege train.

Josephus was won over by the contagious excitement of his fellow comrades. He was offered and accepted the governorship of Galilee. The job included administrative, judicial, and military authority of Galilee. Josephus' main job was to fortify the cities of Galilee and to raise an army to defend it or at least hold off the Romans long enough for Jerusalem to make better preparations for war. In just a few months time as governor of Galilee, Josephus had aroused suspicions of treason, escaped several assassination attempts, and failed to unify Galilee against the Romans. In fact, fighting broke out between John of Gischala and his army and the army that Josephus had raised over Josephus' refusal to sell imperial grain in Galilee for John to rebuild the walls of his city. Despite all the problems that Josephus faced, he did manage to fortify sixteen towns and to raise and equip an army of sixty thousand men. They were no match for the sixty thousand Roman troops of the Fifth, Tenth, and Fifteenth Legions with auxiliary troops that Vespasian led into Galilee. Most of the Roman auxiliary troops were Syrians and Arabs who hated the Jews and were motivated to kill them. As the Roman army entered Galilee, the Jewish forces fled in panic with many including Josephus going to Jotapata.

Jotapata proved to be a good choice for defense since it was surrounded on three sides by high cliffs. The only access point had been heavily fortified on a descending spur of the mountain. As the Romans began their assault on May 21 of 67, Josephus led the Jewish forces in a reckless, unexpected attack that repulsed the Romans. For five more days the Romans assaulted Jotapata, and the Jews continued their attacks with great determination, repulsing the Romans each time. The Romans brought up 160 catapults and ballistae to bombard the defenders as workers built earthworks up to Jotapata. The projectiles thrown by these machines made a constant whizzing sound with the thud of dead bodies hitting the ground often dismembered. Josephus wrote that a man next to him on the wall had his head torn off by a projectile as they looked over the wall. As the Romans built earthworks, the Jews built their walls taller and raided the Roman positions and camp causing much destruction. Josephus also had a protective shield built over the wall to prevent Roman arrows and stones from entering the city or harming the workers building the wall higher.

The Romans were taking heavy casualties and decided to starve the city into surrender. The Jews had plenty of food, but very little water since it was the dry months and Josephus knew that they wouldn't be able to hold out long. He devised a plan for the Jews to soak their garments and to hang them on the walls to give the impression that they had plenty of water to waste. After the Romans saw this, they renewed their attacks because they believed the Jews could withstand a siege indefinitely.

Josephus consulted leading citizens in Jotapata about attempting escape in order to raise a relief army to rescue them, but the people began crying in panic and Josephus gave up the idea. The Romans brought up their battering rams to the walls under the cover of archers and slingers and began battering the city. Josephus saw that the walls were crumbling and consequently, had men fill sacks with chaff and lowered them with ropes to cushion the walls where the rams were battering. The innovation worked until the Romans countered with a sword on a long pole to cut the ropes holding the sacks. Desperate to stop the destruction of their walls, the Jews came out at great cost and burned the battering rams.

The Romans next brought up a siege engine to assault the city. The Jews were exhausted, with heaps of dead along the walls from the constant missiles from the archers and ballistae. Josephus knew the end was near and gathered the people together to inspire them for a courageous last stand. He said, "Let each man fight, not as the savior of his native place, but as its avenger, as though it were already lost. Let him picture to himself the butchery of the old men, the fate of the children and women at the mercy of the foe; seize with both hands the fury which these impending disasters arouse in your breasts, and hurl it upon the would be perpetrators."

As the Romans lowered the drawbridge of the siege engine, the people "shrieked a loud, last shriek." When the drawbridge lowered onto the wall, the Jews, remembering Josephus' words, rushed across it, drove the Romans out of the siege engine and set it on fire. The Romans approached again in a turtle formation of interlocked shields to undermine the stone walls, but the Jews poured down boiling oil and scalded the Romans out of formation as the Jewish archers and slingers finished off the tormented legionaries. The Romans brought up more siege engines to the walls of Jotapata, but, as the gangways were lowered, the Jews poured boiled fenugreek onto the planks which caused the Roman soldiers to slip and slide off to their deaths on the ground below. Losses were nigh on both sides with exhaustion wearing down the defenders.

By the forty-seventh day of the siege, the Romans earthworks overtopped the wall, while other parts of the wall had collapsed. The Romans made a pre-dawn assault and found the exhausted Jews sleeping. The Romans, in revenge for their ordeal showed no mercy to any man, woman, or child. Many people were thrust down the ravines near the citadel. Many gathered at the edge of town and committed suicide. Many others were crushed trying to escape in the narrow alleyways. Josephus estimated that over forty thousand inhabitants were massacred, and over twelve hundred were sold into slavery. The Romans themselves had lost the equivalent of an entire legion (over five thousand men) in the siege.

The Romans began searching for Josephus whom they believed was responsible for the whole Jewish rebellion. Corpses and prisoners were searched, but he could not be found. Josephus and forty others hid in a cave in a deep pit for two days before being detected on the third day. Vespasian sent two tribunes to offer Josephus safe conduct if he would come out. Josephus was told that Vespasian admired him for his heroic deeds and would spare him if he came out. As Josephus got up to go surrender, the other Jews surrounded him with swords in their hands and wanted to know how he could go surrender after inspiring so many fellow Jews to die fighting. The Jews in the cave decided to commit suicide rather than submit to the Romans. In this predicament, Josephus suggested that they should draw lots for the order of death. The first to die would be killed by the next to die with a sword until all had died. It just so happened that Josephus drew the last lot. After all had been killed except him and one other, they decided to surrender to the Romans.

Josephus was brought before Vespasian while the Roman soldiers crowded around demanding his death. Vespasian quieted the soldiers and spoke to Josephus of his admiration for how he had led the defense of Jotapata. Josephus said he should not be sent to the emperor in Rome, as was the custom with captured enemy leaders, because he was with the emperor already. Josephus told Vespasian that he would soon become the next emperor of Rome. Vespasian heard from other captives that the Jews at Jotapata believed Josephus to have prophetic abilities. Vespasian treated Josephus well, but forced him to remain with the Roman army in chains.

After resting his men for twenty days, Vespasian led the Romans on to conquer the greater part of Galilee with Jewish resistance simply melting away until they reached Gamla in the Golan Heights. The city was built on the side of a steep slope that was part of a rugged mountain with deep ravines on two sides and a deep precipice at the rear. The houses of Gamla were on the side of a steep slope, tiered one upon another. It had a wall which was situated in front of the city below the houses. The town had a spring located within it and could hold out indefinitely if the defenses held out.

The Romans surrounded Gamla and began building earthworks toward the highest tower in the wall in front of the town. The Jewish defenders attacked the Romans, but were driven back behind their walls. The Romans then brought up three battering rams to pound the city walls. Soon the Romans broke through the wall and swarmed into the city. The defenders broke and fled to the upper parts of Gamla as the Romans pursued them. Without warning, the Jews counter attacked and pushed the Romans down the slopes, slaying them as they became trapped in the narrow alleyways and as they stumbled down the steep terrain. The Romans were not able to resist the Jews above them or to force their way back through the mass of their oncoming comrades. They took refuge on the roofs of the Jewish houses which came close to the rising ground. Suddenly, the houses began to give way under the weight of thousands of soldiers. House collapsed on house down the slope like dominoes. Roman soldiers tried to leap off houses as they collapsed only to land on the next collapsing house. Thousands of Romans soldiers were buried and crushed to death from the disaster. The Jews, with renewed courage, came charging down the hill, killing every wounded and isolated Roman that they could find. Vespasian and his son Titus were themselves nearly surrounded and killed as they and a small number of Romans managed to get out of Gamla alive.

The undermining of the corner tower at the siege of Gamla in Galilee led to the fall of this town. Many Jews jumped to their deaths from cliffs at the end of the battle to avoid the humiliation of rape, slavery, and crucifixions that the Romans were sure to give out to any survivors.

The Romans were in a state of despair because of the scale of the disaster. Over four thousand Romans were killed in this attack. A few days after the disaster, three Roman soldiers silently undermined Gamla's main tower by pulling five large stones from the tower's foundation. The tower came crashing down, opening a large breach in the wall. The Romans waited to make their final assault, not wanting a repeat of the earlier disaster. That final assault took place in October of 67 A.D. in the pre-dawn hours. Once again, panic gripped the city; men snatched up their children and dragged their wives wailing behind them as they ran up the slopes of the city. The Romans began taking heavy casualties as they approached the citadel at the summit. They finally managed to climb into the citadel under the cover of a storm and continued the slaughter sparing no one as fear gripped the population. The Jewish men gathered their wives and children and in desperation plunged them off the cliffs to their deaths below rather than to have to see them raped and murdered by the Romans. Josephus claims that over five thousand Jews jumped from the cliffs to their deaths with the Romans slaying another four thousand inhabitants. According to Josephus, only two women and a man survived by hiding in the ruins of Gamla.

The last city in Galilee that still held out against the Romans was Gischala. As the Romans approached, John of Gischala led ten thousand people in a stampede toward Jerusalem. The Romans pursued and killed six thousand and took three thousand women and children as prisoners to be sold into slavery. Only John and the most able men made it to Jerusalem to continue the war from there.

A flood of refugees converged on Jerusalem to be near the one place where they believed God would be present, the Temple. There was great tension in Jerusalem between the poor and the rich. The wealthy Jews were angry because the records of indebtedness were burned down at the beginning of the revolt, and it made it difficult to collect debts. There was also a split in the Sanhedrin, where the Pharisees supported the poor by wanting to end all indebtedness and wealthy Sadducees who argued for debts to be paid and reconciling with Rome.

Fighting broke out in Jerusalem between the Sicarrii and the Zealots when the Sicarrii leader Menahem showed up at the Temple dressed in royal robes and claiming to be the messiah. The Zealots killed Menahem and forced the Sicarrii to leave Jerusalem. After that, twenty thousand Idumaean Jewish warriors from southern Judea stormed through Jerusalem after the Zealots allowed them to enter, killing 8,500 people and the high priest Ananus because of some rumors that Jerusalem was going to be turned over to the Romans. Later, the Idumaeans found out that the rumor was untrue, and fifteen thousand left in disgust,

At that point, a three way civil war broke out for control of the Temple area among the Zealots led by Eleazar, the forces of John of Gischala, and a new rebel leader named Simon Bar Giora. Thousands more died in the fighting between the factions. To make matters worse was that several years' worth of provisions was burned in order to keep any of the factions from getting them.

In 68 A.D., Nero committed suicide and the next year would be known as "the year of the four emperors," as Sulpicius Galba, Marcus Salvius Ortho, and Aulus Vitellius were either assassinated or committed suicide. On December 9, in the year 69, Vespasian was declared emperor by his troops after his son, Mucianus, had taken over Rome with troops that Vespasian had sent. Vespasian pardoned Josephus and gave him the family name of Flavius because his prophecy came true.

Vespasian's son, Titus, took over as commander of Roman forces in Judea with the addition of the rebuilt Twelfth Legion and more Syrian and Arab auxiliaries to increase the Roman numbers back up to sixty thousand to replace the losses from the Galilean campaign. The Romans had never conducted a siege on a city as large as Jerusalem (Carthage and Alesia covered a smaller area) and this presented quite a challenge. In May of 70, Titus moved the Roman army around Jerusalem to begin the siege after occupying most of the rest of Judea. As Titus and some cavalry moved toward Jerusalem to reconnoiter the walls, Jewish soldiers dashed out of the women's gate and surrounded him. The Jews killed several of Titus's entourage of officers and body guards before he fought his way back to the Roman army.

The Romans then set up their camp and began building fortifications to protect their positions. The Fifth, Twelfth, and Fifteenth Legions camped on or near Mount Scopus; approximately one mile from Jerusalem, and the Tenth Legion camped a little less than a mile from the city on the Mount of Olives. The legions had piled up their weapons and were busy building fortifications around the camps. The Tenth was caught unprepared as thousands of Jewish attackers from the city rushed out of the gates to cut down hundreds of Romans as they scrambled to gather their weapons. Wave after wave of Jewish attackers routed the Romans in panic as they were nearly cut off and surrounded. Titus gathered his forces on Mount Scopus and counter-attacked, but was repulsed from the Mount of Olives and was almost captured again. The Romans retreated, leaving Titus surrounded and fighting desperately to survive. In shame, the legionaries rallied and rescued Titus while eventually driving the Jews from the Mount of Olives.

This Jewish victory was short-lived though because that very night the factions in Jerusalem began fighting again. The fighting was triggered when the forces of John of Gischala snuck into the Temple disguised in prayer robes and then attacked the worshippers, taking over the Temple area from the Zealots and the supplies to withstand the siege. After hearing the Jews fight all night, Titus sent Josephus to seek surrender terms from the Jews. The Jews who had thought that Josephus had died as a hero at Jotapata began cursing him as a traitor and tried to kill him on several occasions when he had approached the walls to negotiate surrender. Josephus would always carry the burden of being labeled a traitor by his own people until the day he died.

The Jewish forces inside of Jerusalem consisted of ten thousand men led by Simon Bar Giora along with five thousand Idumaeans, who held the Upper City and part of the Lower City. John of Gischala held the Temple and the fortress Antonia with six thousand men and twenty-four hundred Zealots in a tenuous alliance. The common people were constantly plundered for provisions so that they suffered the most during the siege. The Romans moved their fortified camps to within a few hundred yards from the walls and could hear constant fighting between the Jewish factions in the city who seemed bent on self-destruction.

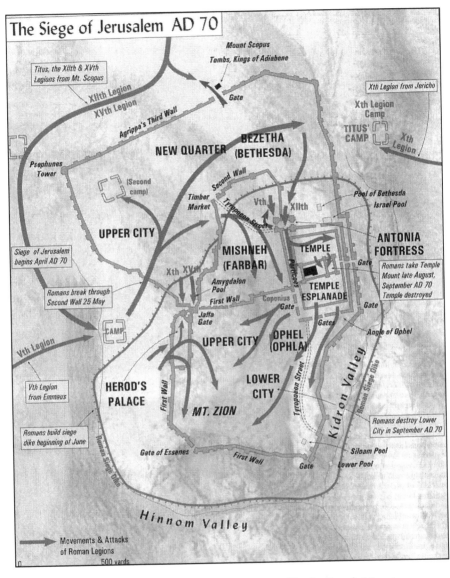

The Romans assaulted the Upper City followed by the Temple Mount
and then the Lower City in the Siege of Jerusalem that proved to
be one of the most difficult sieges in Roman history.

The Romans had worked tirelessly to construct huge earthwork embankments up to the third wall in the Upper City. The forces of Simon Bar Giora tried to hinder the Roman efforts, but they were halted by the ballistae and thousands of archers that were positioned near the earthworks. There was the constant whiz, thud crack of projectiles slamming into bodies and walls that kept the defenders back. The forces of John of Gischala and those of the Zealots wanted to come out of the Temple area to help fight, but they could not for fear that Simon Bar Giora's men would attack them and take over the Temple. After finishing the earthworks, the Romans brought up battering rams and began pounding the Upper City walls causing a cry of fear throughout Jerusalem. The factions once again decided to unify to fight the Romans. For fifteen days, fighting raged around the rams as Jews attacked out from the gates. When the Romans finally finished breaching the wall, the Jewish defenders retreated to the second wall as the Romans swarmed into the Upper City and established a new camp.

The Romans breach the Upper City walls of Jerusalem.

The Romans brought up battering rams and projectile throwers as legionaries tried to scale the walls. The Jews fought back savagely through gates to the outside walls for fear that the crumbling second wall would not hold up much longer. After four days of desperate fighting, the Romans had made a small breach in the wall. Titus and over a thousand legionaries charged through the breach and into the small unfamiliar streets of the Second Quarter of the city. The Jews attacked from every house and rooftop, surrounding Romans in isolated groups. Most of the soldiers were butchered in the streets. Only Titus and a few men escaped alive back through the breach. The Jews savagely fought for possession of the breach for several days before the Romans secured it. Instead of moving into the Second Quarter again, the Romans took control of the whole northern stretch of the second wall and then destroyed it so that they would not be trapped again.

The siege took on an increasingly cruel nature as Jews would pretend to surrender and then kill the Romans sent to accept their surrender. In return, the Romans crucified thousands of captured Jews in creatively demented ways to maximize pain. Josephus mentions that many Jews watched in horror from the walls as family of all genders and ages were screaming in agony in horribly long deaths. As conditions and famine got worse, Jews tried to escape only to be captured by Roman cavalry and crucified at five hundred a day around Jerusalem's walls. Syrian and Arab auxiliary troops cut open the stomachs of over two thousand Jews to search for gold coins that they often swallowed to pick out of their excrement later. At long last, the people of Jerusalem came to the realization that there was no escape and only death awaited them.

Titus combined his legions into two groups and began raising earthworks against the Temple via the fortress Antonia and against another section of the Upper City protected by the Old Wall. The Jews brought up 340 projectile throwers that had been captured at the beginning of the revolt. As the Romans toiled to build up their earthworks, the Jews bombarded them with projectiles of all sorts. The Romans could hardly build their earthworks because of the constant fire and attacks by the Jewish forces. After seventeen more days of constant fighting and working, the earthworks were completed to the fortress Antonia and the Upper City. In the meantime, the Jewish forces had tunneled pits under the Roman earthworks at Antonia that brought them down after their support beams were burned. Jewish forces dashed out of their walls at the Upper City and burned down the battering rams and siege engines. The wood in the earthworks also caught fire and came down at the Old Wall as well. The Jews poured out in waves driving the Romans back into their camp before a counter-attack by Titus repulsed them.

In the meantime, the Jews from the Upper City captured a large number of Roman cavalry horses left outside the walls to graze and butchered them for food. Only the Jewish soldiers were given any meat despite the begging and crying of the women and children to share in the food. Titus discovered that there were numerous tunnels leading out of Jerusalem that were being used to bring some supplies into the city. Titus had his army build a 4.5-mile wall with thirteen forts in an incredible thirteen days to completely isolate Jerusalem. The situation became increasingly desperate with the alleyways filled with the unburied corpses of people of all ages that had died from famine. All law and moral conduct had collapsed as brigands roamed the streets stealing what little food that could be found. Jerusalem had deteriorated into a place of madness, yet cattle was set aside and fed to continue the daily sacrifices in the Temple.

In July of 70 A.D., the Romans gathered more wood and supplies from areas miles away from Jerusalem to rebuild the earthworks against Antonia and the Upper City. As the Romans built these earthworks, many of the Jews were so weak from famine; they could do little to hinder the work. The earthworks up to Antonia and the Upper City were completed in Twenty-one days. The stench of rotting bodies was more of a hindrance to the Romans than the Jewish attacks who were hindered by piles of their own dead and weakness from famine. Battering rams were brought up to Antonia, but made little headway against the thick brick walls of the fortress. That same night a tunnel that the Jews were digging collapsed and took a portion of the wall with it. The Romans quietly climbed the walls two days later in a pre-dawn assault as the Jews slept. The startled Jews retreated from the fortress Antonia to the Temple. For twelve hours the Jews and Romans fought in desperate hand to hand fighting for control of the Temple's outer courts as the priests offered sacrifices. At one point, a centurion named Julianus single handedly fought his way into the inner court of the Temple. Julianus was killing all comers until he slipped on his nail studded boots and crashed to the floor where the Temple guards hacked him death. This desecration of the inner court of the Temple seemed to galvanize the Jews who pushed the Romans back into Antonia with both sides having taken high losses.

The next night, the Romans brought up elite troops for a night assault on the Temple. As the Romans were preparing to attack, the Jews launched their own pre-emptive attack into Antonia. Both sides had thousands of men waiting to get into the battle because of the limited fighting space inside the fortress. The battle lasted for most of three days with no advantage to anyone. On the third straight night of fighting in Antonia, the worn down Jews retreated over the walls of the fortress onto the top of a massive wooden portico colonnade that led into the Temple. Hundreds of Romans swarmed on top of the portico in pursuit of the Jews. The Jews set on fire the pitch resin that covered the roof of the portico. The flames spread so rapidly that most of the Romans became trapped and died screaming for help from their comrades in Antonia, who helplessly watched in horror at the inferno.

In August of 70 A.D., the Romans pounded at the Temple walls with battering rams, but made no impact on the huge, perfectly bonded stones. The Romans then sent waves of attackers to scale with ladders the sixty-two foot tall walls of the Temple. Most of the Romans were thrust back headlong to their deaths, but some legionaries did get a foothold on the walls and planted legion standards there. The Jews counter-attacked and killed or threw the Romans over the walls and captured several legion standards, the ultimate insult to the legionaries. The Romans then set fire to the Temple gates which took all night to burn down. The Romans rushed the burned gate, and for several more days the Jews and Romans fought for control of the outer courts of the Temple until the exhausted Jews fell back into the inner courts.

The Romans continued their assault into the inner Temple region, but were repulsed. In the attack, the massive curtain that covered the Holy of Holies caught on fire. The Jews tried desperately to put out the fire, but were prevented from doing so by the Temple guards who could only allow the High Priest into this area because it was so sacred. A battle ensued between the Temple guards trying to save the sanctity of the Temple and the other Jewish soldiers just trying to save the Temple from burning down. In the chaos, the Romans sensed their opportunity and attacked. As the Romans entered the inner Temple court, they became an uncontrollable mob as Jewish resistance collapsed. Heaps of corpses mounted higher and higher around the altar with a stream of blood flowing from the altar and down the steps of the Temple. The Romans set on fire another wooden portico which burned alive over six thousand women, children, and elderly seeking refuge on top of it. Titus tried to stop the killing, but lost all control of the vengeful legionaries. When the carnage finally stopped, the Romans gathered many gold coins and religious objects and sacrificed to their eagle standards in the Holy of Holies. The entire city was screaming and wailing in mourning for the destruction of the Temple. Titus raped a woman on the alter and had the Temple destroyed and only left the Western Wall as a place where the Jews could mourn its loss. Josephus states that the destruction of the Temple took place on August 10, the anniversary of the destruction of the first Temple by the Babylonians in 586 B.C. Josephus goes on to state that this destruction was no accident and that God was judging the Jews for their bickering, lack of compassion for the poor, and the bad treatment of holy men that God had sent to Jerusalem.

The next day, the Romans occupied the Lower City as the remaining Jews retreated into the Upper City section still under Jewish control. The Jews in the Upper City resisted for four more weeks as the Romans built earthworks and brought up siege engines to assault these last holdouts. On September 8, 70 A.D., the final assault took place as the Jews resisted for a time before terror and fear filled them. The Romans slaughtered most everyone in the Upper City from dawn until dusk. At dusk, the legionaries just got tired of killing people and spared the last thousand or so, mostly women and children. A tent was set up inside the Temple outer court as a brothel where most of the surviving Jewish women in Jerusalem were raped. The Romans also found over two thousand horrendously smelling corpses that had starved to death and gold treasures in the massive underground system of tunnels.

Nine hundred Sicarii on Masada held out for three more years when, in 73 A.D., they committed suicide before a final Roman assault could be made. Josephus claims that throughout the entire Jewish War over 97,000 Jews were captured and 1,100,000 were killed from all causes out of a population of 2,700,000 in Judea from Roman census records. The Romans lost 60,000 out of 120,000 legionaries and auxiliaries that had participated in the war.

The captured Jewish women from throughout Judea were separated from their families and loaded on ships to be taken to brothels in Rome. The women of one such ship jumped overboard in mass suicide when told of their fate by a smiling legionnaire. Children were sold in open markets around the empire. Most of the captured men were killed in the gladiator games. Those too old or feeble to fight were fed to the wild animals featured in the mornings of the gladiator games. Those men who could fight were sent into mock battles in the afternoons wearing their Jewish uniforms and weapons against well fed and well trained gladiators (Gauls, Britons, and Germans mostly) who played the "Romans." The few Jews who survived these mock battles were promoted to celebrity as "main event" gladiators who would fight toward dusk. Josephus states that 2,500 Jews perished in the games in Caesarea alone. Josephus was forced to attend a celebration of Rome's victory at the Temple of Capitoline Jove in Rome where he watched John of Gischala and Simon Bar Giora being scourged, tortured and beheaded to great applause. Simon had tried to escape Jerusalem by wearing white powder and pretending to be a ghost. Josephus could only think of his good fortune that he didn't share in this humiliating death for his part in the war. Several hundred thousand of the remaining 1.6 million Jews remained in Judea with close to 600,000 forced to relocate by the Romans.

Josephus lived in comfort in Rome and wrote and dedicated a number of books to a friend named Epaphroditus. Epaphroditus was also a friend of the Apostle Paul (Philippians 2:25-30) until Paul was executed in Rome in 67 A.D. Josephus claims that it was Epaphroditus that encouraged him to write the *Jewish War* and his other books. In 95 A.D., sometime after Domitian had succeeded Titus as emperor, Epaphroditus and likely Josephus were executed for their Judeo-Christian beliefs and refusing to sacrifice to the emperor. Perhaps this was Josephus' way of proving to himself that he was not a traitor to the Jewish people after all. There is no record of Josephus again after 95 A.D. Christians love to read the works of Josephus because he is a Jewish, non-Christian source who provides helpful information on such New Testament figures as Herod the Great, Herod Agrippa, John the Baptist, Pontius Pilate, James the Apostle, and Jesus Christ, whom he says "was perhaps the Messiah concerning whom the prophets have recounted wonders." Josephus is the only historian who gives credible information on the Jewish War and supporting information on the tumultuous first century A.D.

BIBLIOGRAPHY

Feldman, Louis H.*Josephus and Modern Scholarship*. New York: Walter de Grutzer Co., 1984.

Johnson, Steven. *Josephus: His Life, the Jewish War, and His Credibility*. Dissertation presented to the Faculty of Arts and Sciences in the Department of History at Winthrop University, 1998.

Josephus, Flavius. *The Jewish War.* Translation and ed. Gaalya Cornfield (Grand Rapids: Zondervan, 1982).

Josephus, Flavius. *Josephus: The Complete Works.* Grand Rapids: Kregel Publications, 1960. (Translation by William Whiston).

Madden, Thomas F. *Empires of Trust.* Cambridge: Dutton Publishing, 2008.

Rogers, Cleon. *Topical Josephus.* Grand Rapids: Zondervan, 1992.

CHAPTER 5

Hadrian's Nightmare: The Bar Kokhba Revolt 132 – 136

As the smoke rose over the ruins of Jerusalem after the vicious siege by the Romans in 70 AD, plans were being put in place to move large groups of Jews to other parts of the Roman Empire. This was an effort to get the Jews to forget their precious smoldering temple in Jerusalem which only consisted of one undestroyed wall and to try to assimilate them toward becoming in all things Roman. Emperor Vespasian decided that of the surviving 1.6 million Jews left in Judea and Galilee after the war that 600,000 would be forced to relocate mostly to Libya (Cyrene) and the island of Cyprus. Smaller groups of Jews would relocate to Egypt, Syria, and the western part of Roman occupied Mesopotamia (Iraq). Unknown to the Romans was that this relocation of Jews would not lead to peace, but to further efforts to overthrow the hated pagans as soon as an opportunity presented itself. The opportunity presented itself in the year 115.

In 115, the Emperor Trajan after previously having conquered Dacia (Romania) decided to attack and to take land from the Parthian Empire (eastern Iraq and Iran). Living in Parthia was close to another million

Jews left there from the Babylonian exile (597 – 538 BC) who hated the Romans for having destroyed their sacred temple in Jerusalem. Jews in the Roman Empire began requesting that the Parthian King Osroes to give support for another rebellion against Rome. King Osroes knew that Trajan was going to invade the Parthian Empire and agreed to support the Jewish revolts against Rome. He had even thought that a renewed Jewish Revolt could allow him to conquer and add Judea, Syria, Egypt, and Libya to the Parthian Empire at Rome's expense. King Osroes told the Jewish representatives to occupy and distract the Romans as much as possible in Judea, Libya, Egypt, and Cyprus until he could defeat Emperor Trajan's army. King Osroes said that he would then bring the Parthian army to rescue the Jewish forces and that the nation of Israel would be reestablished as a protectorate nation within the Parthian Empire. He promised to rebuild the Jewish temple in Jerusalem as well. Even though the nation of Israel would not remain free under this plan it was better than the humiliation of living under the Romans so Jewish leaders began making plans to begin their revolt after Trajan had started his invasion of Parthia. A small number of Jewish scholars and rabbis criticized this plan because it relied on trusting the Parthians rather than God for victory. Israel had met disaster when an earlier plan spoken of in the Book of Kings had called for trusting the Egyptians rather than God for victory which had turned into a disaster.

Trajan invaded the Parthian Empire with the best veteran legions from the Roman Empire while leaving only inferior foreign auxiliary troops to garrison most of North Africa and the western Mediterranean area. Trajan's legions in just a few months had successfully captured and annexed Armenia as well as to have defeated and deposed King Osroes after the capture of the Parthian capital Ctesiphon. It was at this time that the Jews in Libya and Cyprus over took and massacred the poorly trained and lead auxiliary forces in their garrison forts. The Roman auxiliary forces were made up of previously conquered Syrians, Arabs,

Germans and Britons that felt little enthusiasm to fight and die for the Romans if not forced to fight and then only if they were supported by veteran Roman Legions. These easy early victories created a false confidence in the Jewish rebels that they could destroy any Roman veteran forces that were sure to come.

The Jews in Libya under a leader named Lukas that many there and in Judea had recognized as the messiah attacked and massacred almost the entire population of 200,000 Romans and Greeks that had been living in Rome's Libyan colony. Years of ridicule and mistreatment from the Greeks and Romans had built up such anger and rage in the Jewish community that they only wanted blood vengeance against their neighbors. The revolt and violence spread to Egypt as well. The idea among many prominent Libyan Jews such as Lukas was to create an Israeli empire based out of Jerusalem that encompassed the area from North Africa to Syria and which also included Cyprus. The revolt spread to Egypt where the city of Alexandria was seized as the frightened Roman auxiliaries fled the city without a fight. On Cyprus, the Jews quickly overcame the frightened garrisons and then massacred over 240,000 Greeks living on the island as they also destroyed their pagan gods and temples. In Judea, the Jewish rebels captured the city of Lydda and made it a base for operations to retake Jerusalem which was the only city that had a veteran Roman legion to garrison it out of fear of a possible revolt, but Trajan did not anticipate how widespread this Jewish revolt had become.

Trajan first became aware of the revolt when Jewish rebels had captured a number of cities in Turkey, Syria, and western Iraq and began attacking supply caravans that were to provide supplies and replacements to finish the conquest of the Parthian Empire. Trajan had to abandon his gains and the enemy capital which was quickly reoccupied by the Parthians that could not believe their luck that a disastrous defeat had turned into a great victory without them having to have won any battles against their arch enemy. The cities in Turkey, Syria, and western Iraq were quickly and brutally recaptured by the Roman legions. Trajan had a heat stroke on the return journey and died after boarding a ship in Turkey to take him back to Rome.

Hadrian became the new emperor in 118 and sent his grizzled veteran legionnaires to retake the rebel stronghold at Lydda in Judea. Lukas came to lead the revolt in Judea as the Jewish messiah to try to direct the rebellion. Lukas decided to pull all the rebel forces into the well fortified city to stake everything on a desperate siege battle to buy time as they held out hope that the Parthians would come to their rescue. In the meantime, the Parthians did not want to risk provoking the Romans to invade again so they sent emissaries to discuss making peace with Emperor Hadrian. Hadrian was actually very generous because he gave up claim to any Parthian territory that had been conquered by Trajan including Armenia if the Parthians would not attempt any aide in the form of troops or supplies to the Jewish rebels. The Parthians then ceased to even answer the frequent and frantic calls for help from the various Jewish rebel groups who by now had realized that there was a big difference between fighting Roman auxiliaries and fighting legionnaires.

The Jewish rebels in Lydda held out in vicious fighting along their walls and in desperate sorties to slow Roman progress in the siege for over three months before a Parthian emissary at the request of Hadrian came to give the bad news that no rescue was coming and to try to seek terms from the Romans. Lukas and the Jewish rebels knew that there was no hope of terms with the Romans, so they vowed to die as free men. The rebels had successfully destroyed and stopped the construction of two earthen and wood siege ramps from desperate and fanatical sorties during the siege. Roman siege towers were also burned down at great cost to the Jews in suicidal attacks out the gates of their fortifications. Hundreds of Jewish defenders attacked in waves oblivious to the clouds of arrows and stones fired by Syrian archers and slingers until the siege engines were consumed in fire.

After several months of fighting, the Romans had breached the city walls in several places by using turtle shield formations of legionnaires that undermined the walls of the city by pulling out the foundation stones with picks and iron bars that caused sections of the walls to collapse. Hundreds of Roman soldiers in the turtle shield formations were burned alive in this grim business by scalding oil that was poured down on them from above followed by torches that set the legionnaires on fire. After weeks of undermining the walls of Lydda at great cost, the Roman legionnaires made a final predawn attack at the breaches in the walls as archers and slingers kept the defenders back. Once inside the city, the Romans spared no Jewish man, woman, or child as Lydda was ransacked and destroyed. Lukas and the last Jewish rebels in the citadel had only broken swords and shields to defend with and were forced to surrender who were then tortured and crucified. The Talmud pays homage to the Jewish defenders of Lydda and praises them as having died as heroes while opposing Roman bondage.

As the Romans were conducting their siege of Lydda, other veteran Roman legions defeated the Jewish forces in Libya, Cyprus, and in Egypt. The rebels fought bravely in several pitched battles, but were no match for the veteran Roman legions that brutally reestablished control of the lost provinces. Tens of thousands particularly in Libya and Cyprus were crucified as several hundred thousand Jews were put to the sword without mercy. There was virtually no Jewish presence in either Libya or Cyprus after 118.

In the year 130, Emperor Hadrian visited the ruins of Jerusalem that had not been rebuilt after its destruction in the first Jewish War. Hadrian listened attentively as the Jewish rabbis and scholars told him of their great sorrow over the destruction of their temple and Jerusalem. Hadrian then pleased the Jewish community very much by promising to rebuild the Jewish temple and Jerusalem. What he failed to tell the Jewish leaders was that the temple would be rebuilt as a shrine to the god Jupiter and to himself and subsequent emperors as gods as well. Jerusalem was to be rebuilt as a Roman city called Aelia Capitalina complete with a red light district with brothels that would be adjacent to the temple and a coliseum for gladiator games. The ten percent tax that Jews used to pay for the upkeep of their temple in Jerusalem would be reestablished to pay for the rebuilding and the maintenance of the new pagan temple to Jupiter and the emperors. The next year the plan for the temple became public after Roman legionnaires began clearing and plowing up the foundation of the temple in order for construction to begin on the new pagan temple. Roman soldiers had to put down riots in Jerusalem and forbid any Jews from living in or even to set foot into Jerusalem again except for one day each year to attend Tisha B'Av to wail against the one wall left from the previously destroyed Jewish temple. To add insult to injury, Hadrian also forbid the Jewish practice of circumcision. To keep the peace, the elite X Fretensis and the VI Ferrata legions were stationed in Jerusalem to maintain strict order. The population of over one million Jews that still lived in Judea and Galilee began speaking of rebellion again if the messiah would finally come to rescue the Jews from Roman tyranny.

The Talmud states that Rabbi Akiva was the head of all sages at this time and was given great respect in Judea and Galilee. Rabbi Akiva had been preaching that the long awaited messiah was alive and well and living among them just waiting for the right time to reveal himself. He stated that the time had come for the messiah's one world government and the destruction of the Roman Empire because God was ready to smite the Romans for their desecration of the Temple Mount. In 131, Rabbi Akiva announced that the long awaited messiah was a handsome tall rugged looking man named Simon ben Kosba who was descended from King David. Simon ben Kosba was believed to have a special favor from God because he was the only Jewish warrior believed to have escaped the Siege of Lydda. Rabbi Akiva anointed this messiah king with special frankincense and myrrh oil which was only to be used to anoint and to coronate the true messiah. Rabbi Akiva gave Simon the name Bar Kokhba which means Son of a Star which connected him to a prophecy in Numbers 24:17 that stated that a star or scepter would rise out of Israel to crush their enemies. Unlike previous men to have been proclaimed as messiahs, most of Judea and Galilee came to believe that Bar Kokhba was the true messiah and came to rally to him as a unified nation.

There was a backlash though against Christians at this time that had come to have been viewed in Judea as a sect of Judaism and had been allowed to worship in the synagogues with Jews. The Christian idea that Jesus of Nazareth was the suffering servant messiah from Isaiah 53 to take their sins away was debated and not just dismissed by many Jews at this time. The historian Eusebius (263 – 334) states that there was a debate among the Christians and the Jewish scholars about who the messiah was supposed to be according to scripture. Was the messiah the suffering servant of Isaiah 53 to sacrifice himself for the salvation of Israel or was he the scepter or star of Numbers 24 that would smite the enemies of the Jews with war or was he both? There was anger among many Jews that the Christians did not want to rally around this new messiah nor to get involved in the revolt to come and there was a sadness among Christians that their message which had been getting wider support in Judea was being rejected to embrace the warrior messiah. This was when there became a true separate identity and message between Judaism and Christianity. Despite the differences over the identity of the true messiah, Eusebius states that Bar Kokhba convinced a number of Christians to join their Jewish brothers in the war against Rome.

Bar Kokhba was a capable and at times a brilliant commander. He rallied all the leading men of war in Judea and raised a Jewish army of over 200,000 troops who were very motivated to fight and die for

their warrior king messiah. Bar Kokhba pointed out to his commanders and leading men that the first Jewish War was plagued by dissen-
sion and a three way civil war as the Romans were outside battering
Jerusalem's walls and gates down. The second Jewish War was plagued
by no coordination between the Jewish forces in Libya, Cyprus, Egypt,
Mesopotamia, and Judea so that gains could not be consolidated and the
various Jewish forces could not come to each others aide. The mistake
was relying on the Parthians to come to everyone's aide. Bar Kokhba
went on to say that the Jews could not depend on the nations for protection. After speaking of the mistakes made in the previous revolts,
he asked for suggestions from his commanders on how to approach
fighting the Romans. All of the Jewish commanders favored attacking
the two legions in Jerusalem in a siege. Bar Kokhba pointed out that
the Romans had repaired the walls of Jerusalem and these defenses
would cause great losses among the Jewish forces. No, the Jewish forces
would attack all caravans laden down with supplies for the two legions
in Jerusalem. The way to defeat the Romans would be to first to cut
off their supplies. After a couple of months, the Romans would have
to come out of Jerusalem or would have to send a relief force to fight a
battle at a place that favored the Jewish forces if they were to open their
supply lines again. The Jewish commanders saw the brilliance of Bar
Kokhba's plan and agreed this would work.

Starting in 132, Jewish forces ambushed and captured every supply
caravan sent to bring supplies to the Roman legionnaires in Jerusalem.
Small garrisons of Romans were cut off as well, overwhelmed, and mas-
sacred. Emperor Hadrian at first did not appreciate the danger that
Bar Kokhba's revolt was to Rome's eastern empire. Hadrian dispatched
Publius Marcellus to lead the veteran XXII Deiotariana and the IX
Hispana legions along with 20,000 Syrian auxiliaries for a total army
of 30,000 – 35,000 to force open Rome's supply lines to their legions in
Jerusalem from Syria. Both Roman legions were noted for their efficient

brutality in combat. The Syrian auxiliaries were noted for their special hatred toward the Jews and were equally hated in return for cutting open the stomachs and intestines of over 2,000 Jews at the siege of Jerusalem. The Syrians cut open Jews to look for gold coins that some had swallowed so that they could later bribe their release from captivity. The Syrian auxiliaries also seemed to enjoy crucifying Jews of all ages and sexes in creative ways to maximize pain in both of the previous Jewish revolts and this was not forgotten.

Prior to the revolt, the Romans had hired Jewish blacksmiths to repair and to produce Roman armor, swords, and shields for the occupying legionnaires. What the Romans did not know was that these Jewish blacksmiths were also reproducing thousands of pieces of armor and weapons for secret Jewish armories for the day that the Jews would rise up again against their hated masters. Over 40,000 sets of Roman style armor and weapons had been made secretly and stored away for the next rebellion against Rome. The Jewish forces painted light blue stars of David on their shields with blue or white cloaks to distinguish their own forces from the red cloaks that the Romans wore. It was a shock though for the Romans in the early battles of the Bar Kokhba Revolt to see Jewish units armed and looking just like Roman legion units and using similar tactics in battle. The Jewish insurgents had drilled to advance behind a wall of shields while driving the enemy back with their short gladius swords being leveled to jab into an opponent's ribs or stomach in much the same way as the Romans had done.

In the Fall of 132, Publius Marcellus lead the two Roman legions with their Syrian auxiliaries south into the Golan Heights where Bar Kokhba had 40,000 Jewish troops in Roman armor standing in battle formation halfway up a large hill at the end of a valley. The valley was surrounded by large hills on the sides (the exact location of this battle is not known). Marcellus hesitated, but then ordered his entire force which he believed was superior to the Jewish forces to march straight toward the rebels. As the Romans started up the hill toward the Jewish army, Bar Kokhba ordered his entire force to attack briskly down hill, but without losing formation and maintaining their lines. The Jewish forces crashed into the Roman line and began driving them down hill without breaking discipline. The Romans and Syrians were being driven back when hundreds of shofars (a ram's horn that sounds like a trumpet) were blown from across the hills of the valley on both sides. Then the sound of 80,000 screaming Jewish warriors came as they swarmed down on both flanks of the Roman army. Terror gripped the Romans and the Syrian auxiliaries who broke ranks and tried to run away, but there was no where to go. The depredations and humiliations of the previous 70 years were remembered that day and no Roman or Syrian nor the commander escaped or was taken prisoner. The Jews lost only a few hundred men from the opening moments of the battle.

A few Roman scouts arrived at the site of the battle to witness the final moments of the disaster and hurried back to Jerusalem to tell the Roman governor of Palestine, Tineius Rufus, about the destruction of the relief force. Having not been supplied in months and being at their wits end, Rufus ordered his two legions to evacuate Jerusalem to move south to safety in Egypt before Bar Kokhba's forces in the Golan Heights could return from their victory to stop him. The Roman evacuation of Jerusalem started in an orderly way, but waiting to ambush these forces were close to another 80,000 Jewish warriors who weren't as well equipped or disciplined as the forces equipped and disciplined like the Romans were. These Jewish forces harassed and attacked the Romans all the way south into the Sinai Peninsula. The exhausted Romans lost all of their baggage and their catapult and ballista artillery that had to be abandoned. Of the 15,000 Roman troops and auxiliaries that left Jerusalem, close to 5,000 were killed by the constant hit and run attacks by the Jewish forces that lasted for several days during the retreat.

Hadrian did not take the news of the double disaster well. He ordered that the XXII Deiotariana and the IX Hispana legions were to be disbanded and never rebuilt because he wanted the shame of this defeat and the men who had died in it to be forgotten forever. Also, the name of Publius Marcellus (he is known from Jewish sources) was to be erased from all sources so that his name would be forever forgotten and not associated with defeat as had the names of other defeated Roman commanders such as Publius Varus who was only remembered for also getting 30,000 men massacred at the Battle of Teutoburg Forrest in 9 AD. Hadrian wanted a cover up of just how bad the situation in Palestine was. The cover up in a lot of ways has remained to this day because very little is commonly known even today about the Bar Kokhba Revolt.

Hadrian called for 12 veteran legions with auxiliaries (120,000 men) to be gathered from all around the empire to put this revolt down without mercy. A draft would raise another 120,000 men as replacements. Hadrian recalled his best general, Sextus Julius Severus from Britain which had been considered the main problem area of the Roman Empire before the revolt in Judea had broke out. All of the top generals and men that the empire had to offer were to be involved in the retaking of the Palestine. The Romans had not made this massive of an effort to defeat an enemy since the Punic Wars from several hundred years earlier. Julius Caesar had not even used these numbers of troops and effort to conquer Gaul (France) for Rome.

Hadrian's plan was for Severus to lead the best 35,000 troops that the empire had to move down from Syria to subdue the Golan Heights and Galilee before moving to place Jerusalem under siege. Despite previous misgivings, Tineius Rufus would lead 60,000 troops north from Egypt to act as a vice to force all of the Jewish forces back toward each other. Roman naval forces were to use their 30,000 legionnaires and marines to take coastal cities and to be used as replacements for losses as well. War was to be waged on the men, women, and children of Galilee and Judea's villages and towns. Mercy was not to be shown. The fact remained that Bar Kokhba had a formidable force of 200,000 Jewish troops that were confident after experiencing victory. The Roman forces would not be ready to implement Hadrian's plan until the summer of 134.

Bar Kokhba entered Jerusalem during Yom Kippur in October of 132 to great cries of triumph and praises to their long awaited messiah. The Jews had great celebrations throughout Judea and Galilee to mark the beginning of the renewed nation of Israel. Israel enjoyed a time of peace throughout 133 and toward the beginning of 134. Bar Kokhba as messiah was supposed to establish a one world government based out of Jerusalem, but this messiah was not in a hurry to pick a fight to conquer Rome to make this to happen. In fact, he was hoping that Rome would just leave the new Israel alone. A number of Jewish commanders felt that their forces should seize both Syria and Egypt since most of the Roman forces in both provinces had been defeated and they were ripe for the taking, but these ideas were overruled in the hope that peace could be achieved. After the great celebrations had ceased, many Jews feared the return of the Roman legions.

Spies had informed Bar Kokhba in early 134 that the Romans had large forces in both Syria and Egypt that were about to invade Israel from the north and south. Severus marched his 35,000 mostly elite legionnaires with Syrian archers and slingers into the Golan Heights where he found Bar Kokhba with his well armed 40,000 Jewish troops facing him halfway up a large hill. Severus had received word that there were hordes of lightly equipped Jewish warriors with a fanatical fighting spirit poised to ambush them behind the surrounding hills. Severus ordered his army into a large rectangle formation that could be defended from any and all directions at once. Severus moved his army to the base of the hill where the Jewish forces were and ordered his ballistae, catapults, and archers to rain arrows and projectiles into the Jewish infantry formations. The Jews then began firing their captured ballistae and catapult projectiles positioned in the surrounding hills back at the Romans. Projectiles created gaps in both sides' lines. Bar Kokhba then ordered the shofars to blast the signal to spring the ambush. Again, 80,000 screaming and fanatical Jewish attackers slammed into the legionnaires from three sides who held their positions and did not panic. Bar Kokhba led his force down the hill and into the Roman ranks. The fighting was desperate as Severus had to lead reserves he had kept in the middle of his formation to plug holes in the lines where his men had been killed in the vicious hand to hand fighting. The Jews fought with a fanatical desperation and killed and wounded thousands of hard fighting Romans, but the Syrian archers and slingers were causing frightful casualties among the Jewish ambush forces that did not wear armor other than an occasional helmet and shield. After taking more than 20,000 casualties, the Jewish ambush forces withdrew. Severus ordered the Roman forces to withdraw after suffering more than 7,000 casualties mostly from fighting the better armed Jewish forces who also had taken similar losses as well.

In the south in either southern Israel or Jordan, 60,000 Roman legionnaires and auxiliaries who had marched north from Egypt attacked a Jewish force of 40,000 who fought hard for an hour when they feigned retreat. Some of the Roman forces thinking that they had won the battle broke ranks and charged after the fleeing Jewish forces. The Romans charged headlong into a rocky desert pass where another 40,000 Jews were waiting in ambush. The Jews charged in and massacred close to 10,000 Romans who had rushed into the ambush. The rest of the Roman forces fell back to their fortified camps in the Sinai. Tineius Rufus was so angered at the legions that had broke ranks that he ordered them to go through decimation which involved one out of every ten legionnaires to be put to death by their comrades for not maintaining order on the battlefield. Decimation was decided by lots and was the greatest humiliation for a legion unit and pretty much guaranteed that discipline would be maintained in the future.

Severus ordered Tineius Rufus to not fight any more battles on ground of the enemies choosing where the Jews had the advantage and could set up ambushes. Severus ordered his commanders to try to avoid large battles, but to instead to strike villages to massacre all the inhabitants and to destroy any supplies that could be used by the enemy to aide their cause. The Romans began advancing deeper into Jewish territory where they would establish fortified camps that the Jews were reluctant to attack as smaller fast moving Roman forces attacked and killed Jewish families on farms and in villages. The Jews began sending out smaller forces to try to intercept these smaller Roman forces before they could massacre the Jewish noncombatants.

There were many small battles (sources say that there were 52) fought across Judea and Galilee where both sides won and lost battles. As hard as the Jewish forces tried, they could not prevent many of the massacres of Jewish men, women and children in the targeted villages. These smaller battles on open ground tended to favor the Roman cavalry forces to ride down and kill Jewish foot soldiers that did not have much in the way of cavalry themselves. The Jewish forces out of fear for their own families began dispersing to defend their own towns and homes which started a phase where more than 50 fortified towns and 985 villages were razed by the Romans with most inhabitants being massacred or captured to be sold into slavery according to Roman historian Cassius Dio (150 – 235). Bar Kokhba seemed to lose his confidence and was at a loss of how to turn the tide of war. As a messiah, he had no miracles to offer to help his beleaguered followers as the Romans converged on Jerusalem.

In 135, Bar Kokhba gathered perhaps as many as 20,000 Jewish defenders to defend Jerusalem as the Roman forces converged to place the city under siege. The Jews put up a spirited defense of the walls of Jerusalem for several weeks, but Severus ordered all sections of the city to be attacked at once so that the Jews could not concentrate their defenders in any one area as had been done in the long and costly siege of 70 AD. Bar Kokhba realized that Jerusalem was lost and made his escape to the fortress city of Betar where the Talmud says that 80,000 men, women, and children gathered for a last defiant stand. The Talmud also mentions that the slain in Jerusalem were piled up on the walls, in the streets and in every home where the bodies were left to decompose. The streets of Jerusalem were slippery from the blood and entrails spilled there. The members of the newly reestablished Sanhedrin were tortured to death including Rabbi Akiva who was flayed alive for his part in starting the war by naming Bar Kokhba as the messiah.

There is no record of Bar Kokhba claiming or whether he believed that he was the messiah. Some in their disappointment and anger toward Rabbi Akiva began referring to Bar Kokhba as Bar Kozeba (son of a lie). It had to have been evident that he had no miracles to offer his loyal followers at this point, yet he and his followers were determined to expend their lives dearly at the cost of Roman blood in a last stand at Betar.

Bar Kokhba made his last stand at the fortress of Betar.

The Siege of Betar lasted several months and was particularly bloody for both sides. Betar was considered the best fortified city in Judea which sat on top of a large hill that was steep on all sides. The Jews lost thousands in the many sorties out of the fortress to hinder the Roman siege work. The Romans and the Jewish forces each lost close to 20,000 fighting men in the battles outside the walls of Betar. Most of the fighting in the siege was around a wood and earthworks ramp that was being built up to the top of the wall so that Roman legionnaires could storm and take the city in a final bloody assault. The Jewish forces sortied out of the fortified walls several times a day to halt work on the ramp, but despite their best efforts, the ramp continued to slowly progress under the covering fire from archers and slingers until it came right up to the walls of Betar.

The Jews in the city had long been out of food and had grown weak. An old moldy piece of bread had been found and was offered to Bar

Kokhba who gave it instead to a boy who had bravely brought water under fire to the men defending the walls. Bar Kokhba knew that the next dawn would be the final battle. He ordered the men to find their wives and children and to pray with them and to hold them one last time before slitting their throats so that they would not be raped and enslaved to serve the pagans and their gods. After this was done and the weeping had stopped, the men went back to sleep at their defensive positions. Bar Kokhba prayed and wept at his own Gethsemane and Golgotha which had been the lot of the Jewish messiahs. Perhaps, he learned that being a messiah means pouring one's blood out for one's followers. After his weeping and praying, Bar Kokhba put on his purple royal robe and his shiny armor that had gold engravings in Hebrew on it and he slept with the reserve force that would be lead from the interior of the city to force back the Romans once they broke into the city from the ramp.

The final Roman assault on Betar during the Bar Kokhba Revolt.

As the sun rose in brilliant colors over Betar in early 136, there was a short time of silence as each man sought to make peace with God and to again pray for His mercy on what every man knew was their last day on Earth. The silence was suddenly broken by thousands of arrows from Syrian archers and projectiles from catapults that thudded loudly against the walls with loud cracks and took heads and torsos off of men's bodies that stood on the walls. The 10th Legion (Legio X Gemina) led the assault and marched up the ramp with a siege engine in a tight formation and quickly gained control of the wall and began pouring into the city. Bar Kokhba lead the reserve forward that crashed into the Romans with such force that they were driven back for a time, but more Romans continued to march up the ramp and into the city so that the exhausted Jewish forces started losing ground as more and more Romans pushed there way into the city. It was clear from his royal purple robe and the impressive looking armor who the messiah was supposed to be. The Roman who could bring Severus the head of Bar Kokhba was promised a bag of gold coins and a nice Italian villa. Bar Kokhba's body guards sold there lives with blood as they fought to defend their messiah. Then Bar Kokhba fought alone and according to Jewish sources killed 12 Romans before he was slain by a centurion veteran from Gaul (France). By sunset of that day, all of Betar's defenders had died with swords in their hands. The 10th Legion that had lead the assault that day had been practically wiped out in this last desperate battle.

Emperor Hadrian was so sickened by the losses that his forces (80,000 – 100,000 dead) had taken in the war that he refused to have the customary celebration with gladiator games in Rome. It was the only victorious war in Rome's history that was never celebrated. The Bar Kokhba Revolt was the greatest threat to Rome since the Spartacus slave rebellion. Many surviving Jews believed that God had avenged them when Hadrian became ill and died two years after the revolt.

Dio Cassus said that based on Roman census records that 580,000 out of the over 1 million Jews living in Palestine/Judea had perished in the war. The surviving Jews were then sent to live mostly in Europe in the final Diaspora. Judaism changed from the worship of Yahweh (God) dependent on the temple and a sacrificial system to a worship based on the study of the Torah and the Tanakh (Old Testament). The Jewish communities in Europe thrived and increased until they reached a population of 8 million by 1938. From 1938 until 1945, the Nazi Germans killed over 6 million Jews during the Holocaust. Most of the remaining 2 million Jews came back to establish the nation of Israel in 1948 to fulfill Bar Kokhba's dream for a return of a strong Jewish state. Bar Kokhba is remembered today as a patriotic freedom fighter in Israel's long struggle for a return to nationhood.

BIBLIOGRAPHY

Axelrod, Alan. *Little Known Wars*. Fair Winds Press, Beverly, Massachusetts, 2009.

Babylonian Talmud. Jerusalem, Ben Zvi Institute, 1988.

Dio's Rome, Volume V. – www.gutenburg.org

Eusebius, Ecclesiastical History. Catholic Encyclopedia, Advent Publishing, 1917.

Freund, Richard A. *Secrets of the Cave of Letters: Rediscovering a Dead Sea Mystery.* Humanity Books, Amherst, New York.

Jerusalem Talmud. Jerusalem, Ben Zvi Institute, 1988.

Jewish Encyclopedia: Bar Kokhba and the Bar Kokhba War.

Josephus, Flavius. *The Works of Josephus*. Peabody, MA: Hendrickson, 1980.

Morgan, Julian. *Hadrian: Consolidating the Empire*. New York: Rosen Central, 2002.

Neusner, Jacob, ed. *History of the Jews in the Second Century of the Common Era*. New York, Garland, 1990.

Richard Marks. *The Image of Bar Kokhba*: Pennsylvania State U, Press, 1994.

Yigael Yadin. *Bar Kokhba:_The Rediscovery of the Legendary Hero of the Second Jewish Revolt against Rome*. Random House, New York, 1971.

CHAPTER 6

The Mongol Conquest of China: 1205 to 1279

The Mongol conquest of China was the longest and most difficult conquest of any the Mongols conducted during their many successful invasions between 1190 and 1294. It took the Mongols an incredible seventy-four years to conquer the three nations of Xi Xia (Hsi-Hsia), the Chin (Jin) Dynasty, and the Song (Sung) Dynasty that made up China during the thirteenth century. The Mongols had overrun Central Asia, Russia, and had attacked Eastern Europe in the early thirteenth century while they were still in a slow drawn out series of wars to conquer China. The Mongols fought as a cavalry army of horse archers who rode around and weakened their enemies by firing tens of thousands of arrows into them and then sent in heavy cavalry armored with chain mail and armor to finish them off.

The deeper the Mongols advanced into China the more they had to cross and control rivers and lakes with ships and to conduct sieges which involved the types of warfare that were totally unfamiliar to them. They had to use captured Chinese troops to help them fight on ships and in sieges. Chinese census records from the early thirteenth century show that the three kingdoms in China at this time had over 100 million people living in them. When the Mongols would destroy one Chinese army of a hundred to two hundred thousand troops they often soon faced another army of similar size and then another. The Chinese ability to field such large forces slowed considerably the Mongol conquest.

The Mongols Empire was the largest in history.

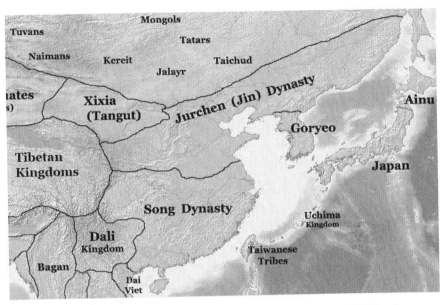

China in the early thirteenth century was split into the nations of Xi Xia, the
Chin (Jin) Dynasty in the north and the powerful Song Dynasty of the south.
It took the Mongols 74 years to conquer all three Chinese nations.

In 1205, Genghis Khan began looking south into China after he had
unified the Mongol tribes. The Mongols who had been discussed earlier were also known as the Xiongnu to the Chinese and as the Huns
to the Romans after they migrated to Europe. The Mongols were looking to conquer China rather than to be content to just raid for wealth
and women. The Mongols attacked Xi Xia which was south of the Gobi
desert in western China in 1205 by first taking its border settlements.
In 1209, 75,000 Mongols faced a large army of 150,000 Xi Xia troops
near their capital at Zhongxing. The Xi Xia had over 100,000 armored
pikemen and crossbowmen in large phalanxes in the center of the battle
line with 25,000 Tangut cavalry on each wing who fought the same way
as the Mongols. The Mongols had taken large casualties in an earlier
battle with the Xi Xia pikemen by charging their pike wall and were
determined to not repeat the mistake. Their light cavalry rode parallel

to the Chinese pikemen and crossbowmen firing thousands of arrows into them as most of the Mongol forces fought with the Tangut cavalry on the flanks. The Mongol and Tangut cavalry also rode parallel to each other firing thousands of arrows back and forth, causing thousands of casualties on both sides. Each side's cavalry also feigned retreat, but neither of them fell for the ruse. Finally, the Mongols attacked the Tangut cavalry with their heavy cavalry and with their light cavalry close behind firing arrows in support. The Tangut cavalry broke and retreated which left the huge phalanxes of the Xi Xia pikemen vulnerable. The Chinese pikemen had formed a giant rectangle that faced in all directions as they took repeated volleys of arrows which killed and wounded tens of thousands while the Mongols stayed mostly out of range of the Chinese crossbows. Eventually the Xi Xia pikemen lost unit cohesion. At that point, the Mongol heavy cavalry attacked the remaining demoralized and exhausted Chinese from all sides to finish most of them off.

The Mongols were unbeatable as horse archers on flat terrain. The horse archers would fire clouds of arrows for hours before the Mongol heavy cavalry would charge in to finish off the remaining disorganized, wounded, and demoralized enemy with lances, swords, and maces.

The Xi Xia capital of Zhongxing presented a problem for the Mongols who had little experience in sieges. In an earlier siege of the walled city of Volohai, the Mongols attempted a few suicidal assaults with scaling ladders which failed with heavy casualties. Genghis Khan then offered to lift the siege if the city provided the Mongols with a thousand cats and ten thousand swallows in cages. The puzzled citizens of Volohai granted the request but lived to regret it. Soon, the cats and swallows fled back into the city with wool that had been set on fire tied to each of them who then in turn set the city on fire. As the defenders were occupied trying to put the fire out, the Mongols scaled the undefended walls and massacred the city inhabitants.

Genghis Khan knew the trick would not work again. He also did not want a costly assault of the walls of Zhongxing, so he decided to break and release water from dikes on the Huang River to flood out Zhongxing. This plan backfired though when the Mongol camp and troops were swept away by the raging flood which drowned hundreds of Mongols and then left over two feet of standing water for miles around the city. The Mongols retreated, but returned in 1210 when the Xi Xia Emperor, Li Anquan agreed to give his daughter to Genghis Khan as a wife and to pay tribute to the Mongols as a vassal state. Xi Xia rebelled in 1218 and 1223 because they tired of providing the Mongols with so many men to fight in their wars of conquest, but the Mongols brutally put down all of these rebellions.

In 1210, an emissary of the Chin emperor appeared before Genghis Khan and asked for his submission and for tribute to be paid to the Chin (Jin). Genghis Khan answered that it was the Chin who needed to submit and pay tribute to him and then he turned to the south and spat on the ground as a gesture of defiance. With his flank secured by the conquest of Xi Xia, Genghis Khan was ready to attack the mighty Chin (Jin) Dynasty. In 1211, thirty thousand Mongol troops under Genghis Khan's greatest general, Subotai, assaulted the Great Wall.

The Mongols brought up thousands of archers who cleared an area of wall allowing others to scale the Wall with ladders and take possession of sections of it.

The Chin brought up reinforcements who recaptured the lost sections. Thousands died on both sides as the fighting continued back and forth like this for several days. The Chin brought up most of their army to back up the forces that were defending this section of the Great Wall.

What the Chin didn't know was that Subotai's attack was a diversion. Two hundred miles to the west, Genghis Khan with ninety thousand Mongols was crossing the Wall at its end in the Gobi Desert. The Ongut tribe, who had much in common with the Mongols, defended this section of the Wall. They defected to Genghis Khan and allowed the Mongols into China unmolested. As Genghis Khan's ninety thousand cavalry poured into China, Subotai's force left the Wall and headed west to join him. The Chin forces were out of position and scrambled to try to cut off the Mongols from Beijing.

Genghis Khan's cavalry caught close to 200,000 Chin troops on open ground near Badger Pass where the Chin hoped to block the Mongols' advance. The Chin formed up for battle with the pike phalanxes and crossbowmen in the middle and the armored heavy cavalry on the flanks. The outnumbered Mongol heavy cavalry engaged in a hotly contested battle on the flanks with the Chin cavalry as the densely packed Chin phalanxes and their crossbowmen held off the Mongol horse archers. At that point, Subotai's hard riding army arrived and struck the flanks and rear of the Chin army. After the Chin cavalry was defeated, the Chin pikemen who were made up of half militia conscripts broke and tried to flee but were cut down by the Mongol cavalry.

After this victory, Genghis Khan then separated his army into three forces that burned, pillaged, raped, and murdered the populations of ninety cities over the next six months. Despite the awful destruction, the Chin would not surrender and Genghis Khan became frustrated by the enormous size and scope of conquering a nation like Chin, so he entered into negotiations with the emperor and agreed to not attack any more cities. The Mongols had captured well over a hundred thousand Chinese military and civilian prisoners who now had no use to them so Genghis Khan had them executed.

Over the next year, the Chin moved their capital from Beijing (Peking) to Kaifeng which was much further south and began rebuilding their armies. Genghis Khan was angered by this and looked for an opportunity to attack the Chin again. In the spring of 1213, the Chin attacked the Mongol allied Khitan tribe in Manchuria. Genghis Khan came to the aide of his Khitan allies and attacked the Chin armies in Manchuria who fell back to their fortifications at Nankuo Pass. The Mongols were blocked from attacking Beijing by the well fortified Chin positions at Nankuo Pass and by the eastern sections of the Great Wall.

The Mongols headed into the pass, fought for awhile and then retreated as a ruse. The Chin forces, wanting to trap the fleeing Mongols, left their fortified positions in pursuit. The Mongols led the Chin out of the pass and into their own trap in which most of the Chin army was destroyed. Those Chin troops that had not pursued the Mongols fled their fortified positions and retreated to the Great Wall with the Mongols right behind. The Mongols caught and destroyed the remaining Chin troops as they tried frantically to retreat through the Great Wall. The Mongols captured and passed through the opened gates of the Great Wall that the Chin were trying to retreat through.

The Mongols moved south to besiege the over one million residents of Beijing. With walls and moats extending for over fourteen miles around the city and nine hundred towers, Beijing was a tough nut to crack. The Chin defenders in Beijing had double and triple crossbow ballistae and trebuchet catapults that fired clay pots filled with something similar to naphtha incendiaries that exploded and consumed with fire whatever they hit. The Chin also had one of the first biological-poison gas weapons in history. They fired round projectiles bound in wax and paper of 70 pounds of dried human feces with ground up poisonous herbs, roots and beetles packed in gunpowder. The projectiles were lit from a fuse and fired from a trebuchet which created on impact a cloud of toxic fumes that killed or disabled the unfortunate persons that breathed in the poison dried feces into their lungs.

The Mongols moved their lines back on a number of occasions to get out of range of these weapons because of the many casualties the gas clouds produced. The Chin also had clay pot fire bombs filled with incendiaries to throw from the walls as well as hot oil to pour down on attackers. The Mongols launched attacks against the walls with ladders, but lost thousands who were burned from the incendiaries and the hot oil. They next forced captured Chin soldiers to build and push forward siege engines as well as to lead the attack as human shields for the attackers. Chinese sources say that Chin soldiers would recognize family and friends and didn't want to kill their comrades leading the Mongol attack.

Many Chin prisoners were killed anyway from errant crossbow fire aimed at the Mongols and from the bombs used to burn down the siege engines before they could be used to get into the city. The Mongols and their Chinese human shields also dug trenches covered by cow hide up to the walls to undermine them, but the Chin dropped clay pot fire bombs from chains onto the trenches when they got close which exploded with such force that it left only a crater and no intact remains of the attackers. The Mongols had over sixty thousand deaths from the siege, half of which were Chinese that were increasingly relied on to act as human shields, but also to be assault the walls from siege engines. The Mongols increasingly relied on the Chinese to do the worst of the fighting in its sieges in China. The siege of Beijing dragged on for a year as starvation and disease began killing people on both sides of the walls, but the defenders had the worse of it with over a million souls to feed. Two Chin relief columns loaded down with food were defeated and captured by the relieved Mongols as the defenders were forced into cannibalism.

In June of 1215, the Chin commander escaped to Kaifeng where he was executed by the emperor for leaving his post. The desperate people of Beijing then opened the gates of the city to the Mongols who charged in and ransacked the city while massacring hundreds of thousands in revenge for their ordeal. The city was set on fire in the midst of the chaos which made the streets of Beijing slippery from the blood and grease of the dead that dripped down from the burned buildings. Over sixty thousand young women who feared being raped ran to a part of Beijing the Mongols had not yet reached and threw themselves to their deaths off of the high walls or hung themselves from the walls or from trees. A year later, the ambassador of Khwarezm described seeing slippery streets from the grease of burned people and mountains of bones of the dead in piles inside and outside of what had been the greatest city in the world.

Between 1205 and 1215, the Mongols killed over five million Chinese in the conquest of western and northern China with most of China still to be conquered. Despite the overwhelming victories, the Mongols were trapped in a long war of attrition in China.

Rather than finish the conquest of the Chin, Genghis Khan became sidetracked in 1217 in the destruction of Khwarezm (Iran, Pakistan, and Afghanistan) in an Islamic holocaust where over a million more people were massacred by the Mongols. During the campaign to conquer Khwarezm, the Mongols brought thousands of Chinese engineers, siege engines, and their crews with assault troops to conduct their sieges to reduce the Islamic fortifications.

Genghis Khan, however, wasn't finished with China. While he concentrated on Khwarezm, he sent an army under his general Muhuali to attack the outer cities of the Chin. In 1223, Muhuali with 100,000 troops attacked Chang'an, defended by 200,000 Chin who often sallied out in force in what was a very difficult and costly siege. Muhuali became ill and died. As soon as this happened, the Xi Xia troops abandoned the Mongol army and left for home which forced abandonment of the siege.

Genghis Khan returned to hunt down and kill the Xi Xia troops that had abandoned the Mongol army. At this same time, the Chin were also fighting the Song (Sung) Dynasty of southern China. In 1227, Genghis Khan died in the midst of planning another massive invasion of Chin. His son Ogedai Khan ascended the throne and sent envoys to the Chin who they promptly executed.

Subotai was sent to conduct one last effort to conquer the Chin for Ogedai in 1231. The Chin armies all faced north to prevent Subotai's 120,000 Mongols from crossing the Yellow River. Subotai sent a general named Tuli with 30,000 Mongols on an arduous journey to cross through the western Chinese mountains of Sichuan and through Song territory (with permission) and into southern Chin territory to face the capital of Kaifeng unopposed.

The Chin panicked thinking this force was the main Mongol army. They repositioned the majority of their troops to the south and pursued the Mongols with a massive force of over 300,000. The 30,000 Mongols had planned a retreat into the Sichuan Mountains as the huge Chin army followed. They fought a rearguard action with their archers in the rough mountainous terrain killing thousands of Chin. The Mongols led the Chin higher and deeper into the snow covered mountains. Tens of thousands of the unprepared Chin froze to death or fell off of the icy trails.

The Mongols circled back through passes in the mountains and destroyed the Chin baggage trains which caused starvation and added to the suffering that the Chin troops were enduring from the cold. Once Subotai knew that the main Chin army was in the mountains, he moved his 120,000 Mongols across the Yellow River against the much smaller Chin force left behind. Subotai's army moved to trap the Chin on the plain outside the capital. The Chin realizing too late that they were not facing the main Mongol army began desperately trying to get their forces out of the mountains to face Subotai and to defend the capital. The Chin retreat turned into a rout as Tuli's and Subotai's Mongol forces massacred the entire Chin army without mercy on open ground within sight of Kaifeng.

The Mongols had learned well how to conduct sieges from their Chinese prisoners and built an incredible fifty-four mile wooden wall of contravallation to hem in Kaifeng's over one million frightened inhabitants in their capital. In addition to the almost 150,000 Mongols that were conducting the siege, the Song supplied 300,000 troops to help finish off their Chin enemies.

For six days, the Mongol and Song armies assaulted Kaifeng's wall, but took thousands of casualties from a dreaded weapon called a "ho pao," a long bamboo tube filled with incendiaries that was placed in the ground. It could be lit with a fuse or thrown into siege engines from holes in the walls. It exploded with such force that it left craters in the ground and burned everyone around it. As many as fifty thousand Mongol and Song Chinese troops died in assaults against Kaifeng's stout walls. So it was clear to Subotai that a long slow siege would be required to reduce the Chin capital.

As it happened, plague soon broke out in Kaifeng. Subotai withdrew his forces to let the dread disease destroy his enemies while the Mongol and the Song armies remained plague free. Within a month, the Chin emperor committed suicide while the Mongol and Song armies once again assaulted and broke into Kaifeng and began massacring the survivors. Ogedai Khan ordered the massacre stopped and aide brought to the suffering people. Subotai wanted to massacre the entire surviving Chin population of over thirty million people (10 million Chin had already died) and to turn Chin land into grazing land for Mongol horses, but Ogedai Khan again overruled him because his Chinese advisors convinced him that the Chin population would provide taxes, craftsmen, and soldiers for future Mongol conquests.

One Chin army of a hundred thousand remained under a new claimant to the Chin throne. This army held out until 1234 before being destroyed by combined Mongol and Song forces. This ended the Chin Dynasty forever.

In 1235, the Song fielded their armies to occupy Chin cities that they understood the Mongols would give to them for their part in the war. These were former Song cities that had been lost in previous wars with the Chin Dynasty.

The Mongol forces refused to give these cities up and repulsed the Song using the same weapons and methods of defense they had learned from the Chin. This started another very long war in China between the Mongols and the Song that would last 43 more years and would cause over 10 million more Chinese deaths before the Mongols could claim victory.

In 1236, the Mongols captured the city of Xiangyang in Sichuan Province. The Mongols and the Song fought for control of Sichuan mostly around the city of Chengdu until 1248 before the Mongols had solid possession of this area. By 1248, the Mongols had killed hundreds of thousands of Song Chinese and had reduced many cities to rubble in Sichuan. One reason that the war was just fought in Sichuan and for so long in this early phase of the war was that the war with the Song was just a sideshow for the Mongols. Most of the Mongol efforts were directed toward the western parts of the empire.

In 1251, Mongke was elected as Great Khan and wanted to intensify the war with the Song Dynasty. In 1253, over a hundred thousand Mongol and Chinese allies captured Dali and Yunnan and crossed through Laos in a very difficult and costly journey to attack the Song Empire's southern flank. In 1254, the Mongol army and over one hundred thousand Song troops with a thousand war elephants fought a desperate battle near the border with Laos. The Mongol horses wouldn't charge the Song elephants, so the Mongols dismounted and fired flaming arrows to kill and enrage most of the elephants who became uncontrollable killing men on both sides. The battle degenerated into a chaotic bloody hand to hand battle of attrition. Both armies virtually annihilated each other with twenty thousand Mongols retreating back into Laos. In 1257, Mongke made the mistake of invading Da Viet (North Vietnam) and lost most of the rest of his army and horses to disease in the intense tropical conditions there.

In 1258, Mongke Khan pulled together over 300,000 Mongol and Chinese soldiers to face in Sichuan a massive army of over 400,000 Song troops. In 1259, both sides met at the Battle of Diaoyucheng with huge cavalry battles on the flanks and a giant infantry battle in the middle between the Mongol-Chinese and the Song troops. During the battle, Mongke Khan collapsed from cholera and dysentery and died. The battle ended in stalemate with over 100,000 dead from both sides including Song general Wang Jian. The new commanding Song General Jia Sidao collaborated with Genghis Khan's grandson, Prince Kublai, and worked out a deal where the Song army could occupy Sichuan, but under Mongol authority.

After the Mongol forces left Sichuan, General Jia Sidao reneged on his agreement with Prince Kublai and reoccupied Xiangyang and returned Sichuan to Song control. It would take the Mongols until 1273 to recapture the city. The Song Emperor Lizong was also facing a number of peasant uprisings and was suspicious of the intentions of Jia Sidao. In 1260, General Jia Sidao took his army back into Song territory and established himself as prime minister with a new young emperor named Zhao Qi who would serve as a puppet ruler. After Prince Kublai had left Sichuan, he took his army to Mongolia to make his claim as the new khan of the Mongol Empire. In 1260, Kublai Khan became the khan of the Mongols. Eleven years later, he established the Yuan Dynasty in China with himself as emperor.

Kublai Khan sent envoys to the Song in 1260, but they were imprisoned. In 1265, a Chinese allied naval force destroyed a hundred Song ships in a river battle and Mongol troops defeated the isolated and cut off Song army to regain control of part of Sichuan again. The Song were so difficult to conquer because southern China was covered with large walled cities protected and supplied by rivers. The Mongols couldn't fight the Song with their tried and true horse archer tactics. Instead, they had to employ huge numbers of Chin Chinese to conduct sieges and to fight in river fleets with the Mongols fighting as archers and cavalry. The key to conquering Song China was the twin fortress cities of Xiangyang (Hsiang-yang) and Fancheng. Both fortress cities had over five miles of 20 foot thick walls with one hundred yard wide moats which covered the convergence of both the Han and Yellow (Yangtze) Rivers. Kublai Khan's forces weren't ready to assault these cities until a large river fleet and enough siege machines and trebuchet catapults had been built for a long siege.

In 1268, the Mongols built fortifications down river from Xiangyang on the Han River to cut off re-supply of the city by ship. Most Song ships were still able to run by the Mongol forts to re-supply and to reinforce Xiangyang and Fancheng until five hundred allied Chinese ships were brought in to block the passage between the Mongol forts. Over thirty-two miles of siege lines consisting of wooden walls and fortifications were built around both Xiangyang and Fancheng on both sides of the Han River. The Mongols and their Chinese engineers set up their trebuchets about one hundred yards from the walls of both cities and began firing explosive incendiary clay bombs, and the exploding bio-chemical projectiles they had learned about from the Chin at the Siege of Beijing. The Song also fired incendiary bombs and bio-chemical projectiles at the Mongols as well, which caused great destruction and loss of life on both sides. Lulls developed in the bombardments on both sides when men died or ran away from their posts to get away from the bio-chemical clouds.

Soldiers from both sides could be seen running and screaming in agony to jump into the moat or river to end their torment from the ghastly Chinese incendiaries. The Mongols had to eventually pull back because they were getting the worst of the bombardments given that their wooden siege walls and trebuchets would burn up from the bombardments leaving the Mongols with no cover as compared to the stout rock and masonry walls that the twin cities provided for the Song.

In 1269, Kublai Khan sent twenty thousand more troops to replace losses from the previous year of fighting. It was also at this time that over three thousand Song Ships attacked the Mongol forts on the Han River in an effort to break the blockade. Over five hundred Song ships were sunk with the loss of two thousand men by Kublai Khan's brilliant admiral Liu Cheng (with five hundred ships) who had defected to the Mongols from the Song. Many of the Song ships were consumed by the clay pot incendiary bombs being hurled from the Mongol fortifications. Other ships were abandoned due to the choking gases when they were hit by the exploding bio-chemical projectiles. Heavily armored Mongol and Chinese storm troopers boarded Song ships as they beheaded hundreds of soldiers and sailors. The river had turned a bright red from the great quantities of blood and all of the dismembered bodies floating in the water.

In 1270, Kublai Khan sent seventy thousand additional Mongol and Chinese troops and five thousand ships to bolster the siege forces. A Song land force of 200,000 tried to relieve the twin cities, but they were defeated with huge casualties when they assaulted a firing line of dis-mounted Mongol archers backed by trebuchets that had been brought from the siege lines. More than 50,000 Song troops were cut down try-ing to cross large fields of flooded rice paddies before their army turned retreated. The besieged Song tried several unsuccessful attempts to break out, but were defeated each time with thousands of casualties. In 1271, a hundred Song ships broke through a boom across the Han River to bring three thousand soldiers and much needed supplies to Xiangyang.

The siege dragged on and on with no real advantage for either side when Kublai Khan decided to bring Muslim engineers, captured during the Siege of Baghdad in 1258, to China to build a giant 40 ton trebuchet, 18 yards high with a ten-ton counter weigh. It was capable of hurling a two-hundred-pound projectile over two hundred yards to breach the walls of Xiangyang and Fancheng.

Kublai Khan decided to concentrate his forces and firepower on Fancheng rather than to take Xiangyang. In late 1272, the Mongols set up their giant trebuchet two hundred yards from Fancheng and began firing two hundred pound projectiles that cracked loudly against the city's masonry walls with great force as the inhabitants screamed in fear. After a few days, it opened a thirty yard breach as Mongol storm troopers met Chinese defenders as they fought desperately for control of the breach. For days, men fought and died in the vicious battle of the breach. The Mongols on several occasions had to pull the mounds of dead back to even be able to fight in the breach.

The Song were able to continuously throw more soldiers into Fancheng to defend the breach from a pontoon bridge that connected to Xiangyang across the Han River. The Mongols called off the assault on the breach to widen it further with their giant trebuchet. At the same time, their river fleet attacked the pontoon bridge. Desperate fighting developed on the bridge and on Song and Mongol ships. The Song burned several Mongol and Chinese ships with incendiary bombs fired from trebuchets when ships that were tied to the bridge were hit and the fire spread to the pontoon bridge and consumed it. Hundreds on both sides were trapped on the bridge and were burned or drowned when they fell or jumped into the river with their armor on.

With Fancheng cut off from reinforcements, the Mongols assaulted the widened breach. The disheartened defenders held the breach for several hours before resistance broke and the Mongols poured into the city and began massacring the inhabitants. The Mongols took the last three thousand Song soldiers and seven thousand inhabitants to the walls facing Xiangyang and in full view slit the prisoner's throats and threw them off the wall and into a mountain of bodies.

The Mongols dismantled their giant trebuchet and repositioned it across the Han River facing Xiangyang. Its first shot collapsed a tower in a great crash. At that point, Kublai Khan offered to spare the inhabitants and to reward the Song commander if he would surrender the city. Xiangyang did surrender, opening the Song heartland to the Mongols. The siege had lasted five years from 1268 to 1273.

Right after the bad news of the fall of Xiangyang reached the Song capital at Hangzhou, the thirty-four- year-old Emperor Zhao Qi died and his four-year-old heir, Zhao Xian, became the new emperor. The grandmother, Empress Dowager Xie, set herself up as regent after discrediting and removing from power the Prime Minister Jia Sidao.

In 1274, the Mongols with 200,000 infantry (with half being Chinese) and 800 large ships and 5,000 smaller ones (74,000 Chinese sailors) under the Mongol General Bayan faced a formidable Song army numbering over 700,000 soldiers and sailors with 4,500 ships that were still in scattered garrisons around the Song nation. The Mongol army headed down the Han River and was again blocked by two fortresses connected across the river by a chain and defended by 100,000 Song soldiers. Rather than get into another siege that could last years, the Mongol and Chinese army carried their ships on poles around the fortresses with a blocking force of Chinese infantry and Mongol archers to hold off the Song forces that sallied out to try to stop them.

After a few weeks, the Mongol and Chinese had successfully bypassed the fortresses and were in the flood plains of the Yellow River (Yangtze). The Mongols now faced on the Yellow River the impregnable fortress Yang-lo, the Song fleet, and the maze of lakes and inlets that defend Wuhan. The Mongols sacrificed several thousand Chinese troops on a frontal attack on Yang-lo supported by part of the fleet, while most of the Mongol army carrying a number of ships bypassed the fort and Song fleet and crossed the Yellow River upstream. The Mongol and Chinese fleet came down the Yellow River and attacked the Song fleet from both front and behind. The Song fleet was so packed together on the Yellow River that incendiary clay pot bombs fired from catapults set much of it on fire. Thousands perished in the flames. Fortress Yang-lo and the cutoff Song troops surrendered the next day.

In an effort to redeem himself by stopping the Mongol juggernaut, Jia Sidao set out in 1275 from the capital of Hangzhou at the head of 100,000 Song troops and another fleet of 2,500 ships chained together to block the 2 mile wide Yellow River at Jiankang. A massive cavalry and infantry battle took place on both sides of the river. The Mongols and Chinese pushed back the Song army and boarded their ships from both ends of the river as they beheaded thousands of Song troops and captured 2,000 ships in another overwhelming victory. Jia Sidao was later assassinated by a Song officer for the defeat.

The Empress Dowager Xie sent daily offers of land and wealth to Bayan and Kublai Khan to try to salvage some form of the Song Dynasty, but the Mongols were only interested in unconditional surrender. The city of Changzhou which was close to the capital refused an offer to surrender peacefully and was burned and all of its inhabitants massacred. With only untrained militia forces left to defend it, the Song capital was in a panic with many people fleeing. Thousands of women and their families committed suicide together rather than to endure the humiliating rapes and murder that the people of Hangzhou knew would come. Over a hundred beautiful royal courtesans drowned themselves rather than be given to Kublai Khan as wives.

On February 21, 1276, the boy Emperor Zhao Xian came out of Hangzhou and bowed down to Bayan and toward the north in obeisance to Kublai Khan and turned over the capital and the Song Empire to the Mongols. The Mongol troops were ordered to not rape or harm the people of Hangzhou and gave the people much needed food items. The people of the occupied Song Empire were told to continue their normal lives and to buy and sell with Song money which would still be recognized as legal tender. The Empress Dowager Xie and her grandson Zhao Xian were treated well in Beijing by Kublai Khan's wife Chabi.

But the war wasn't over. Before the capitulation, the younger brothers of Zhao Xian (Prince Zhao Xia and Prince Zhao Bing) were taken toward the coast where every soldier and boat was gathered to continue Song resistance. As the Mongol and Chinese armies moved south in pursuit of the young princes, multiple thousands committed suicide in fear of what the Mongols would do to them. The city of Tanzhou (Changsha) put up a desperate fight, but the Mongol trebuchets breached the city walls for a last Mongol assault and massacre. Before the Mongols could take the city, the people of Tanzhou began committing mass suicide. Men slit the throats of their families before slitting their own throats while others drowned themselves in wells. Thousands hanged themselves from trees in the city or burned their homes with themselves inside.

Upon entering the city, the Mongols found tens of thousands of dead from suicide. Several thousand people who hadn't killed themselves earlier jumped into the Xiang River to drown. Untold thousands committed suicide in this way as the Mongol army continued toward Guangzhou (Canton), China.

In 1278 and 1279, the Song loyalists with the two princes had gathered a formidable force of 200,000 troops and a fleet of 1,000 large Song warships that were stationed in the waters off of Guangzhou. The Song did not have a land base to work from so they roped together their ships into a solid water fortress. On March 19, 1279, 300 Mongol and Chinese ships attacked the Song fleet unexpectedly in an early morning fog. The

Mongols had built archery platforms where they could sweep the decks of the Song ships of their soldiers and crews followed by storming parties of heavily armored Mongol and Chinese troops to capture the Song ships and then to continue the same tactics on the next ships. The sea turned red with the blood and bodies of tens of thousands of dead. About mid-day, it was clear that the Song were defeated and tens of thousands of Song troops including officials with the two young princes jumped into the sea with weights tied to them to drown themselves rather than to submit to the Mongols. Chinese sources say that 100,000 Song troops and ship crews died in the battle or committed suicide with another 100,000 that were captured and later executed.

This last battle ended the Song Dynasty and completed the Mongol conquest of all of China. It had taken seventy-four years and the lives of twenty-five million Chinese to complete.

Two years before Kublai Khan died in 1294, the census he ordered recorded the population of China as seventy-five million. This was down from the one hundred million recorded early in the thirteenth century. The ramifications of the Mongol conquest of China were felt for some time because the population of China would remain at seventy-five million until the sixteenth century when a population boom took place during the Ming Dynasty. After the Ming overthrew the Mongols in 1368, they became obsessed with improving and lengthening the Great Wall.

BIBLIOGRAPHY

Davis, Paul. *Besieged.* Oxford University Press, Oxford, 2003.

Dictionary of Wars. Editor, George Childs Kohn, New York; Checkmark Books, 2007.

Gabriel, Richard. *Genghis Khan's Greatest General:_Subotai the Valiant.* Greenwood Publishing Group, Westport, CT., 2004.

Haskew, Michael. Jorgensen, Christer. McNab, Chris. *Fighting Techniques in the Oriental World_.* Amber Books, Dubai, 2008.

Li Bo, Zheng Yin. *5,000 Years of Chinese History.* Inner Mongolian People's Publishing Corp, 2001.

Man, John. *Genghis Khan.* Bantam Books, London, 2005.

Man, John. *Kublai Khan.* Bantam Books, London, 2006. (Man provides very good information on the Chinese incendiary and biological-gas weapons that I mention in the article.)

Turnbull, Stephen. *Genghis Khan & the Mongol_Conquests 1190-1400.* Osprey Publishing, New York, 2003.

CHAPTER 7

Death by A Thousand Cuts:
Kublai Khan's Nightmare in Syria, Japan, Burma, Vietnam and Java

From 1206 to 1294, the Mongols created the largest empire that had ever existed. The Mongols at the height of their power had conquered much of Russia, Eastern Europe, Central Asia, China, and parts of the Middle East and Southeast Asia. The Mongols created this massive empire with horse archers who were virtually unbeatable on the steppes and flat grasslands that most of their empire sat on. It was under Kublai Khan's Reign from 1260-1294 that the Mongols began seeing their power decline with defeats against enemies that wouldn't fight in the Mongol way or on terrain that favored their horse archer tactics. Kublai Khan bankrupted the Mongol Empire by continually launching expensive expeditions into areas that didn't suite Mongol tactics and brought continual defeat. These failed Mongol invasions weakened the Mongol Empire so that when Kublai Khan died in 1294, the empire split into four sections.

The first real defeat that the Mongols faced was at the Battle of Ain Jalut in Syria on September 3, 1260. An army of 20,000 Mongols with some Georgians and Armenians left the pasture lands of Armenia and ventured into the hot deserts of southern Syria. As the Mongol horde traveled through the desert, many Mongols were suffering from heat exhaustion in their hot leather armor. Many of the four Mongol horses that each Mongol warrior took on campaign (so that they would always have fresh mounts in battle) were dying from heat exhaustion. There was no water and grazing land available for the horses that started dropping dead after a few days in the desert.

On September 3, the Mongol force arrived at Ain Jalut in southern Syria completely worn out with each warrior having only one or two exhausted Mongolian steppe horses. In battle formation near the village of Ain Jalut was a force of 10,000 elite Mamluk horse archers from Egypt mounted on large Arabian Stallions with another 10,000 mounted Mamluks hiding behind some hills to the rear to ambush the Mongols. As the exhausted Mongol army moved into battle formation, the Mamluks were riding up and firing new small caliber hand canons which startled and terrified the Mongol horses. The battle raged with each side riding parallel to the other firing thousands of arrows which caused high casualties on both sides. After a couple of hours of hard riding and trading volleys of arrows, the Mamluks used the old Mongol ruse of faking retreat back to the hills with the Mongols following close behind in the false belief that they were winning the battle.

The Mamluks hidden behind the hills saw that this was the time to spring their ambush and charged into the Mongols from all sides with swords, maces and lances. The Mongols attempted to break out of the trap, but the overheated Mongol horses that had not been changed for fresh horses could barely trot at this point. The Mamluks charged into the fray yelling, "My Islam! My Islam!" as they rode down and engaged all of the disorganized groups of Mongols. The Mongols put up a desperate fight and killed quite a number of Mamluks before they were cut down to a man. The day had been very bloody for the Mamluks as well, who had lost thousands in the battle.

Kublai Khan didn't take news of the defeat well and sent another Mongol expedition into Syria in 1262 which was also beaten in a very similar battle at a village called Homs. Kublai Khan wanted to send a third army into Syria in 1263, but Berke Khan in the Caucasus region refused to join this third invasion and stated that the Mongols had no business in Syria and that he wasn't going to send his men there to die. Hulagu Khan's army was sent to fight Berke Khan in the Caucasus instead and there never was another attempt to take control of Syria by the Mongols again. This campaign showed the Mongol extent of power in the southwestern part of their empire was just inside of the desert regions of the Middle East. The Mongols were great steppe fighters, but not great desert fighters. These defeats led to several efforts by other Mongol warlords to attempt to break away from the Mongol Empire in Central Asia even during the reign of Kublai Khan.

Kublai Khan's next obsession was the conquest of Japan in 1274 and 1281. Kublai Khan had received the submission of Korea (Goryeo) shortly after becoming Khan of the Mongol Empire in 1260 (Korean rebels continued to resist Mongol control until 1270) and had mistakenly thought that Japan was a vassal state of Korea. In 1266, Kublai Khan sent emissaries to Japan asking why the Japanese had not already recognized themselves as a vassal state and sent tribute to the Mongols as Korea had done. The emissaries returned without a reply. In 1268, 1269, 1271, and 1272 Mongol emissaries returned empty handed from Japan again. Kublai Khan then ordered an invasion fleet to be prepared to force Japan's submission in blood and fire.

In 1274, an army of 23,000 Mongol, Chinese and Korean soldiers was ready to cross over to Japan in 300 large ships and 500 smaller ones manned by 6,700 mostly Korean sailors. On Oct. 5, 1274, the Mongols cleared the beaches of Japanese samurai warriors at Tsushima Island (half way between Korea and Japan) by launching exploding shells from catapults from their ships. The Mongols formed a type of phalanx with several thousand warriors on the beach and moved inland. A number of samurai warriors attempted to challenge individual Mongols to one on one duals through heraldry when they were shot through by Mongol arrows. Finally, the Mongols accepted the challenge of a samurai warrior named, Sukesada, who went on to kill 25 Mongols in individual combat including a 71/2 foot tall giant before he was pierced and killed by three arrows by his frustrated enemies. The Mongols advanced as the samurai warriors attacked into a wall of arrows. The samurai fought to the death, killing a number of Mongols despite being wounded with arrows protruding from each warrior. The Mongols went on to storm a samurai castle while killing all the inhabitants of Tsushima except for a few women.

On Oct.14, the Mongols made short work of 100 samurai and the fishermen of Iki Island before storming the castle. A samurai named, Sozaburo, was asked by the island's Daimyo (warlord) to escape with his beautiful daughter, Katsura, so that she wouldn't be raped. The last 36 samurai in the castle held off the Mongols in order to give the Daimyo and his family time to commit suicide while the castle burned down around them. The young women of the island were then stripped and ravaged before being nailed by their hands to the bows of the Mongol ships. As they tried to pass by the Mongol fleet, Katsura was killed by several arrows and only Sozburo escaped alive from Iki Island.

Throughout Japan, a call for prayer to the ancestors for a miracle went out from all of the Shinto and Buddhist shrines and temples. On October 19, 6,000 samurai gathered on the beach of Hakata Bay on the Island of Kyushu to face the Mongol horde. The samurai were shocked to see the bodies of the women from Iki Island nailed to the bows of the Mongol ships and realized what Japan faced if they didn't stop the Mongols on the beaches. The Mongols launched exploding catapult shells and poison tipped arrows to get several thousand warriors onto the beach at Hakata Bay. The samurai attacked and fought desperately while taking and causing heavy casualties. The Mongols had taken and burned the village of Hakata, but then retreated to their ships for the night because of the heavy casualties and little headway that they had made that day. That night a typhoon or storm called a Kamikaze or "Divine Wind" came up and destroyed the Mongol fleet and saved Japan. Over 22,500 of the total Mongol force died in the waters off of Hakata Bay when their ships were swamped or collided with each other or against the rocky shoreline. Most of the 7,200 survivors were Koreans whose ships left the Mongol fleet on the evening of Oct. 19 when they saw that a very bad storm was coming. All of Japan gave thanks at the shrines and temples for their miracle victory.

Typhoons called the Kamikaze or divine wind destroyed
the Mongol fleets in 1274 and 1281.

Enraged, Kublai Khan sent 5 emissaries again in 1275 to demand that Japan submit to him. The emissaries were beheaded and their heads were displayed in defiance. Kublai Khan then sent 5 more emissaries in 1279 to demand Japanese submission and again these were beheaded as well. A massive invasion fleet of 4,500 ships was ordered to be built and ready in a year, but the ships weren't ready until 1281. In order to fill Kublai Khan's order for 4,500 ships, the Chinese and Korean shipyards had to hastily build ships with many defects because they didn't have time to properly build them. In addition, the shipyards had to impress many flat bottomed river boats into service because they couldn't build so many ships in such a short amount of time. River boats often floundered and sank if they encounter rough and choppy seas, but Kublai Khan was impatient and threatened death for the overseers if the deadlines weren't met. Expecting another invasion in 1280, the Imperial Court in Kyoto, Japan ordered all shrines and temples to pray for another miracle.

In the Spring of 1281, 40,000 Mongols, Chinese, and Koreans in 900 ships left from Korea and 100,000 Mongols and Chinese soldiers left for Japan from southern China in a thirteenth century version of shock and awe. The Mongol fleet from Korea anchored at Hakata Bay, but they couldn't get a foothold on the beaches because the Japanese had built a sea wall along the entire bay and the samurai defended it well. The Mongols set up a camp on Shika Island which was just off of Hakata Bay. The samurai then came on boats at night to the island and ambushed the camp taking over 2,000 Mongol heads and driving thousands into the sea before withdrawing. The samurai were also came out into the bay in boats that would hold 20-40 warriors and attacked individual ships and beheaded everyone on board before returning to land. Each morning the Mongols would find several ships with all headless corpses on board. The Mongols decided to counter by chaining their ships together in a mass in the bay. The samurai then sent fireboats into this Mongol mass of ships. Many ships were burned and hundreds of Mongols died before they could unchain and disperse the fleet.

The rest of the 3,500 ships with its 100,000 soldiers arrived from China and it was decided to try to land 30 miles up the coast of Kyushu to Imari Bay. The Samurai army followed the Mongols along the coast and met them in force at the beaches of Imari Bay. A two month battle ensued daily on the beaches where both the Mongols and the samurai took heavy casualties in desperate hand to hand fighting. The Japanese also continued their nightly raids by boats loaded with samurai warriors and from fire ships on the Mongol fleet.

The Mongols had become demoralized with hundreds and sometimes thousands of daily casualties. The Korean sailors noticed that a typhoon was coming again and the Mongol fleet tried to make it out to sea to avoid the rocks of Imari Bay, but they didn't make it. The ships were jammed into each other where they broke up. Other ships were broken on the rocks and shipwrecked on the beaches of the bay. Thousands of Mongol survivors who were washed onto the beaches were beheaded when they were found by the samurai. It was the worst naval disaster in history with over 130,000 Mongols, Chinese and Koreans who had died. Only perhaps 10,000 Koreans who manned some of the sturdier built ships survived the disaster. All of Japan gave thanks at the temples and shrines for this second miracle Kamikaze wind that saved Japan. In 1284, a defiant Kublai Khan ordered ships to be built for a third invasion of Japan, but he had to cancel the invasion in 1286 because the Mongols were already overcommitted to already planned invasions of Burma and Vietnam. The Mongol tax coughers went bankrupt from just too many expensive and risky invasions to meet Kublai Khan's ambitions.

In 1273, Kublai Khan sent emissaries to demand Burma's submission. The emissaries were treated well by King Narathihapate and sent back without a reply, but he had a second group of emissaries executed. The Burmese then invaded the Thai state of Kaungai which was a protectorate of the Mongol Empire. In 1277, 12,000 Mongol horse archers entered the mountainous jungles of Burma and camped near the village of Baoshan. The Burmese advanced against the Mongols in the jungle with 200 elephants and 20,000 infantry. The Mongols had never seen elephants before and were quite frightened by them. The elephants were making a lot of noise and the terrified Mongol horses refused to charge the beasts and were throwing hundreds of their riders to the ground. The Burmese elephants crashed into the disorganized Mongol line causing havoc. The unhorsed Mongols were picked off by Burmese archers from the castles on the backs of their elephants. The mounted Mongols regrouped a few hundred yards back and dismounted to form a firing line of archers. The Mongol archers then concentrated hundreds of arrows into the charging elephants who in pain and in rage turned on the Burmese infantry and trampled many while smashing their castles that they carried on the trees in the jungle before they ran off. The Mongols gathered their horses out of the jungle and rode down and killed many of the routed Burmese infantry.

Both the Burmese and the Vietnamese used war elephants in battle
that also looked and fought in much of the same way in war.

The Mongols continued their advance through the hellish jungles when the heat and disease began decimating the Mongol army and their horses. The Mongols abandoned Burma after half of their men and 2/3rds of their horses died from disease and returned to China to present Kublai Khan with 12 elephants as his only reward for this invasion.

Kublai Khan needed to save face from his earlier defeats and ordered a force of 10,000 Mongols to again invade Burma in 1283. The Mongols dismounted from their horses and with archery defeated the Burmese army and elephants at the Battle of Bhamo. King Narathihapate's army then fled to the jungles to fight a guerrilla style war. The Mongols again began taking heavy losses from disease in the hot, humid tropical climate of Burma. An agreement was reached for the Mongol army to leave Burma before their entire force would die from disease. Kublai Khan put a brave face on at court, but he knew he hadn't really won anything in Burma.

In 1286, the Burmese King Narathihapate was assassinated by his son, Thihathu, and the Mongols wanted to exploit the chaos that this caused in Burma. Kublai Khan sent his grandson, Essen-Temur, to re-conquer Burma. In 1287, Essen-Temur with 7,000 Mongol archers defeated 30,000 Burmese who attacked across a large field of rice paddies near the Burmese capital of Pagan. The Mongols then looted Pagan's 5,000 Buddhist monasteries and temples of their gold and silver. The Burmese once again retreated to the jungles and prayed for revenge for the desecration of their temples and once again disease began decimating the Mongols and forced a withdrawal. The Mongols tried to subjugate Burma again in 1299, but by 1301 they had to withdraw with the same results as before. The tropical jungles and climate of Burma was another natural barrier to Mongol world conquest that Kublai Khan never seemed willing to accept.

In 1279, Kublai Khan began also looking at the two kingdoms of Vietnam, which were Da Viet (also known as Annam and North

Vietnam), and Champa (South Vietnam) for subjugation. The Mongols had briefly occupied Da Viet in 1257, but had to retreat due to the many deaths by disease. Kublai Khan had found out that former Song Dynasty officials were living in Champa and he demanded the return of these former enemies and submission to the Mongols. Kublai Khan's real motivation was to control the lucrative spice trade that came from Java through Vietnam and into China. Champa had sent some nice gifts to Kublai Khan in 1279 and 1280, but no signs of submission. In 1282, Kublai Khan sent 5,000 Mongol troops in 100 ships under a commander named Sodu to Champa's capital at Vijaya (Qui Nhon today).

The Mongols found the capital mysteriously abandoned and thought that they had won an easy victory, but King Indravarman V of Champa had set up several camps deep in the jungles and mountains of South Vietnam. Sodu took his 5,000 men into the jungles to find the enemy sanctuaries. As the Mongol force was moving single file through elephant grass, the unseen Cham warriors began firing arrows and bolts from crossbows through the elephant grass killing over 200 enemy warriors. More Mongols came up and began chasing the Cham warriors who fell back again unseen when another 200 Mongols fell into pits with sharpened dung covered bamboo stakes that impaled bodies and feet. Those wounded Mongols not killed died within days from infection caused by the dung on the bamboo that pierced their feet. Sodu and the Mongols pushed on and continued to be ambushed by an unseen enemy and then entered into an area containing hundreds of pits with sharpened bamboo with dung on them or boar traps that impaled one to three men. Then the rains came and the Mongol's leather armor became soaked and rotted and had to be thrown away. Disease was taking a toll as well. Sodu retreated back to Vijaya with only 2,500 men and no real contact with the Cham other than to see shadows that would ambush them and then disappear.

Sodu sent for reinforcements. Kublai Khan sent his best commander, Ataqui (who had helped to defeat the Song Dynasty in 1279) with 15,000 more Mongols. These also entered the jungles to look for the Cham sanctuaries in the central highlands of South Vietnam. The Mongols were allowed to travel unmolested for several days when at dusk one evening the Cham ambushed the long column of Mongols in the jungle. Cham archers and crossbowmen launched a rain of arrows and bolts on the unsuspecting Mongols followed by a Cham attack by warriors armed with spears, shields, and battleaxes called pheaks. The Mongols rushed up thinking that they had their decisive battle when the Cham suddenly pulled back and retreated through preplanned paths. The Mongols came on with a vengeance when they found themselves falling into hundreds of tiger pits which impaled hundreds. The Cham launched more arrows and bolts into the chaos and confusion the ambush caused. The Mongols tried desperately to get out of the trap, but became confused in the tangle of trees and vines in the jungle and found themselves stepping into hundreds of smaller pits with bamboo stakes that impaled their feet.

Mongol troops fell back and established a makeshift camp for the night without being able to gather their many wounded. The Cham gathered the Mongol wounded in the dark and tied them to trees and began using their favorite Chinese torture of "death by a thousand cuts." The Mongols went mad listening to the agonizing cries of the Mongol wounded as they were tortured. A party of over 100 Mongols ventured into the dark to try to rescue their tormented comrades only to fall into the sharpened bamboo pits and to get lost in the jungle. Those not killed were then captured and tortured as well. The next day the horrified Mongols found the area abandoned with hundreds of shredded and mutilated Mongol bodies tied to trees. The unnerved Mongols then returned quite shaken to China. Kublai Khan's dream of a lucrative Southeast Asian empire was becoming a nightmare.

Kublai Khan then decided to march a much larger army across Da Viet (North Vietnam) to crush Champa. Da Viet was mistakenly thought to be a Chinese vassal state even though the Mongols had never received tribute from this nation. Da Viet sent no reply to Kublai Khan's demand that the Mongol army be allowed to cross into Champa. In 1285, 300,000 Mongols crossed into Da Viet (Annam) and found empty houses, villages and cities all stripped of food. The Vietnamese fell back to the city of Thanh Hoa which was 170 miles into the jungle in the southern part of Da Viet. The Mongols began starving because they had planned on living off the land. Immediately, the intense tropical heat and disease began killing men and horses at an alarming rate. Small scale guerilla attacks began killing groups of Mongols occupying posts and foragers looking for something to eat.

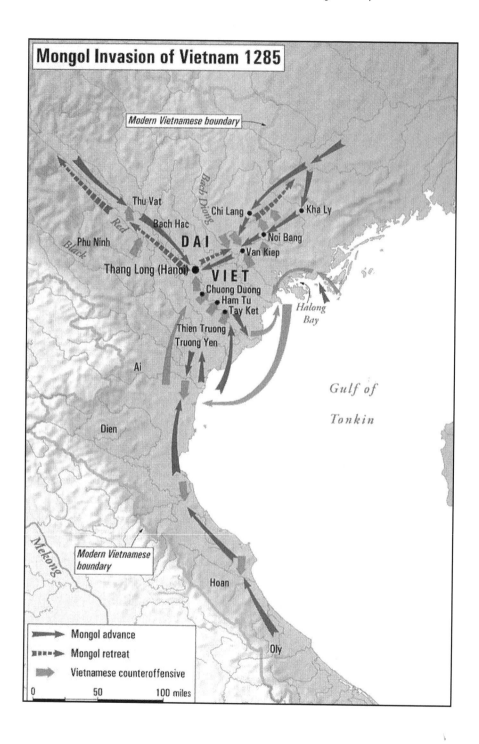

Mongol Invasion of Vietnam 1285

Modern Vietnamese boundary

Thu Vat

Bach Dương

Chi Lang

Kha Ly

Bach Hac

Red

Phu Ninh

Black

D A I

Noi Bang

Van Kiep

Thang Long (Hanoi)

V I E T

Chuong Duong

Ham Tu

Tay Ket

Halong Bay

Thien Truong

Truong Yen

Ai

Gulf of

Tonkin

Dien

Mekong

Modern Vietnamese boundary

Hoan

Oly

Mongol advance

Mongol retreat

Vietnamese counteroffensive

0   50   100 miles

On June 14, 1285, a large fleet of Vietnamese river barques (a long canoe like boat 20 feet long with paddlers on the sides and two rows of warriors armed with spears, battleaxes, and shields in the middle from stem to stern) attacked the Mongol river fleet at Chuong Duong about 20 miles up the Red River from Da Viet's capital of Thang Long (Hanoi). The Vietnamese swarmed aboard the much larger Mongol ships and captured most of the fleet with bloody fighting with spears and battleaxes. On land over 100,000 Vietnamese warriors with 1,000 elephants led by King Tran Hung Dao attacked by land the city of Chuong Duong. The outer Mongol hilltop outposts with earthwork and wooden fortifications were overrun by the attacking hoard of Vietnamese and elephants. Surviving Mongols ran to the main fortifications at Chuong Duong being chased by the Vietnamese. Elephants with metal plates on their heads were brought up to the gates and were used as battering rams to break down the wooden gates of the fortifications. The Vietnamese charged in the broken gates and massacred over 50,000 Mongols in bloody street fighting. The elephants were particularly useful in smashing Mongol barricades and houses that were used as strongholds in the city. The Mongols just could not get enough archers to concentrate on the elephants to stop them or the swarming Vietnamese warriors either.

On June 24, 1285, Sodu brought up 100,000 more Mongols from Thang Long by land along the Red River to the Tay Ket River to try to recapture Chuong Duong, but found his way blocked by thousands of bamboo pits that covered the trails to the city. Suddenly, the Vietnamese ambushed the entire Mongol force in column against the river with their army and elephants as the Da Viet river fleet landed warriors from behind along the river thus surrounding them. Sodu was beheaded and over 50,000 Mongols died and another 50,000 Mongols were captured in the battle. The Mongols had lost another 50,000 men and most of their horses to disease. The other half of the Mongol army retreated back to China.

It took Kublai Khan two years to rebuild his army in southern China from this disaster for another invasion. The Mongols planned a two pronged assault by land and sea with overwhelming forces led by Kublai Khan's son Toghan to lead the sea component of the invasion and to serve as the overall commander. In early 1288, 250,000 Mongols invaded Da Viet by land and found only scorched earth as all of the Vietnamese people withdrew to the jungle sanctuaries around Than Hoa. Disease and low rations began taking a toll again on the Mongols and their horses as they advanced. The second force of 80,000 troops on 500 large ships and over 1,000 smaller ones (that were originally to be used on the aborted 3rd invasion of Japan) was to head up the Bach Dang River from Hai Phong to bring much needed supplies and to link up with the land force.

The Vietnamese knew that the invaders of their country never studied their history. The Vietnamese never changed their strategies and basic tactics in warfare from 111 B.C. all the way to the 20th century. The Vietnamese were students of the writings of the Chinese military philosopher Sun Tzu. They felt that the principles in Sun Tzu's *Art of War* worked whether they were fighting the Chinese in 111 B.C. or the Mongols in 1288 A.D. or the French and Americans in the 20th century. The Vietnamese believed in Sun Tzu's precepts that, "All war is deception" and "He who lies in wait for an enemy that will not wait himself, will be victorious."

King Tran Hung Dao decided to use the identical battle plan that the Da Viet had used in the 1st Battle of Bach Dang when the Vietnamese had decisively defeated the Chinese fleet to win independence in 938. On March 22, 1288, the entire Mongol fleets headed up the Bach Dang River at high tide. Hidden in a well concealed cave on an island in Halong Bay was 1,000 Vietnamese with thousands of iron tipped wooden stakes. The Vietnamese watched silently in the cave as the armada of Mongol ships went by as the Mongols cheered their commander Toghan.

Once the Mongol fleet had passed, it became low tide in the bay and the water was only around one or two feet deep or less in most places. The Vietnamese came out of the cave and began covering the entire harbor with thousands of iron tipped stakes that were 6 to 12 feet long and one foot thick facing up river in a zigzag pattern so that at high tide the stakes would be just under the surface of the water. The Vietnamese river fleet hid in the jungle with their boats on the river banks until the Mongol fleet had passed. The Vietnamese river fleet began harassing the Mongol fleet from behind and then pretended to retreat back toward the mouth of the Bach Dang River. The Mongols sensed victory and gave chase to the Vietnamese. The retreat was timed as it had been in 938 in order to cross over Halong Bay at high tide, but just before low tide which occurred rapidly in this area. The Vietnamese river fleet began skirmishing with the Mongol fleet directly over the stakes in Halong Bay for when the Mongol ships began getting stuck on the stakes as the tide receded. The Mongol ships were impaled in around 6 to 12 feet of water and the Vietnamese river fleet retrieved fire rafts on the beaches and directed them into the Mongol ships setting them on fire as they set other ships on fire by shooting flaming arrows into their masts. The Mongols on these ships then were killed with pheak axes as they jumped into the receding water to escape the flames.

Suddenly, 100,000 Vietnamese warriors on foot charged out of the jungle into the bay screaming and surrounded each boat to set on fire while firing arrows and throwing spears. The Mongols were cut down as they jumped from the burning ships. Elephants were brought out to knock over other impaled Mongol ships on their sides so that the Vietnamese could behead the Mongol warriors as they tumbled out. The Mongol defeat was total with few of the 80,000 Mongol and Chinese soldiers and sailors surviving. Toghan managed to escape on a small boat. Mountains of Mongol heads were created in the middle of Halong Bay. The high tide came in and washed the heads, the great pools of

The Second Battle of Bach Dang gave the Vietnamese a decisive victory over the Mongols in 1288.

blood, and the dismembered bodies out to sea. The Mongol land force which had been decimated by disease and starvation had to turn back because the fleet had most of their food and supplies.

More than 80,000 Mongols and allied Chinese died at the mouth of the Bach Dang River.

Toghan had to face his father, Kublai Khan, with the bad news of the total defeat to Da Viet. Toghan entered Kublai Khan's palace in Beijing and knelt before his father and with head lowered told him about the disaster. Chinese sources say that Kublai Khan's face turned red as he screamed in rage. Kublai Khan cried out, "Don't they know that I am Khan of all that is under Heaven? I will crush them! They will come to beg me for rice and I will give them none!" Kublai Khan berated his son and ordered the army and navy rebuilt with plans for a larger simultaneous invasion of both Champa and Da Viet to be made.

By 1292, with a bankrupt treasury, only 20,000 men and 1,000 small ships could be mustered for another invasion. With so few men and ships available another invasion of Vietnam had to be scrapped. Kublai Khan had another idea about how to subjugate Vietnam. Kublai Khan wanted to capture Java to get control of the Southeast Asian spice trade at its source. Kublai Khan imagined that the Vietnamese would then come and repent to him to restore the lucrative spice trade through Vietnam. Kublai Khan then thought that he could get the Vietnamese to accept an occupation army and once that was established he would punish the Vietnamese for refusing to submit to him. It was decided that the invasion force would be sent to the island of Java (Indonesia).

Kublai Khan's emissary was not well received in Java by King Kertanagara who had him branded on the face with a big "NO!" in Chinese so that Kublai Khan would be crystal clear about his answer concerning submission to the Mongols. In 1293, the Mongol fleet with 20,000 men and a year's supply of grain left for Java. In the meantime, King Kertanagara was killed in a war with the neighboring state of Kediri and replaced by his son-in-law Raden Wijaya. On the way the Mongols received the submission of Malay and Sumatra. When the Mongols arrived at Java, King Wijaya asked for help defeating Kediri in return for submission. The Mongol commander, Shi-pe led a seaborne attack on Kediri killing 5,000 and executing their king.

King Wijaya then invited 200 of the top Mongol warriors and officers to the city of Majapahit in the interior in order to receive gifts as a sign of his submission to Kublai Khan. The 200 Mongols were ambushed and killed by King Wijaya's warriors deep in the jungle. The Mongol army was also moving toward Majapahit and camped in a clearing in the jungle unaware of the ambush of their top men. The Javanese warriors under King Wijaya surrounded and attacked the camp while killing 3,000 Mongols. The remaining 17,000 Mongols abandoned most of their equipment and fought a running battle for 150 miles back to their ships while losing several thousand more men. Shi-pe realized that he wasn't going to defeat the Javanese in the jungles where they preferred to fight and that he didn't have the numbers of men or equipment to conquer Java. Shi-pe received 70 lashes when he returned to give a report to Kublai Khan of the failure of the expedition to Java.

Most of what Kublai Khan wanted to accomplish had been a miserable failure other than the final conquest of the Song Empire in China in 1279 and the putting down of a number of Mongol rebellions. Kublai Khan had grown fat with poor health and died in 1294. Chinese sources report that his last words were, "Don't they know that I am Khan of all that is under Heaven?" The Mongols were at their best on the massive steppes of Eurasia, but they were just out of their element in Southeast Asia and at sea. After Kublai Khan's death in 1294, the Mongol Empire was bankrupt and greatly weakened from Kublai Khan's obsessions with the conquests of Syria, Japan, and Southeast Asia which caused it to split into four smaller empires.

THE THIRD, FOURTH, AND FIFTH KAMIKAZE DIVINE WINDS OF WORLD WAR II

To this day, the Japanese see the Kamikaze "Divine Wind" of 1274 and 1281 as miracles provided from their ancestors (the Japanese religion of Shintoism combines ancestor and nature worship). So when Japan was threatened again by the 5,000 ships of the U.S. fleet in 1944-1945, the Japanese once again prayed in mass at the country's many Shinto and Buddhist shrines for another Divine Wind to save Japan.

On December 17, 1944, the Japanese prayers were answered when Typhoon Cobra rocked the U.S fleet in the Philippine Sea. All of Japan rejoiced when they heard on the radio that the American fleet was under attack by another Divine Wind. The U.S. fleet lost 3 destroyers and 870 men as well as sustained a lot of damage from the 140 mph winds and the 70 degree rolls that wrecked the interior of the ships and got the Americans praying themselves. It took several weeks for the battered U.S. fleet to repair the damage before continuing their advance against Japan. On June 5, 1945, another Kamikaze typhoon hit and damaged the U.S. fleet, but didn't lose any ships that time and sustained less damage.

Japan had asked their young pilots who had replaced the dead veteran pilots to make themselves the new Divine Wind as Kamikaze suicide pilots which attacked the American fleet from September 13, 1944 to August 15, 1945. During this time approximately 3,912 Kamikaze attackers sank 34 navy ships and damaged 368 more U.S. ships. Over 9,700 American sailors were killed or wounded in the Kamikaze attacks. Despite the prayers and sacrifice of the Japanese people, over 4,600 U.S. ships continued toward the Japanese home islands and to victory over Japan in World War II.

BIBLIOGRAPHY

Delgado, James. *Kamikaze: History's Greatest Naval Disaster.* Random House, 2009.

Karnow, Stanley. *Vietnam: A History,* Penguin Books, 1983.

Kennedy, Hugh. *Mongols, Huns, and Vikings.* Weidenfeld Military Press, 2002.

Man, John. *Kublai Khan.* Bantam Books, 2007.

Nicole, David. *The Mongol Warlords.* Brockhampton Press, 1998.

Rossabi, Morris. *Kublai Khan: His Life and Times.* University of California Press, 1990.

Saunders, J.J. *The History of the Mongol Conquests.* Routledge & Kegan Paul Ltd, 1971.

Time-Life Books. *The Mongol Conquests.* New York, 2000.

CHAPTER 8

Conquistadors and Indians: Spain's Doomed Apocalyptic Expeditions Through Southeastern North America from 1526 to 1568

In 1492, when Christopher Columbus discovered Hispaniola (modern day Haiti and the Dominican Republic), the island held over 300,000 Native American Indians. By 1508, 240,000 Indians had died from war, mistreatment through slavery, from disease, and mass suicide. The pre-Columbian Native American population of the Americas was (according to University of Wisconsin-Madison Geographer William Denevan) at 54 million. The breakdown of the indigenous population of the Americas before 1492 was 15 million in the Aztec Empire in Mexico, over 15 million in what is today the United States, 2 million in what is today Canada, 10 million in Central America and over 12 million in South America (6 million in the Inca Empire).

The deadliest weapon that the Spanish Conquistadors possessed in their conquest of the Americas was not their armor, swords, halberds, horses, crossbows, canons or harquebus muskets, but it was disease (mostly smallpox). The Indians who caught smallpox from the Spanish had no immunity to any diseases that the Europeans brought to the New World and died at an alarming rate of 80 to 85 %. The Conquistadors under Hernan Cortez had a difficult time conquering the Aztec Empire until smallpox wiped out over 12 million Aztec Indians between 1519 and 1521. The smallpox epidemic traveled and spread faster than the Conquistadors could conquer these civilizations. The Inca Empire was in the midst of a civil war when a smallpox epidemic killed over 4.8 million Incas before Francisco Pizzaro with 160 Conquistadors conquered it in 1532. Until 1540, the area that is today the United States and Canada had not been touched by European disease because of the limited European contact with this area and the deserts of northern Mexico that stopped the northern spread of European diseases.

Pre-Columbian Indian North and South America was not a wild uninhabited and undeveloped place. There were thousands of Indian villages with cultivated fields and orchards that made the Americas a place of abundance. The Amazon rain forest in what is today Brazil was a cultivated paradise with millions of inhabitants. The evidence of the Amazonia Civilization was discovered recently as large areas of the Brazilian jungle had been harvested for its wood which revealed the remains of this great civilization. Spanish Conquistadors describe traveling down the Amazon River for months seeing village after village and large cultivated fields and orchards as they spread the diseases that would destroy this civilization and cause it to be reclaimed by the jungle. Along the Mississippi River for a thousand miles was the great Mississippian Civilization that had millions of inhabitants. The armies of these great Indian civilizations could field tens of thousands to hundreds of thousands of warriors so it is amazing how a few hundred to around a thousand Conquistadors could have conquered these huge armies. It just wouldn't have been possible without disease.

Spain had become the top world power from their conquests of the Americas and the huge quantities of gold and silver that Spain was receiving from primarily Mexico and Peru. Survivors from the first three failed Conquistador expeditions to Florida and South Carolina between 1526 and 1543 claimed that these areas contained gold and silver as well, even though these survivors had not actually brought back or had seen any gold and silver themselves. The Spanish just reasoned that if Mexico and Peru had gold there must be gold in the American Southeast (U.S.) as well. It was only after the fourth and fifth failed expeditions to Florida and South Carolina in 1558 and1568 did Spain accepted that there wasn't gold to be had in the American Southeast.

The first doomed expedition to the American Southeast was led by Lucas Vazquez de Ayllon to look for gold and to start the first attempt at a colony in what is today South Carolina in 1526. Lucas Vasquez de Ayllon was a plantation sugar planter on Hispaniola who led an expedition of 600 Conquistadors and colonists on six ships to start a colony and to look for gold. The Indians fled at the site of the armored Conquistadors and their terrifying horses which no Native American had ever seen before (there were no horses in the Americas before they were brought over by the Spanish). The Native Americans had learned to fear the Spanish in 1521 when 70 Chicora Indians had been captured in South Carolina by other Conquistadors and were then taken to Hispaniola as slaves. Ayllon established the site for the colony near Pawley's Island, SC and named the colony San Miguel de Gualdape. Shortly after establishing the colony, Ayllon died from a tropical disease. From the moment that Ayllon died, the Conquistadors and settlers began arguing over what the mission of the colony should be. Some wanted to start the work of capturing Indian slaves and building plantations, while the Conquistadors wanted to move inland and look for gold. Still others wanted to turn back to Hispaniola.

The 200 Conquistadors who wanted to move inland to look for gold headed into the interior of South Carolina and were ambushed by a large force of over 1,000 to 2,000 Chicora and Catawba Indians in a swampy area of mangrove trees. The Conquistadors at first held off the Indians by their harquebus and crossbow fire, but the Indians kept up a constant fire of hundreds of arrows from their 5-6 foot long bows. The Conquistadors were losing men dead and wounded and could not keep up a fast rate of fire from their slow loading and cumbersome harquebus's and crossbows. The Indians started moving closer and began rushing groups of wounded Conquistadors and killing them with their war clubs though at a high cost in dead and wounded from the steel Spanish swords. Finally, there was a final rush with war cries from the Indians who killed most of the 200 Conquistadors at a high cost of hundreds of their own warriors in dead and wounded. Only a few wounded and frightened Conquistadors made it back to San Miguel de Gualdape to tell of their ordeal.

The over 400 remaining Conquistadors and settlers at San Miguel started starving when they ran out of the provisions they had brought. Any party of Spanish that went outside of the stockade fort at the colony to hunt or fish was killed or captured by the Indians. Many men were dying from disease as well. Those Spanish that were captured were roasted alive to great screams of agony in the Indian camps outside of the fort. Some of the roasted men were then offered to the Spanish to fill their starving stomachs. The horrified Conquistadors and settlers started arguing about what to do when a battle broke out as the colony split and colonists and conquistadors began firing their weapons at each other and then came to blows with swords, halberds, and lances. The Indians watched in amazement to see the Spanish killing each other in the battle. The remaining 150 settlers and Conquistadors that survived the ordeal left the next day and returned to Hispaniola. The colony had lasted right at three months.

The Narvaez expedition was an attempt to colonize Florida and to look for gold from 1527-1528 by Panfilo de Narvaez and 600 Conquistadors and six ships. In 1527, the Narvaez expedition stopped in Santo Domingo to purchase horses for the expedition to Florida when over 100 Conquistadors deserted after they heard about what happened to the Ayllon expedition in South Carolina. Narvaez couldn't get all of the supplies he needed from Santo Domingo so he sent two ships to Trinidad to obtain them. As the ships were returning they sank in a hurricane and took another 60 men, most of the supplies and a number of horses to the bottom of the Caribbean.

On April 12, 1528, Narvaez landed north of present day Tampa Bay with 400 Conquistadors and 80 horses, but they had lost another ship laden with supplies. The expedition claimed Florida for Spain and located an Indian village and traded for venison, fish, and skins for clothing. The Indians had knowledge of the events in South Carolina in 1526 and abandoned their village that night. Narvaez sent a brigantine to explore Tampa Bay, but the ship and its crew disappeared. Narvaez was asking Indians about where to find gold, but communication was a problem. Finally, Narvaez came to understand that the powerful Apalachee near present day Tallahassee were believed to have gold. The Apalachee were part of the powerful Mississippian Empire alliance system and fought in organized column formations of archers and shock warriors that used war clubs with wooden balls carved in to kill by blunt force trauma. Some warriors used war clubs that had sharpened tomahawk like stones down the sides to form blades on one or two sides of the club.

On May 1, 1528, Narvaez, decided to split his forces and to march north to Apalachee with 300 Conquistadors and to send the four remaining ships with almost 100 men to carry most of the supplies. The land force starved for almost two weeks when they captured a Uzita Indian village and enslaved the Indians. For three days the Conquistadors ate the Indian food supplies and raped the women. The Spanish had large mastiff war dogs (75-125 pounds) that they let attack and eat a number of Indians to force compliance to their wishes. Chief Hirrihigua's beautiful young wife became violent and killed the Conquistador that was attempting to rape her in her lodge with a hidden war club. In retaliation, the Spanish cut Chief Hirrihugua's nose off and then forced him to watch as his beloved wife was torn apart and eaten by the war dogs. After these three days of hell, the Indians were then forced to carry the Conquistador's equipment up to Apalachee territory. Chief Hirrihugua managed to escape with another one of his wives, his daughters and some of his warriors.

In the meantime, the ships got lost and couldn't find the land force and returned to Santo Domingo. At the urging of Narvaez's wife, over the next year the ships kept looking for the land force but never found them. On one such attempt to find Narvaez, a landing party was attacked by Uzita Indians and everyone was killed except for Juan Ortiz who was taken captive. Juan Ortiz was then taken to Chief Hirrihugua and was tortured slowly over the next several months. The only kindness shown to Ortiz was from the daughters of Chief Hirrihugua when they would bring him food and teach him their language. The chief decided to have Ortiz roasted alive and as Juan was screaming in the fire on a spit, the daughters of the chief begged for his life. They told the chief that Ortiz was not involved in the rapes and abuse of their people, so the chief relented and had Ortiz released. The daughters of the chief had to nurse him back from his burns and eventually helped him escape when the chief changed his mind about roasting Ortiz again. Juan Ortiz then made his way back toward Tampa Bay and remained there with one of the tribes and became a warrior.

As Narvaez's men continued to move north, the Conquistadors were finding that the Indians had abandoned their villages. On June 25, 1528, the expedition entered Apalachee territory and captured a village of forty lodges. The Conquistadors terrorized the village by taking food, raping women, and demanding to know where their gold was located. The next day over 200 warriors began shooting fire arrows onto the roofs of the lodges which set the village on fire. Then 200 more Indians began firing arrows from the opposite side of the village. Though the Conquistadors fired back they only killed two warriors because the Indians moved too fast from tree to tree to be hit. As the column moved toward the Apalachee capital, the warriors switched to fast shock attacks with war clubs to isolate and kill Conquistadors from one section of the column at a time and then fell back into the forest before the other Spanish could come up to counter-attack. In these attacks, the Conquistadors could only fire one shot from their crossbows or harquebus's before they had to fight in hand to hand fighting.

Narvaez decided to withdraw to the coast to look for their supply ships. As the Conquistadors were walking through chest high water through a swamp, the Apalachee began showering them with arrows. The Spanish couldn't fire and load their weapons in the swamp and were taking many casualties with wounded men falling and disappearing into the water. The Conquistadors finally reached dry ground and were able to form a firing line and drove off the Indians with volley fire. For two more weeks the Conquistadors mostly traveled through swamp land while being harassed by the Apalachee Indians. Some of the Spanish fell into quick sand pits that swallowed them rapidly in their heavy armor. The Spanish finally made it to the abandoned coastal village of Aute where they plundered 640 bushels of corn and found oyster beds for food. Twice the Apalachee massacred groups of ten men gathering oyster shells at low tide in the bay. The Spanish were then forced to eat their horses to survive and began building five boats to take them to Mexico.

The Conquistadors left Florida with 242 men and sailed along the coast. The Apalachee gave warning along the coast so that the Spanish were always being watched by groups of Indian warriors allied with the

Mississippian Empire. On a number of occasions the Conquistadors would land along the Gulf of Mexico to forage for food and each time they were met by Indians that would ambush and harass them. This forced the Conquistadors to ride out storms in their boats rather than to try to meet the Indian war parties waiting on the beaches. Three boats were sunk in storms taking all on board to a watery grave. In October of 1528, a hurricane dumped the last 80 men on a barrier island near Galveston, Texas. Starvation, disease, and Indian attacks killed most of these last survivors including Narvaez. In 1536, only three Spanish men and a Moorish slave had made it to Mexico alive after they had long been given up as dead years before.

Hernando De Soto came to the New World in 1514 when he was 18 to make his fortune as a Conquistador. De Soto had participated in the conquests of Panama, Nicaragua, and was with Francisco Pizzaro when he conquered the Incas in 1532. De Soto had become rich from the conquests, but he wanted to take credit for a major conquest on his own. De Soto theorized as others had that if there was gold in Mexico and in Peru that there must be gold in what is today the Southeastern United States. De Soto knew little of the two previous attempts to colonize the Southeast and to find gold there and had traveled to Spain in 1535 to petition King Charles for full rights to the lands and gold that were to be found.

King Charles gave De Soto four years to conquer the Southeast and made him governor of the area with rights to a huge portion of the wealth to be had there. The catch was that De Soto was to finance the expedition from his own money. De Soto used all of his money from his fortune to marry a relative of Queen Isabella and to organize an expedition of ten ships and 620 Conquistadors (the best troops included many elite Portuguese who had experience fighting the Moors in North Africa). The soldiers on the expedition were not paid, but were to receive a large portion of the gold that De Soto was sure that they would find in the American Southeast. De Soto met Cabeza de Vasca in 1537 that was one of the survivors of the doomed Narvaez Expedition and begged him to go with him back to Florida. De Vasca said that the only way he would go back was if he had command of the expedition and that the men would be controlled. There should be no raping and abuse of the Indians. De Vasca insisted that nothing positive could be accomplished in the Southeast as long as the Indians viewed the Spanish as enemies. De Soto stated that he learned how to deal with Indians in Panama and Peru, but he needed someone who had been to Florida to come on the expedition. De Vasca said that he couldn't go back and turned down a large amount of money offered by De Soto to accompany the expedition.

In May of 1539, De Soto's expedition landed near present day Bradenton, Florida with 620 men, 220 horses, 200 pigs, and 50 large mastiff and greyhound (a larger breed than is commonly known today) war dogs that were bred and raised for killing. After a few days the Conquistadors came across a party of warriors that were approaching them. The Conquistadors were starting to charge when one of the warriors started yelling at them in Spanish to not attack. It was Juan Ortiz who looked just like an Indian. De Soto was very happy to have Ortiz join the expedition because he knew the land and could speak the languages of the Indians. When the Indians were asked about where gold could be found they always said that there was lots of gold up north in Apalachee to get the Spanish to leave and to go somewhere else.

The Conquistadors began moving north while encountering Indian ambushes along the way that killed and wounded a number of men. De Soto's men took food from the mostly abandoned villages and they captured several Indians daily to feed to the war dogs who had been trained in Cuba to eat the blood and flesh of Native Americans. The dogs would also be allowed to run down and eat groups of Indians that the Spanish saw running away from them. It became an amusing sport for the Conquistadors to watch as the war dogs would first tear open and eat the intestines of the Indians as they lingered screaming in pain, before devouring the rest of the unfortunate individual. Other captured Indians were forced to carry the Conquistador's equipment as slaves. The Catholic priests who had accompanied the expedition to convert the Indians to Christianity protested at this barbaric behavior, but De Soto ignored their pleas.

As De Soto moved north he sent word to the chief of the Ocale tribe (Ocala, FL.) to ask for his submission and for the tribe to come out of hiding or to be hunted down by his horsemen and dogs. The chief sent word back that he knew what kind of murders, thieves and rapists that the Conquistadors were and that his men were going to kill and decapitate two Spaniards for every day that they remained in his territory. Over the next several days, Ocale warriors killed isolated Conquistadors who were out scouting or foraging. Every night the heads of the slain Conquistadors were thrown into the Spanish camp and their body parts were found hanging in the trees in the morning. De Soto didn't linger long and began moving north again toward Apalachee and continued capturing and enslaving Indians to serve as guides and porters. Women were also taken from their husbands and fathers and repeatedly raped on a daily basis. The Conquistadors left a trail of the blood of the Native Americans throughout the expedition through the Southeast.

As De Soto started entering Apalachee territory near what is today Gainesville, FL. They started running into Indians that started telling the Conquistadors about the fate of the Narvaez expedition and that they would end up the same way. De Soto had kept the details about the Narvaez Expedition to himself, but now many of the Conquistadors wanted to turn back. De Soto said that there was no turning back and reminded his men about what Cortez and Pizzaro had accomplished in Mexico and Peru. Toward the end of August and into September of 1539, the abandoned Indian villages had also been stripped of any corn or food so that De Soto's men were only getting a little pork from the pigs that they had brought.

Conquistadors and Apalachee Indians fight a pitched battle in Florida.

On September 15, 1539, De Soto's army reached the Indian village of Napituca. The chief of Napituca had arranged to meet De Soto on a plain outside of the village to arrange for the release of another captured chief, but Ortiz tipped him off that it was a trap. De Soto took only six men with him to the meeting, but had his army ready to attack from the village. As the meeting commenced, over 400 Napituca warriors began maneuvering in separate column formations of archers and shock troops armed with large war clubs as a show of force. Suddenly, the Indians shot and killed De Soto's horse with 7 arrows and De Soto and his companions were fighting for their lives. The Conquistador cavalry came out of the village and charged and broke up the column formations of warriors while impaling on their lances over 40 Indians. The Indians ran and dived into two lakes that were close by and began treading water in the deep middle to stay away from the Conquistadors. De Soto had his men surround the lakes until morning of the next day. Some Indians drowned themselves rather than submit, but over 300 Indians including the chief were just too worn out from treading water all night and surrendered to the Spanish.

The chief was then brought in chains to De Soto when the chief shrieked a loud war cry and bashed De Soto in the face so hard with his chains that De Soto went unconscious for half an hour and began bleeding from his nose and mouth. The warriors outside also then let out a war cry and attacked the Conquistadors with their fists and chains as well. Some Conquistadors were killed and wounded when the warriors grabbed their swords and halberds which were lying around the village before being killed themselves. The Conquistadors then cut off the noses and hands of all of the remaining warriors and people. Dogs were allowed to eat as many Indians as they could. De Soto couldn't eat or speak for several days after the attack as the army recovered in the village.

On October 1 and 2, 1539, the Conquistadors were crossing the same swamp that Narvaez's men had been ambushed in and found themselves also under attack by the Apalachee warriors. For two days, the Conquistador infantry slowly fought their way through the swamp under constant fire from arrows. Finally the Conquistadors had fought their way out of the swamp and unleashed their cavalry who rode down and lanced hundreds of warriors. The Apalachee burned their villages and fled to the swamps.

De Soto's men set up a winter camp at the Apalachee capital of Anhayca (Tallahassee, FL.) during the winter of 1539-1540. The Apalachee ambushed and killed small groups of Conquistadors that left

Anhayca to scout or forage. The Spanish in turn cut off the noses and hands of any Indians that they captured. The war dogs were allowed to hunt and eat Indians in the forest. Captured Indians were also tortured to give the location of their gold only to find out that there was no gold anywhere in Florida. Some pearls were recovered from one of the lodges and the captive Indians said that gold mines and lots of pearls could be had in Cofitachequi (Columbia, South Carolina). So De Soto's army then began marching through Georgia and into what is today South Carolina. The expedition priests reminded De Soto that the purpose of the expedition was to convert the Indians to Christianity. De Soto ordered his men to restrain themselves from abusing the Indians as they marched through Georgia. The expedition had a peaceful journey through Georgia and into South Carolina where the Indians freely provided food and guides for the expedition.

On May 1, 1540, the Conquistadors reached South Carolina and were met by the beautiful Lady of Cofitacheque (niece of the chieftainess) being carried on a liter that crossed the Congaree River on large canoes who then presented De Soto with a large necklace of pearls. At first things were cordial as the Indians provided the Spanish with food, but then the Conquistadors demanded women and looted hundreds of pounds of pearls from the Indian temples. Also found in the temples were some armor and weapons from the doomed Ayllon Expedition which was proof that this expedition did indeed come to South Carolina. De Soto then demanded gold and was given copper instead which caused him to become angry, so he took the Lady of Cofitacheque hostage. Three days later she escaped with some of the looted pearls. The son of the chieftainess was told to take De Soto to her, but he committed suicide by piercing his own throat with an arrow rather than to comply with such a request. De Soto was then told that the gold that he so desired was located in the land of the Mobile Indians (central and southern Alabama).

De Soto's conquistadors left a trail of death and destruction in
their failed quest to find gold in the American Southeast.

So De Soto's army moved through North Carolina and the area of
what is today Chattanooga, Tennessee and into Alabama. The Indians
of these areas abandoned their villages, hid their food, and fought small
scale hit and run attacks to encourage De Soto's men to keep moving. De Soto was able to move through the land of the powerful Coosa
Indians (northern Alabama) by taking the chief and his sister hostage.
The Coosa chief sent warriors and warning to the Mobile Indians after
De Soto started raping his sister daily and made her ride on his horse
with him.

On October 18, 1540, De Soto's army reached the town of Mabila
(some chroniclers say Mauvila) in what is today central Alabama among
the powerful Mobile tribe under 7 foot tall Chief Tascaluza (Tuscaloosa).

The towns of the Mobile Indians were fortified with round stockade fortifications and the warriors fought in the Mississippian style of warfare which used separate column formations of archers and shock warriors armed with war clubs to fight on open ground. De Soto demanded women and slave porters to carry their equipment from Chief Tascaluza after a cordial meeting between them. Chief Tascaluza said that these would be provided at the Mobile capital at Mabila as well as accommodations for the Spanish army. Mabila was located in a large stockade fort with 15 foot high walls with towers about 150 feet apart and slits for firing arrows. Chief Tascaluza met De Soto and his advance guard cordially inside Mabila as 20 beautiful women danced for the Conquistadors. After the dance was finished, the women disappeared as the Conquistadors argued about who was going to take which dancer for himself. Chief Tascaluza then disappeared into a lodge and refused to come out to talk anymore with De Soto. De Soto was angered by this and wanted to know where their gold and women were. The Conquistadors told De Soto that the lodges they looked into were all packed with armed warriors and the only women that they could see were armed with bows as well.

A warrior then came out of one of the lodges and aimed his bow with a notched arrow at a Conquistador, but before the Indian could fire, a Spanish captain lopped off the man's arm and shoulder with his sword. The Indians came swarming and screaming out of the lodges and began attacking the Conquistadors. The Conquistadors inside Mabila formed into small circled shield formations to defend themselves from the hundreds of arrows being fired at them and made for the gates to get outside where the rest of the army was. De Soto and the Conquistadors managed to get outside of the gates of Mabila while losing 5 dead and several horses while a group of 12 Spanish were trapped in one of the lodges. Most of the equipment of the Spanish was brought into Mabila by the Indian slaves who joined the Mobile Indians in the battle.

The Indians began holding up the equipment and supplies of the Spanish and flaunted it toward them from the walls of their stockade fortifications. As the Spanish were trying to get organized, the Indians charged out of the gates of Mabila and into the Conquistadors in column formation with war clubs which drove them slowly across the field. A number of Spanish were killed and wounded before the Conquistador cavalry recovered and forced the Indians to retreat back into Mabila. For the next four hours, the Indians and Spanish counter attacked each other outside the fortification again and again with many dead littering the battlefield. The Indians had been taking huge casualties to the superior Spanish arms and armor, yet they continued to close in to fight with their war clubs. De Soto then dismounted most of his cavalry since they were the best armored to lead an assault to take Mabila by storm. The Conquistadors used axes to open the gates and to create breaches in the wall.

The Battle raged back and forth across Mabila with enraged warriors firing arrows and jumping on Conquistadors from the rooftops of lodges with their war clubs and flint knives. Every structure was then set on fire with many Indians and some Spanish being burned to death inside the lodges. Many of the war dogs died defending the bodies of their handlers who fell wounded and dead in the battle. Outside Mabila, some of the other mounted Conquistadors massacred any Indians trying to escape. The trapped Spanish were eventually rescued after fighting desperately for hours. After nine bitter hours of fighting, the battle ended at sundown with the last living Indian warrior hanging himself with his bowstring. Among the dead were Chief Tascaluza and the Coosa Chief and his sister. Most of the Conquistadors collapsed from exhaustion where they stood and tried as best they could to treat their wounds. One elite Portuguese soldier sat down in shock and died with no obvious wounds anywhere.

Over 200 Conquistadors had died in the battle (many died days later from their wounds), and almost all of the remaining Spanish were wounded with over 688 wounds between the close to 380 men left alive. Chroniclers estimated the Indian dead at 11,000 which made this the bloodiest battle in the pre Civil War period of U.S. history. The Battle of Mabila was a disaster for both sides. The Spanish had almost all of their equipment destroyed and 36 horses that were dead or wounded. Many harquebus's, crossbows, swords and lances were broken and needed repaired as well.

On November, 14, 1540, De Soto's caravan from hell continued its march into Mississippi. The Conquistadors spent the winter of 1540-1541 at the town of Chicaza (Columbus, Mississippi). The Chicaza warriors skirmished with the Conquistadors all winter. On March 4, 1541, the Chicaza warriors snuck into the Spanish camp and killed 12 Spaniards and 57 horses. Most of the pigs (over 500 in number) were either burned or escaped and became the descendants of the pigs and wild boars that would populate North America. De Soto's army moved out the next day and on April 28, they reached the village of Alibamos (Mississippi) where 300 warriors were holed up in a round fortification with interior walls to fall back on. De Soto ordered an attack against the fort using axes to get in because he believed that there was food inside that the Spanish desperately needed. The Alibamos Indians fought stubbornly and fell back to the interior walls before retreating. The Spanish had taken the fort at the cost of 15 dead and 15 wounded while only killing 3 Indians. The men were despondent when they saw that there was no food in the fort for all of their effort and sacrifice.

On May 8, 1541, the Conquistadors captured the village of Quizquiz on the Mississippi River and captured food and 300 women whom they raped. The men of the village were out working on distant corn fields. On May 22, 7,000 Mississippian Indian warriors in hundreds of wide 20 yard long canoes were massed at the banks of Quizquiz in a standoff with the Spanish. The Spanish were eventually allowed to cross the Mississippi River after minor skirmishing on large rafts that they had built. The Conquistadors then captured the village of Casque and seemed to get a sincere Christian conversion from these Indians after De Soto said that he was the son of the Son (the Indians thought he meant the Sun). The Indians asked for a sign from De Soto that he was divine by requesting that he heal two blind men and to make it rain. The blind men weren't healed, but it did rain and the Indians saw this as a sign of De Soto's divinity. Then the Conquistadors helped the Casque Indians defeat their enemies the Pacaha, but then De Soto helped the Pacaha defeat the Casque after they had kept some of the captured loot from the Spanish. De Soto left both tribes very angry and confused on July 29 and headed toward the Valley of the Vapors (Hot Springs, Arkansas).

On September 30, 1541, the Conquistadors entered the land of the fierce Tula Indians (Caddo Gap, Arkansas) where they thought they would find gold. The Conquistadors attacked the village of the Tula and had a battle on their hands as the skilled Tula warriors proved difficult to kill. The Tula warriors were able to unhorse cavalrymen by deflecting their lances and then striking them with the long staffs that they fought with. The women fought so hard that the Conquistadors couldn't rape them. One Conquistador who entered a lodge with 4 women found himself tackled and spread eagled as he was beat between the legs with a war club. Other Conquistadors had to kill the women to rescue their comrade. After the warriors retreated with most of the people of the village, De Soto also retreated because he didn't want anymore battles with the ferocious Tula tribe. The bitter winter of 1541-1542 was spent in the area of Little Rock, Arkansas. It was here that Juan Ortiz died and with him the ability to communicate with the Indians.

On April 19, 1542, De Soto's men moved into southern Arkansas desperately looking for gold and food without success. On April 28, a sickly De Soto headed for the Mississippi River again where he demanded that Chief Quigualtam of the powerful Mississippian Natchez tribe come to submit to him and to bring him gold. Chief Quigualtam sent a reply that he doesn't submit or give tribute to anyone that it was De Soto that needed to submit to him. De Soto flew into a rage from his sickbed at the arrogance of this chief and ordered the town of Anilco to be attacked. Over 100 Indians were massacred by the Conquistadors and 80 women and children were captured in the attack. De Soto then became sicker and died on May 21, 1542 and was secretly buried in the Mississippi River. The Conquistadors tried to hide De Soto's death from the Indians who wouldn't attack them because many believed that he was the son of the sun.

The Conquistadors then wanted to go overland to Mexico via Texas, but became lost and turned back to the Mississippi River where they spent the winter of 1542-1543 where most of the Indian slaves died from disease. By June of 1543, the Conquistadors finished building seven brigantine ships to escape down the Mississippi River to the Gulf of Mexico. In June, the Conquistadors started down the Mississippi River after butchering most of the remaining horses for food for the journey (a number of horses escaped during the expedition and began populating North America with its first horses).

On July 4, 1543, Chief Quigualtam sent 2,000 warriors in 100 large canoes to attack the Spanish fleet on the river. The Conquistadors sent 25 heavily armored men to disperse the Indians in 4 canoes, but the Spaniards were overwhelmed and most fell into the river and drowned under the weight of their armor. Only 4 men could throw off their armor and swim back to the brigantines.   The Natchez canoes harassed the Spanish ships for three days while wounding over 50 Conquistadors in the attacks. The Conquistadors didn't have any working harquebus's left and only 7 working crossbows to defend themselves with. Other Mississippian nations harassed and attacked the Conquistadors until they reached the Gulf of Mexico on July 18, 1543. Around August 3, 1543, 257 Conquistador survivors landed in Mexico to safety.

The De Soto Expedition was one of the most devastating events in American History mostly because of one unnamed Conquistador who contracted smallpox that was left in an Indian village in northern Alabama after the battle of Mabila. The Indians who had never contracted any European diseases before tried to help the man who eventually died from the disease. Smallpox then traveled from village to village throughout North America over the next 20 years killing between 12 and 14 million Indians in what would be the United States and 1.6 million Indians in what would be Canada. Most Indians who died had never even seen a European from where the diseases came that led to their apocalyptic end. Most of the tribes mentioned by the De Soto chroniclers including the Apalachee, the Natchez, and the Mississippian Civilization didn't even exist 20 years later.

In 1558-1559, another Spanish expedition of 1,500 colonists under Tristan de Luna was sent to form a colony at Pensacola Bay, Florida. Tristan de Luna was told that there were many Indian villages (Apalachee) to take food from to subsist on. The expedition started badly when seven ships were destroyed by a hurricane in 1558 at the entrance to Pensacola Bay killing over 500 colonists. Then when the other 1,000 colonists began searching for Indian villages to take food for the colony, all they found were ruins of many villages and very few Indians. Illness, malnutrition, and starvation began killing many settlers at Pensacola. Finally, in 1559, the last 200 surviving settlers returned to Havana, Cuba. By the time that St. Augustine was finally established as Spain's first colony in Florida in 1565, the Southeast was covered in the ruins of tribes of people that no longer existed.

In 1566-1568, Spain made one more attempt at establishing a colony in the Carolinas when Juan Pardo led 125 Conquistadors to establish the colony of Santa Elena on present day Parris Island, South Carolina. The Conquistadors found that there weren't near as many Indian villages as De Soto's chroniclers had described that they had found in South Carolina. At Cofitachequi (Columbia, S.C.), Juan Pardo found only ruins of this once great Indian civilization. In 1568, Juan Pardo spread his 125 Conquistadors over six base forts spread throughout South Carolina and

North Carolina. The surviving Catawba and Yamasee Indians (from the smallpox epidemic) overwhelmed these forts and massacred the garrisons. In 1568, only one survivor made his way back to St.Augustine, Florida to tell the tale of the last Spanish attempt to establish a colony in South Carolina.

BIBLIOGRAPHY

Adorno, Rolena. *Alvar Nunez Cabeza de Vaca: His Account, His Life, and the Expedition of Panfilo de Narvaez.*. Lincoln: University of Nebraska Press, 1999.

Duncan, David. *Hernando de Soto.* Crown Publishers, New York, 1996.

Hudson, Charles. *Knights of Spain, Warriors of the Sun.* University of Georgia Press, Athens, 1997.

Jameson, Franklin, Editor. *Spanish Explorers in the Southern United States 1528-1543: Original Narratives.* Texas Historical Association, 1990.

Knight, Clay. *The De Soto Chronicles.* Government Archives Volume I, 1994.

Weber, David. *The Spanish Frontier in North America.* New Haven, CT. Yale University Press, 1994.

Woods, Michael. *Conquistadors.* University of California Press, LA., 2000.

CHAPTER 9

Spain's Conquest of The American Southwest
1539 – 1822

In 1536, three Spaniards and a Moorish slave named Estevanico arrived in Mexico City as the only survivors out of 600 from the failed Narvaez expedition that had landed in Florida in 1527 with 600 Conquistadors. The Conquistadors of this doomed expedition were mostly killed by Florida Indians and by ship wrecks when they made their way to what is today Galveston, Texas in 1528. The 80 survivors of this expedition were then killed and enslaved by Indians in Texas. The last four survivors escaped captivity and made their way across New Mexico, Arizona, and down the west coast of Mexico to Mexico City. Though the survivors had no gold themselves, they told stories of the legendary seven cities of gold that they had been told about from Indians that were supposed to exist in what is today New Mexico. The Spanish officials in Mexico City wanted to see if these cities could be the legendary seven cities of gold that were believed to have been established by a lost group of Portuguese that had escaped the Islamic conquest of Portugal in the Middle Ages. The Spanish wanted to send these four

Narvaez expedition survivors back with a small expedition to verify the existence of the seven cities of gold in New Mexico, but three of them refused to go back. It was decided that a small expedition would be sent with the Moorish slave Estevanico to New Mexico.

On March 7, 1539, a monk named Friar Marcos, Estevanico, and several hundred Aztec and Tlaxcala warriors left Mexico City for New Mexico to search for the seven lost cities of gold. The expedition arrived in New Mexico to find the Pueblo Zuni city of Cibola in the midst of the desert. Estevanico was then sent into the city to ask for permission for the expedition to enter. The Zuni Indians were alarmed by the expedition and killed Estevanico. The Zuni Indians then attacked the Aztec and Tlaxcala Indians outside the city and drove them off. The expedition fought a running battle for several days as they retreated out of New Mexico and returned to Mexico City where Friar Marcos reported that he had seen the seven cities of gold and the Pacific Ocean from a hilltop outside of Cibola.

On Feb. 23, 1540, Francisco de Coronado led an expedition of 335 Conquistadors, 1,300 Aztec and Tlaxcala warriors and Friar Marcos to go to New Mexico and to conquer the seven cities of gold. On July 7, 1540, the Conquistadors and their Indian allies attacked the Pueblo Zuni city of Cibola. Coronado was wounded in the battle, before the Spanish were able to use harquebus musket fire and artillery to clear the walls of defenders and to blast open the gate to the city. The Zuni Indians surrendered to stop the slaughter of their people shortly after the Conquistadors and Aztecs had entered the city. The Conquistadors became even more violent after the city had surrendered because there was no gold to be found anywhere. The Spanish cut off the hands of many Indians and then used their war dogs to tear apart and eat Zuni men, women, and children to get them to tell where they were hiding their gold, but after several days, they came to realize that there was no gold in Cibola. Coronado became angry with Friar Marcos because he had claimed that Cibola was one of the lost cities of gold and the Pacific Ocean was hundreds of miles away according to the Indians.

During the winter of 1540-41, the Conquistadors attacked 12 Pueblo towns on the Rio Grande River thinking that these may be the lost cities of gold. Hundreds of Indians were killed in what became known as the Tiguex War. After the Pueblo Indians surrendered, over 200 were burned at the stake by the Spanish. Coronado ventured as far north as Kansas, but found no cities of gold and returned to Mexico City in 1542.

In 1598, the Spanish established a permanent colony in New Mexico around the city of Santa Fe. In 1607, the Spanish brutally conquered the Pueblo Indians again and forced their conversion to Catholicism. Many Pueblos were forced to become slaves to labor in mines in Mexico. In the 1670s, drought across the West lead to attacks by Apaches from Arizona and other Indian tribes against the Pueblos to take their corn and food supplies. The Pueblos saw that the Spanish were helpless to intervene on their behalf and began sending out war parties to raid the Apache towns as well. The Pueblo also returned to their old tribal religion and began doing the Kachina dance (similar to the ghost dance) all night to contact spirits or their dead ancestors.

In 1675, the Spanish arrested 47 Pueblo medicine men for encouraging the Kachina dance among the Pueblo in place of Catholicism. Three medicine men were hanged, one committed suicide, and the rest were publicly whipped. Pueblo scouts led most of the Spanish soldiers against Apache towns in Arizona as several hundred Pueblo warriors forced the Spanish in Santa Fe to release the forty-three remaining medicine men. One of the medicine men was a man named Pope who began planning a revolt against the Spanish. On August 10, 1680, the Pueblo Indians attacked most of the settlements outside of Santa Fe killing over 400 men, women, and children as well as twenty-one Franciscan monks and priests. Over 3,000 Spanish sought refuge in Santa Fe and were put under siege by 2,500 Pueblo warriors. On August 21, 1680, the Santa Fe militia met the Pueblo warriors in battle outside the city and drove off the Indians with disciplined volley fire from their harquebus's and muskets. The settlers then left for Mexico City. The Pueblos had captured and released several thousand of the Spanish horses onto the Great Plains because they didn't know how to use the animals and saw them as a symbol of Spanish oppression. These released horses became hundreds of thousands by the early 1700s and populated North America. The Plains Indians then developed their hunting and war culture around these horses. In 1692, a few Spanish soldiers recaptured Santa Fe in a bloodless coup after threatening worse Spanish retaliation if the Pueblo didn't submit.

From the early 1700s to 1822, with few Spanish troops available, the Apache Indians were given guns and valuable trade goods by Spanish agents to raid and attack the Comanche and Pawnee Indians in what is today Texas, Oklahoma, Kansas, and Nebraska that had been causing problems in the Southwest as a way of maintaining Spain's authority in this area. The Spanish and their Apache allies had the biggest problems fighting with the Comanche Indians in the northern 2/3 of Texas, Oklahoma, and the eastern third of New Mexico. This area known as Comancheria never really came under Spanish control.

In 1718, the War of the Quadruple Alliance broke out between France and Spain which spread to the Great Plains as French agents from the Louisiana Territory sought to recruit Plains Indians to attack Spanish settlements in the Southwest. In 1718, over half of a force of one hundred Apaches were killed or captured by several hundred Pawnee Indians and their French agents near the Platte River in Nebraska.

This buffalo hide relief shows Pawnee Indians checking Spanish efforts to expand into the American Great Plains in 1720 by massacring most of the Villasur expedition.

In 1720, the concerned Spanish governor sent General Pedro de Villasur with one hundred Spanish soldiers, seventy Pueblo and twelve Apache warriors to capture or kill French agents operating in Nebraska and to recruit the Pawnees to switch to the Spanish side in this war. The Spanish force reached the Platte River in August of 1720 and tried to negotiate with French agents and the Pawnee separately for peaceful relations. On August 13, 1720, the Spanish camped on the Loup River near present day Columbus, Nebraska. At dawn on August 14, the Pawnee warriors and the French agents crawled in close to the camp under cover of darkness and the three foot tall grass that surrounded the camp when they began firing arrows and muskets at the Spanish. Villasur was one of the first to be killed when he was struck by several arrows. The other Spanish soldiers grabbed their muskets and formed a tight circle in the middle of the camp. The French and Pawnees were within 10-20 yards of the Spanish and neither side could miss as they shot at each other. Once it was clear that almost all of the Spanish were wounded from arrows or musket balls, the Pawnee attacked with tomahawks, knives and spears. The wounded Spanish put up a desperate fight as they grappled with the Pawnee warriors before being overwhelmed and killed.

As the melee was going on, eight Spanish soldiers made for and mounted the horses tied to trees to make an escape, but three were pulled off their horses and killed while the other five made it to the Pueblo and Apache camp a short distance away. The Pawnee warriors followed the five escaping Spanish soldiers to the Pueblo and Apache camp where both sides clashed in vicious hand to hand fighting with tomahawks and knives. The Pueblos and Apaches and the five Spanish soldiers then escaped on horseback as they saw more and more Pawnees coming to attack. Over thirty-five Spanish, twenty-one Pueblo, and sixty Pawnee Indians were killed in the battle. The Villasur Massacre as the battle would came to be known had a big impact as the Spanish gave up trying to control the Great Plains after this.

In the 1740s and 1750s, Comanche Indians and Lipan Apaches attacked and burned several Spanish missions around San Antonio, Texas (the Alamo was one) and tortured, maimed, and disemboweled many Spanish settlers, priests and Catholic Indians. The loyal Apaches that raided Texas could not contain the Comanches for the Spanish. The San Saba Mission was destroyed in 1758 near the Red River by a large force of Comanche Indians. The Spanish decided to send a force of 360 Spanish soldiers with 176 recently allied Lipan Apaches under Colonel Diego Parrilla to the Red River in 1759 to force the Comanches to cease hostilities. The expedition reached the Red River and attacked a Comanche camp killing 57 Indians and taking 140 prisoners. On October 7, 1759, Parrilla's force attacked a stockade fort called Spanish Fort that had been occupied by the Comanches near another Indian camp on the Red River. The Comanches kept up a constant fire of arrows and musket balls so that the Spanish could not breach or break into the fort after four hours of fighting. The Lipan Apaches then abandoned the Spanish as over two thousand Comanches began gathering on the Spanish flanks. Parrilla ordered a bayonet attack to disperse the gathering Comanche forces. The Spanish started to attack, but then broke ranks and ran away when they saw how many Indians there were. The Comanches chased and harassed the Spanish for well over a mile killing and capturing over sixty-five men (the captured Spanish were tortured to death later) before Parrilla could get his men to withdraw in a square formation. The Spanish never again tried to send troops against the Comanche Indians. In 1762, the Comanches agreed to stop attacking Spanish territory in return for guns and trade goods as a kind of tribute.

In 1769, the Spanish decided to expand into California and Colorado when they established the first of eight settlements with the Mission San Diego de Alcala. Many Indians hated the Spanish for forcing Catholicism on them and beating and whipping them for minor Catholic infractions. On November 4, 1775, six to eight hundred Indians snuck into the San Diego Mission and burned it down after massacring most of the people living there. In 1781, Yuma and Mojave Indians revolted and killed 131 set-tlers along the southern Colorado River. The Spanish were not able to rees-tablish control of the Colorado area after this. In 1785, a twenty-four-year-old medicine woman led another Indian revolt at the San Gabriel Mission near San Diego. A number of Spanish settlers and monks were killed before Spanish troops put the revolt down and had the medicine woman put to death. After 1807, Spain was preoccupied with putting down revolu-tions in Mexico and Latin America and wasn't able to give the American Southwest much attention. In 1822, Mexico won independence from Spain and the American Southwest went to Mexico until 1848 when the United States took control of it during the Mexican War. The Mexican govern-ment ceased giving the Apaches and Comanches guns and trade goods in return for their good behavior in 1822. The Apaches and Comanches then raided and fought constant wars with Mexico and the United States until the later part of the nineteenth century.

BIBLIOGRAPHY

Day, Arthur Grove. *Coronado's Quest*. Berkeley, University of California Press, 1981.

NebraskaStudies.org – The Villasur Expedition – the site is run by the University of Nebraska.

Hamalainen, Pekka. *The Comanche Empire*. Yale University Press, 2008.

The Handbook of Texas Online – *www.tshaonline.org*- Diego Parrilla 1759.

www.pbs.org- The West

Knaut, Andrew. *The Pueblo Revolt*. Norman: University of Oklahoma, 1995.

CHAPTER 10

England's Pirate Wars: 1568 – 1725

England's almost constant wars with Spain from 1568 to 1713 led to the creation of a force of English licensed privateers and pirates that attacked and captured Spanish treasure ships and cities in the Caribbean Sea region (the Spanish Main). Spain had huge quantities of gold and silver that they had acquired through their conquests of the Aztecs, Mayas, and Incas in Latin America. The Spanish also had a number of gold and silver mines in Latin America that brought a constant monthly supply of wealth to Spain from treasure ships that left Caribbean and South American cities during this time. This wealth made Spain the most powerful nation in the world which put the Spanish at odds with the naval power of England that also was striving to build its' own world empire.

England increasingly turned to privateers and pirates to attack Spanish treasure ships and cities to help finance their own empire. These pirates became the scourge of the Spanish Empire as they captured huge quantities of gold and silver mostly under the umbrella of the English government. England found that when they did have peace with Spain and piracy was no longer needed that their pirates proved very difficult to control. After the Treaty of Utrecht in 1713, England found that they had to fight one last war against the very force they had created to stop the depredations against the Spanish who were no longer enemies.

Spain did not allow any trading between foreign nations and its Caribbean and Latin American colonies. This did not stop a Plymouth, England merchant named John Hawkins from conducting enough illegal trading in 1562 and 1565 in the Spanish Caribbean colonies to make him and his backers immensely rich including Queen Elizabeth. The queen ignored protests by the Spanish ambassador as Hawkins prepared an expedition for a third voyage in 1567. Hawkins third voyage to the Caribbean had serious consequences that lead to a long period of wars between England and Spain. Hawkins had over 400 Englishmen that were of the lowest sort from the streets of London and Plymouth with six ships that left England for the Caribbean. Hawkins landed 200 men on the island of Riochacha who took the island after a brief battle with the island's Spanish militia. A slave then offered to lead the English to the inhabitants buried treasure in the interior of the island if he could join the pirates. Hawkins force laden with treasure forced the island of Santa Marta to trade with them as well.

A hurricane forced the fleet to take shelter on the island of San Juan de Ulua opposite of Veracruz, Mexico. Hawkins fleet arrived at nightfall and was allowed into the harbor and inside the defenses unmolested by the Spanish garrison because they believed this to be the first of 11 galleons that were expected to arrive to take a huge shipment of silver and gold mined in Peru and Chile back to Spain. Once the Spanish realized their mistake they entered into a tenuous truce with the English to allow them to resupply and refit their ships before they left the harbor. Three days later the real Spanish fleet arrived and entered the harbor under much tension between both sides. A battle broke out that night as Spanish Conquistadors boarded old hulks in the harbor that the four English ships were tied up to and took the English ships after boarding them in a bloody battle fought with swords, pikes, and harquebus muskets.

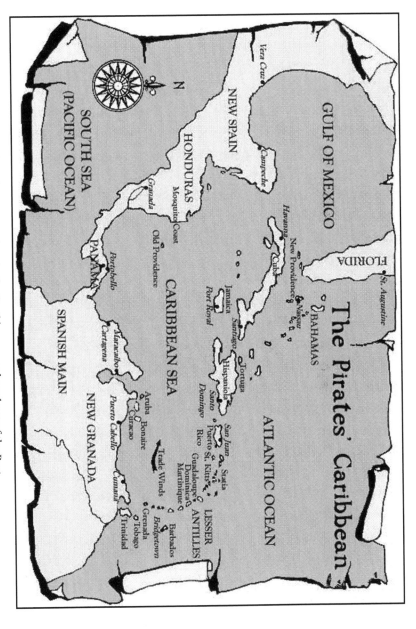

The Pirates' Caribbean

Most pirate campaigns in the Caribbean were based out of the Port Royal, Jamaica, often with the blessings of the English crown.

The English garrison at a harbor battery was also unexpectedly overrun after bitter close quarters fighting. Hawkins escaped with 200 men on two ships. Only one ship made it back to England with only 15 men left alive and little treasure to show for the investors. One of the survivors that returned to England was Francis Drake. The repercussions of Hawkins voyage was the beginning of the Eighty Years War (1568-1648) which pitted Spain against England and Holland.

In 1568, there was a surge in English, French, and Dutch privateers and pirates who attacked and raided Spanish shipping under the protection of their governments. Between 1570 and 1573, Francis Drake raided the Spanish Main with 2 ships and 73 pirates. From 1577 to 1580, Drake circumnavigated the globe as he raided the Spanish from the mostly unprotected west coast of South America including the capture of a gold filled Peruvian treasure galleon named the Cacafuego. Upon his return to England, Drake was knighted by Queen Elizabeth in 1580 for his exploits. The Spanish ambassador demanded that the galleon and its treasure be returned or there would be "grave consequences" for the future of England, but Queen Elizabeth had made so much money from this expedition that she was able to pay off England's national debt.

In 1585, Sir Francis Drake launched a major expedition from England of 29 ships including 2 of Queen Elizabeth's most powerful galleons and 2,300 marines and pirates to attack the Spanish Caribbean in search of Spanish treasure. In January of 1586, Drake's force appeared off the coast of Santo Domingo (Haiti and the Dominican Republic today) which was the jewel of the Spanish crown at this time. Drake ordered boats to be lowered and ships to fire canon opposite of the town as 1,000 marines and pirates were landed several miles away at an undefended beach. The Spanish Conquistadors formed in battle formation on the beach facing the English fleet ready to meet an attack from the sea. Some maroons (runaway slaves who lived in a remote area of the island) at first resisted the marines and pirates in the jungle thinking that the English were Spanish soldiers coming to capture them and return them to slavery. A few English were knifed and speared in the jungle before the maroons were convinced to help the English to find and attack the city of Santo Domingo. As the Spanish were waiting for a seaborne attack, the English marines and pirates with several hundred maroons attacked the Spanish force from the jungle to their rear. Over 200 Spanish were killed and wounded in vicious hand to hand fighting before they broke and retreated into Santo Domingo with the English and maroons hot on their heels who had taken control of the open gate to the city. Soon the flag with the cross of St.George appeared over the city.

Drake demanded an unrealistic 1 million ducats as a ransom for the return of the city to the Spanish. The Spanish said they couldn't come even close to this price as the English burned Catholic churches, tore down buildings, and hung 2 priests in retaliation for the murder of a maroon messenger. Finally, Drake settled for a ransom of 25,000 ducats to return the city to Spanish control.

Next, Drake's force arrived off the coast of the city of Cartagena (Colombia). Again, Drake used the fleet as a pinning force as the marines and pirates landed and stormed the city from its weak landward side. Drake demanded 600,000 ducats from the inhabitants, but excepted 110,000 after his men started dying from malaria and yellow fever. Drake's men also captured a Spanish mule train carrying a huge sum in gold and silver from Panama City that was meant to be kept in Cartagena's fortress vaults. A Spanish rescue fleet arrived several days late after the departure of Drake's fleet to the jeers of Cartagena's population. Drake had lost 750 men from disease and decided to head back to England before he would lose his whole force. On the way he stopped and burned the town of St.Augustine as Conquistadors watched from the walls of the fortress there. The loot brought back to England by Drake amounted to 105,000 pounds in gold and silver. Word of the disaster caused the Bank of Spain and the Bank of Venice (Philip II was its principle debtor) to collapse with all investors losing everything. Germany's top bank at Augsburg refused to loan any money to Philip II because his credit was worthless after this debacle.

Philip II was furious at Drake's pillaging of his colonies and ordered Admiral Don Alvaro de Bazan known as the "Never Defeated" to build a huge invasion armada at Cadiz to invade England. Queen Elizabeth named Drake as her "Admiral of the Seas" and sent him in 1587 with 30 ships to Cadiz where he burned and destroyed 37 ships that had been getting ready for the planned invasion of England. Drake went on to destroy a Spanish castle overlooking Lisbon and captured Philip II's personal ship (San Felipe) loaded with treasures from the orient and 400 slaves who were freed.

In August of 1588, the Spanish Armada of 130 ships loaded with soldiers and supplies headed for the long planned invasion of England. Drake's English fleet used fire ships to scatter the Spanish fleet and then sank five more ships through superior gunnery and avoiding boarding attempts by the Spaniards at the Battle of Gravelines. The Spanish Armada was then battered by an unrelenting storm that sank 51 ships and forced the beaching of 10 more ships on the west coast of the British Isles. Over 20,000 of Spain's best troops went down with the doomed ships. The direct result of this defeat was that pirates began raiding the Spanish Main's shipping at will with very little opposition from Spanish forces. Very little treasure was shipped to Spain between 1588 and 1591 because of these attacks. Between 1588 and 1603, from 100 to 200 privateer and pirate enterprises set out from England every year, averaging 150,000 to 300,000 pounds in Spanish treasure annually.

In 1595, enough treasure was trickling through to Spain from the Caribbean that Spain was starting to rebuild its military forces and conducted a daring raid with 40 ships against the southwest coast of England that burned a number of villages. Queen Elizabeth summoned

Drake and his former commander John Hawkins to lead an expedition of 27 ships and 2,500 marines and pirates to raid the Spanish Main and to recover the 2.5 million ducats that a crippled galleon had brought to San Juan de Puerto Rico during a storm. Drake and Hawkins lost a large landing party that had been captured by the Spanish in a failed raid on the Canary Islands. The English fleet then sailed for Puerto Rico. Hawkins died from dysentery just as the English fleet began trading shots with the El Morro fortress defending the city of San Juan. A shot from the fort barely missed Drake and splattered the blood and brains of several of his leading men as they sat down to eat. Drake then lost several hundred marines and pirates in 2 failed assaults on the El Morro fortress.

Drake told his demoralized men that they would have easy pickings in Cartagena. When Drake's force reached Cartagena they found that the residents had been forewarned and had evacuated the town leaving nothing of value or anything edible behind. Maroons that had helped Drake find the treasure that the Spanish had hidden before when he had raided the Spanish Main had been hunted down and massacred all over the Caribbean and northern South America at the orders of Phillip II. Only a few maroon survivors hid out in the interior jungles and dared not to help the pirates again. Over 800 marines and pirates were ambushed by Spanish Conquistadors and Native American archers and forced to retreat as they tried to take an over land route to attack Panama City from Nombre de Dios, Panama. A broken spirited Sir Francis Drake soon died from disease on board his ship as his defeated fleet returned to England empty handed in 1596. England mourned and Spain celebrated. Spain sent Armada's against England again in 1596, 1597, and 1598, but all were defeated by stormy weather at a great cost in ships and men.

Pirate communities which became known as the "Brethren of the Coast" sprang up along the coast of what is today Haiti and on the island of Tortuga after 1603 being inspired by Drake's incredible successes and riches won by raiding the Spanish Main. The pirates became known as buccaneers after the pork and beef jerky by the same name that they made in their communities. These buccaneer communities attracted the dregs of English, Irish, Dutch, French, Danish, and Flemish societies who operated as pirates under the protection of the English government. Buccaneer communities also took in runaway slaves and fugitive indentured servants as well. All that mattered was if they could work on a ship and fight when the time came. These buccaneers smelled bad from the meat they smoked and looked frightening with grease smeared on their faces to protect them from the sun. They wore bandanas or tricorn hats on their heads with a variety of often dirty mixed clothing items and used a variety of weapon types such as cutlasses, axes, swords, firelock muskets and pistols of various calibers. Women were greatly outnumbered by men in the Spanish Main and were repulsed by the buccaneers and were terrified by the many stories of pirate crew's that had gang raped women on their ships until they had died. It was known that most women taken captive by the pirates were never seen again.

The Spanish tried unsuccessfully on a number of occasions to destroy these communities of pirates. The pirates would fall back into the dense jungle of the island's interior and ambush the Spanish as they searched for them. The Spanish would then kill the pirate's pigs and cattle which just caused them to increase attacks on Spanish shipping. The pirates then built Fort Rocher to defend the pirate colony on Tortuga and as a place to store their captured Spanish treasure. The Spanish failed on several occasions in the early 1600's to capture the fort.

The Dutch also had privateers that employed Englishmen that attacked the Spanish in the Canary Islands, Africa, the Philippines, South America, and the Caribbean. In September of 1628, a Dutch privateer and admiral by the name of Piet Heyn with 31 ships, 679 canons, and 3,300 Dutch and English sailors, pirates and soldiers cornered and captured the entire Spanish treasure fleet of 15 ships in Matanzas Bay, Cuba. It took five days and 1,000 mule carts to unload all of the gold and silver chests in Holland after the soldiers, pirates, and crews had all been given their share of the treasure. The psychological and financial impact of this on Spain was immediate.

Again, the Bank of Spain collapsed on the news of the loss of the entire treasure fleet. In addition, Spain could not secure any credit to make up for the lost treasure. The Spanish Empire was at its lowest ebb in 1629 and was not able to conduct major military operations in its wars for several years after this debacle. The Spanish treasure that was taken by Dutch and English pirates and soldiers financed Holland's War of Independence from Spain for the rest of the war (the Eighty Years War) and helped to give the Protestants victory over the Spanish. The Spanish had provided much of the troops and money for the Catholic League in the Thirty Years War until both wars ended in 1648 at the Treaty of Westphalia. The peace for England would not last long though because war broke out again against its former ally Holland and its old enemy Spain in the early 1650's.

The English Civil War (1642-1649) brought the Parliamentarians to power under the Protectorate of Oliver Cromwell. Another Anglo-Spanish War (1654 to 1660) broke out when the Spanish captured Fort Rocher with 700 soldiers and a battery of artillery in 1654. The Spanish breached the fortification walls with their artillery from some heights above the rear of the fort. The pirates agreed to surrender under terms and opened the gates to the Spanish who stormed into the fort and butchered most of the 330 pirates along with much of the population of Tortuga. The Spanish also captured 12 pirate ships of various sizes and took 500 prisoners to Santo Domingo to work as slaves. Most importantly for the Spanish was the recovery of 160,000 pieces of eight in Doubloons that had been kept in the fort. France took over Tortuga a few years later and used it as a pirate base into the early 1700's. Quite a number of these French pirates were involved in England's pirate expeditions of the late 1600's against Spain.

Oliver Cromwell saw the attack and massacre by the Spanish at Fort Rocher against the mostly English pirates as an attack on England and as an opportunity to gain one of Spain's most lucrative colonies. Cromwell then ordered a fleet of 34 ships, 6,000 soldiers, and 7,000 marines and pirates to put Santo Domingo under siege and to claim Hispaniola as a colony of England in 1655. This expedition was part of Cromwell's grandiose Western Design plan to dominate the Caribbean and to capture Spanish gold from treasure ships by English privateers and pirates.

Over 13,000 English soldiers, marines and pirates were landed 30 miles from the city of Santo Domingo to march through the jungle to attack the city from its landward side on Hispaniola. After 4 days of marching through the jungle the English army was ambushed by 2,400 Spanish soldiers, militia, and vaquero cavalry (cattle herders) armed with lances. Discipline in Cromwell's New Model Army broke down as 3,000 English troops in the vanguard were cut down in a cross fire of musket balls and canon grapeshot followed by charges by the vaquero cavalry who rode down and impaled the fleeing Englishmen on their lances. After the English force was re-embarked back onto the ships, the fleet failed to subdue the Spanish fortifications through bombardment and left to evict the Spanish from Jamaica instead. The naval commander William Penn took over command of the entire operation from Robert Veneables after the debacle at Santo Domingo. On the way to Jamaica, 1,500 English troops died from malaria and 1,500 more troops were drowned when 4 ships went down in a storm. Jamaica had only 1,500 Spanish settlers and no fortifications. Around 600 Spanish militiamen were routed by the 7,000 English soldiers and pirates that had descended on Jamaica. The Spanish population was then forced to evacuate for Cuba. Within a year, the English invasion force had been further reduced to only 2,500 of the original 13,000 men that had left

England due to tropical diseases. Penn and Veneables were locked up in the Tower of London by Cromwell for not capturing Hispaniola and losing so many men on the expedition. The Spanish tried unsuccessfully to take Jamaica back in 1657 and 1658 before ceding it to England in 1670.

In 1655, Port Royal became the new English pirate base and sin city of the world with a harbor that could hold 500 ships. Cromwell had intended the city to be a bastion of Protestant piety and had sent a number of Puritan missionaries there to spread the Christian message. One such missionary left for England on the same ship that he had arrived in Port Royal on saying that the city was nothing but a "den of iniquity for pirates, cutthroats, and whores." Port Royal became rather a pirate paradise which almost exclusively consisted of brothels, gambling houses, taverns, and grog shops with huge amounts of Spanish Doubloons, gold, and silver to be spent. Most pirates could have retired after only a couple of successful Spanish treasure ship acquisitions, but they were so addicted to the life of sin in Port Royal that they stayed in pirating until they died of disease or in battle. England even had a licensing office where ship owners could get a privateering license to conduct their depredations against the Spanish with the English government's approval. By the late 1600's there were thousands of pirates that were based out of Port Royal which meant that the pirates had the numbers and ability to launch major all pirate campaigns against the Spanish.

In 1660, England's war with Spain had ended and King Charles II was restored as king of England after the death of Cromwell. Sir John Modyford was appointed governor of Jamaica and was ordered to halt the pirate attacks against the Spanish. Modyford, who regularly received a cut of the captured Spanish treasure found excuses to allow the pirates to raid Spanish ships and settlements anyway. King Charles sent a number of letters to Modyford to force all of the pirates back to port. Modyford sent letters back to King Charles claiming that the pirates in Jamaica had stopped their attacks, but in truth he continued to approve pirating expeditions against the Spanish because he couldn't control them. A number of expeditions that were approved to be conducted against the Dutch had in fact been conducted against the much more lucrative Spanish islands and shipping.

In 1667, Modyford had sent Sir Henry Morgan to lead the first of his major pirate expeditions against the Spanish when he took a force of 700 buccaneers and 12 ships and attacked Puerto del Principe, Cuba to capture 500 Spanish hostages in the event of a rumored Spanish attack on Jamaica. The residents of Puerto de Principe were warned from a prisoner that had runaway when Morgan landed in southern Cuba to invite 200 more French pirates with 2 more ships to join his expedition. When Morgan's force reached Puerto de Principe, they landed and went toward the city in a difficult jungle route that bypassed a Spanish ambush on the main trail. Once the pirates reached the city they found close to a 1,000 Spanish militiamen in battle formation. The pirates fought a 4 hour engagement where their superior marksmanship and discipline eventually routed the Spanish militia. While the battle was going on, most of the inhabitants had hidden with their valuables in the interior. A few inhabitants were caught and revealed the whereabouts of some of their valuables, but only 50,000 pieces of eight were gathered. This amount didn't come close to paying off the debts for the expedition so it was decided that they would attack Porto Bello, Panama which was considered the Spanish center of trade in the New World.

Many of the pirates complained that the residents could have been forced to give up more treasure had Morgan allowed them to have tortured the Spanish. Morgan vowed that he wouldn't make that mistake again in fear that he might lose the support of his men. The French then left the expedition after an argument where one of their men was murdered before an agreed duel to deal with a dispute with an English pirate.

Porto Bello was well defended with a blockhouse and three castle fortifications that defended the city's horseshoe shaped harbor. The main problem that the Spanish had was that they only had 133 soldiers and no militia to defend the forts. Normally the port was defended by 200 soldiers and 800 to 1,000 militiamen, but sickness and apathy had depleted Spanish ranks. Morgan's fleet came across 6 scarecrow looking pirates in a canoe that had escaped from a Porto Bello castle dungeon. Morgan swore vengeance as he heard their stories of abuse at the hands of the Spanish and more rumors about a planned invasion of Jamaica. The pirate fleet anchored at Boca del Toro as Morgan and 500 of his men transferred to 23 large canoes to sneak up on Porto Bello in a night attack. The pirates disembarked and broke into a blockhouse manned by 5 soldiers and made the mistake of calling out for the men to surrender or be cut down. The Spaniards opened fire and shot a couple of pirates before they were rushed and run through by swords. The firing alerted the other Spanish fortifications that an attack was under way.

The pirates quickly charged across the beach past the walls of Santiago Castle and into Porto Bello and started killing every person they could find to spread terror. After securing Porto Bello, the pirates charged through the shallow surf to take the half finished Geronimo Castle whose 5 defenders surrendered after only taking a few badly aimed shots. Now the pirates turned back toward Santiago Castle with priests and nuns as human shields that carried the pirate's ladders to the walls. The Spanish fired chain shot that cut down 2 priests and decapitated a number of pirates in the assault. The pirates ran past their slow moving human shields with the ladders up to the walls, but were shot by musket fire as they tried to climb the ladders. In the meantime, another group of pirates breached the castle's front gate with wick lit grenades and charged inside the castle. The fighting was desperate with swords, firelock pistols, and cutlasses until the entire Spanish garrison of 74 lay dead. Morgan lost 18 dead and 34 wounded in the battle for Santiago Castle. Many of the wounded pirates screamed and cried in agony with gaping sword wounds and died days later. Then San Felipe Castle surrendered with 44 of 49 men after they had repulsed a pirate assault.

The Spanish sent a militia force of 800 men from Panama City to attack Morgan's men, but the militia was no match for the violent pirates who met this force on an open field outside of the town and made short work of them. Morgan's men raped a number of women and terrorized the people of Porto Bello until they had gathered 250,000 pieces of eight ($12.5 million in today's money). Each man received an equivalent of $12,000 as their share. Morgan returned to Port Royal with evidence in a letter from the governor of the Spanish intentions to invade Jamaica as his men blew their money on prostitutes, rum punch (called kill devil), and in gambling. A number of men died in drunken fights over prostitutes and gambling losses which was normal behavior when the pirates started running out of money after a big haul. The pirates then started asking Morgan when they were going out on another big expedition.

Modyford emphasized the planned attack on Jamaica by the Spanish as to his reason for not reigning in Morgan's attacks on the Spanish Main in his dispatches to King Charles II. King Charles had the 34 gun frigate called the Oxford given to Port Royal to help defend Jamaica from a potential Spanish invasion. Modyford then gave the ship to Morgan to use in his next expedition. In 1669, Morgan gathered together 900 men and 12 ships including the Oxford at Cow Island off of Hispaniola for a war council and a party to celebrate the riches to come when they were to attack Maracaibo in what is today Venezuela. At nightfall, the pirates aboard the Oxford began firing their pistols in a drunken celebration. One of the pistols accidentally ignited the ammunition and powder room in the Oxford and caused the ship to explode. Only Morgan and 10 others survived out of 211 men that were on board the ship. Pirates in the rest of the fleet came out to go through the dismembered remains of the 200 men that had died to take coins and gold rings from their clothes, ears and fingers. Another 200 men and 3 ships left the expedition after this disaster. Morgan continued to Maracaibo with 8 ships and 500 pirates.

The pirates reached an inlet from the Caribbean Sea called Lake Maracaibo and found a Spanish fort at its mouth defended by 9 men and 11 canons. The fort's garrison fired canon shot at the fleet all day before they abandoned their post prior to a pirate assault that night. Morgan's men took the fort and stopped a fuse that was an inch from exploding the fort's powder magazine. The pirates then went on to terrorize and to plunder the towns of Maracaibo and Gibraltar on the coast of the inlet lake for another 3 weeks. When Morgan's fleet of 13 ships (5 ships were captured from the Spanish) approached the mouth of Lake Maracaibo, they found the fort reoccupied and garrisoned by 40 soldiers. In addition, there were three warships that were manned by 500 more Spanish soldiers that blocked the channel that led out to sea. Morgan's fleet withdrew and busily readied themselves for a battle.

On April 25, 1669, Morgan's fleet returned and sent forward a ship covered in combustible materials and full of explosives to bring alongside the 38 gun Spanish flagship called the Magdalena. Once the ship had came next to the Magdalena, over 100 Spanish soldiers swarmed onto the ship and found that its' crew were dressed dummies as 12 pirates dove off the back of the ship and swam to a waiting rowboat. Suddenly, the ammunition magazine of the pirate ship exploded from a time fuse which killed the Spanish troops on board and sank the Magdalena within minutes. The 14 gun Marquesa and the 26 gun San Luis cut their cables to get away from the burning Magdalena and ran aground near the fort. The Spanish soldiers on those ships ran for the fort as Morgan's men refloated and took the Marquesa. Morgan's men then pretended to land pirates near the fort's landward side for an assault by sending the same pirates back and forth from their ships as the men hid in the bottom of the boats on the return trip. The fort's soldiers then moved its entire complement of canons landward to prepare for an attack. Once Morgan saw this, the entire fleet slipped out of Lake Maracaibo and headed for Port Royal with its' ships loaded with Spanish wealth. Spanish ambassadors vehemently complained to King Charles again as Morgan's men made the prostitutes and the bar owners in Port Royal wealthy. Again, Modyford ignored letters from the king to reign in the pirates.

In December of 1670, Morgan with 2,000 pirates and a fleet of 40 ships headed for Panama to take the Spanish gold and silver warehouses at Panama City. The Pacific port would be attacked from the landward side after securing a Caribbean port for the fleet. On January 6, 1671, 400 pirates disembarked to assault a stockade fortification called Fort San Lorenzo that was defended by 360 Spanish soldiers at the mouth of the Chagres River. The pirates were cut down by grapeshot and musket fire as they charged across the beach at the fort. The second attack was turned back with heavy losses as well. After the sun set, the pirates crept along a gully to get close enough to the fort to throw in grenades and firepots that set the fort on fire. Over 150 Spanish soldiers deserted at that point as the over 200 other troops prepared to defend the ruins of their smoldering fort. In the predawn hours the buccaneers assaulted the ruined fort and fought a desperate hand to hand battle with cutlasses, swords, pistols, and musket butts. The entire Spanish force was killed or wounded at the cost of 30 buccaneers dead and 76 wounded. Morgan's fleet anchored and his army disembarked. Morgan picked 1,400 of his best men and headed up the Chagres River in 36 large canoes toward Panama City as the rest of his men guarded the fleet and rebuilt the fort. Morgan's men traveled as far as they could by canoe and headed over land for seven days through the jungle with their weapons and very few provisions. Over 200 pirates died from fever, dysentery and occasional ambushes by the Spanish and their Native American allies during their journey through the jungle.

On January 27, 1671, Morgan's army came to a great plain in front of Panama City filled with cattle that the famished buccaneers slaughtered and ate as they made camp for the night. At dawn on January 28, Morgan's army awoke to see over 2,000 Spanish militiamen in battle formation with 300 cavalry on each flank. Undaunted, 1,200 pirates formed a solid line 2 and 3 ranks deep and advanced against the Spanish army. The Spanish cavalry charged from both ends of the line with over 100 of them being shot down and forced to retreat by accurate musket fire from the pirate line. Then the Indians stampeded cattle toward the rear of the pirate army. The pirates in the rear ranks turned and fired their muskets which forced the cattle and Indians back. The Spanish militia advanced and exchanged a volley with the pirates before throwing down their muskets and running away in terror. The pirates killed many Spanish militia troops as they tried to run away. Over 500 Spanish and only 15 pirates died in the battle. Panama City was set on fire as the residents fled into the jungle. To Morgan's disappointment most of the gold and silver had been taken away by Spanish ships prior to the pirate's arrival. Over 750,000 pieces of eight were acquired through the torture of those Spaniards that the pirates were able to capture to reveal the location of their hidden valuables and from ransoming others. The fortune was packed on 176 mules and hauled back to Morgan's ship. Morgan gave each man only 200 pieces of eight ($36) and then simply abandoned his army and left with the rest of the money without saying anything to the men. The pirates were furious and felt betrayed for all their suffering for Morgan. Many then took their ships and raided along the Spanish Main for more loot to make up for this disappointment.

In April of 1671, Morgan arrived in Port Royal to a hero's welcome. King Charles was livid because he had just signed another treaty with Spain and ordered both Modyford and Morgan to be brought back to England in chains. Hostilities with Spain and Holland resumed in 1672 and both Modyford and Morgan were forgiven. A buccaneer expedition under Basil Ringrose was launched against Panama again in 1680 that captured and plundered some ships, but failed in taking any cities. Morgan returned to Jamaica in 1674 and served as Lieutenant-Governor of the island until his death in 1688. Sir Henry Morgan always resented being called a pirate because he saw himself as a loyal subject doing his duty for England.

For years, Protestant ministers had made their way to Port Royal and preached on the streets and from their pulpits that God's wrath would come down on this sinful city just as it had on Sodom and Gomorrah in biblical times. The pirates mostly just laughed off the warning, took a swig of rum and walked away with their arm around a prostitute. Many pirates joked that they'd rather be in Hell where all their friends surely were having a party. In 1692, Port Royal had 2,000 dwellings with over 6,500 pirates, prostitutes and bar owners that lived there. On June 7 of that year, a devastating earthquake destroyed 2/3rds of the city and dropped it into the sea. Those not killed in the earthquake ran down to what was left of the city not to help and rescue the survivors, but to steal valuables off of the dead and wounded and to rummage through the destroyed brothels and bars. As this was going on a tsunami came into Port Royal and killed most of those looking to take valuables. Over 3,000 people died in the earthquake and subsequent tsunami. Another 2,000 died from disease in the weeks that came after the disaster. There were attempts to rebuild Port Royal to make the city a pirate paradise again, but these efforts ended with a fire in 1703 and another tsunami in 1722. Today, Port Royal sits under between 20 to eighty feet of water at the southern end of Jamaica.

The time from 1692 to 1724 was considered the Golden Age of Piracy when the likes of Black Beard (Edward Teach), Charles Vane, Calico Jack Rackham, and Samuel Bellamy terrorized the seas with their mostly English crews attacking Spanish shipping. The pirates new sin city and base became New Providence in the Bahamas (known as the

Republic of Pirates). Gone were the days when pirate expeditions made major conquests. The Golden Age of Piracy was marked by attacking shipping exclusively for the most part. Blackbeard had seized 20 ships over an 18 month period and had terrorized everyone he had captured. The violent reputations of the pirates of this time caused most ships to surrender without a fight. Many depredations were committed against people captured by the pirates on the high seas. Murder was common and rape was almost always a given when women were found aboard seized ships. The reports of the atrocities by the pirates caused a loss of public support and took away a romanticized view of piracy in England.

Blackbeard was hunted down and killed by the English navy in 1718. Most of the 25,000 pirates operating in the Caribbean had to be hunted down and killed or hanged by 1725.

The British government did encourage privateers during the War of the Spanish Succession from 1702 to 1713 by licensing the pirates as part of their war against Spain and France. Spain demanded that England revoke all privateer licensing and enforced an end to English piracy with the Royal Navy as a provision of the Treaty of Utrecht in 1713 that ended the war. England agreed to end piracy by its subjects because of the great debt that the war caused and because the pirates were not sending the king's share of prize money to England except for a small pittance of the seized wealth. Piracy had become a liability to England and it needed to be stamped out. At first pirates were given the opportunity to be given amnesty by the British government if they turned themselves in and swore to never be involved in piracy again. Some pirates did get out when given this option. Most pirates loved the exciting lifestyle of a buccaneer too much to quit. After 1718, it was clear that the royal Navy would have to enter an intensive campaign to end piracy by its subjects. Between 1718 and 1724, the royal navy hunted down and killed thousands of pirates including Blackbeard in bloody ship battles. Close to 600 pirates were hanged by the Royal Navy during this time as well. By 1725, the Age of Piracy was over with. Pirates still came and went over the next 100 years, but they never lasted long like piracy did under the umbrella of the English government from 1568 until 1714.

BIBLIOGRAPHY

Cawthorn, Nigel. *A History of Pirates* . Chartwell Books, New Jersey, 2004.

Cordingly, David – Editor. *Pirates, a Worldwide_Illustrated History*. World Publication Group, Miami, 1998.

Earle, Peter. *The Pirate Wars*. St.Martin Press, NY. 2003.

Marrin, Albert. *The Sea King.* Athenium Books, NY. 1995.

Steele, Ian. *The English Atlantic: 1675-1740.* Oxford Publishing, London, 1986.

Talty, Stephen. *Empire of Blue Water.* Crown Publishers, NY. 2007. (This book has some excellent maps from Henry Morgan's pirate campaigns).

Williams, Neville. *Francis Drake.* Weidenfield & Nicolson, London, 1973.

Woodward, Colin. *The Republic of Pirates.* Harcourt Publishing, NY. 2007.

CHAPTER 11

Christian Holocaust:
The Thirty Years War 1618 – 1648

The Thirty Years War from 1618 to 1648 was one of the most devastating wars in European history which caused as many as 8 million deaths (these numbers come from European census records) from war, disease, famine, and religious persecution between Catholics and Protestants. Most people know about the Holocaust of World War II, but few know about an equally devastating holocaust between Catholics and Protestants that came out of the Reformation. There were unprecedented casualties in the war from battles that often caused losses of between 20-40 % of all combatants involved in the bloody 17th century style of warfare that mixed medieval swords and pikes with matchlock muskets and canons. The war depopulated whole regions of Bohemia and Germany. There are numerous accounts and illustrations of travelers seeing hundreds and even thousands of civilians hanging dead by their necks from trees in areas that had an army of the opposite Catholic or Protestant religious affiliation pass through the area.

A common site in Bohemia and in Germany during the Thirty Years War was that of hundreds and even thousands of mostly civilians hanging dead from trees. Both the Catholic and Protestant armies committed atrocities against populations that sympathized with the opposite side's faith.

The Thirty Years War eventually pulled in all of the nations of Europe which pitted Catholic nations against Protestant ones. The Catholic League was made up of the Holy Roman Empire (Austria under Habsburg rule), Poland, the southern German states (Bavaria), and Spain who fought against the northern German states, Bohemia (Czech Republic today), Denmark, Sweden, and surprisingly Catholic France. All nations in Europe not mentioned sent troops to fight in the war either as mercenaries or for their religious convictions. For instance, there were over 127,950 English and Scottish troops that fought in the Swedish and French armies for the Protestant cause while 42,587 Irish troops fought with the Spanish for the Catholic League during the war. Mercenaries were used extensively by both sides during the war, but were problematic in that they saw rape, murder, and plunder as their legitimate right to supplement their incomes as paid soldiers. The Eighty Years War which started in 1568 as a war of Spain against Holland and England merged with the Thirty Years War and expanded the war into colonies in the West Indies, South America, Africa, the Philippines, and Indonesia. The Thirty Years War was split into the Bohemian phase (1618-1625), the Danish phase (1625-1628), the Swedish phase (1629-1635), and the French phase (1635-1648).

The Thirty Years War involved large formations of soldiers armed with pikes and supported by musketeers who fired firelock muskets. Most of the armies that participated in the war looked and fought in a similar way as these Spanish troops.

The war was started by conflict in Germany and Bohemia between Catholics against Lutherans and Calvinists that came out of the Protestant Reformation. This conflict often turned into violence and bloodshed particularly against Protestants. The Catholic Church wanted to maintain a monopoly on Christianity and vigorously fought against the Protestant movements and nations that emerged out of the Reformation.

The war was started when a Catholic, Ferdinand II, inherited the throne of Bohemia in 1617. Ferdinand also inherited the Holy Roman Empire as emperor in 1618 which consisted of Austria, Bohemia, Croatia, Hungary and several southern German states (it was not really holy or Roman). The population of Bohemia had only 10% of its population as Catholic and greatly opposed Ferdinand as their king. The vast majority of Bohemians were Lutherans and Calvinists who resented being ruled by a staunch Catholic ruler. Ferdinand II ordered that all Protestants were to either convert to Catholicism or were to leave Bohemia. Angry Bohemians then rose in revolt in 1618 and elected the Calvinist Frederick V as their king and formed a Protestant confederacy with Transylvania and Saxony. Dutch, German, and English money and mercenaries were sent to bolster the Bohemians. An army of Bohemians and mercenaries that resembled more of an armed mob pillaged several Austrian towns near the border and massacred hundreds of Catholics in the process. Many hundreds of Catholics were impaled through the rectum in Transylvania (the favorite torture of a previous king named Vlad Dracul the Impaler from the mid 1400's). Then a war between Catholic Poland and the Ottoman Empire came out of efforts by the Bohemians to make an alliance with the Ottomans. This led King Ferdinand II to gather the Holy Roman army under Count Tilly to march on Prague and to subdue Bohemia.

On November 8, 1620, King Ferdinand and Count Tilly arrived at White Mountain outside of Prague with 25,000 seasoned troops including several thousand elite Polish and Bavarian Cuirassier cavalry arrayed in battle formation. The Bohemian army with 30,000 militia and mercenaries were stationed between three evenly spaced redoubts across the front of their line with a large star fort on the right wing of their army where the commander, Christian I of Anhalt-Bernburg was to oversee the battle. The redoubts and the star fort were to be defended by the more dependable of the Bohemian troops. It was thought that the militia would stand and fight better if they could see that their flanks were protected by fortified positions.

Christian I opened the Battle of White Mountain by sending forward his mercenary infantry and cavalry against the Catholic forces. The fighting was fierce with both sides losing close to 1,000 casualties apiece before the mercenaries retreated back to the Bohemian line. The Polish and Bavarian cavalry then charged the Bohemian left which disintegrated before the relentless charge. At seeing this, the whole Bohemian army broke and ran for their lives leaving their troops holding the redoubts and star fort isolated and cut off. The Bohemians in the redoubts fought on desperately in hand to hand fighting, but were all eventually overrun within an hour. The star fort and Christian I then surrendered as well after all other resistance had ceased. The Bohemians lost over 5,000 casualties to the Catholic forces losses of 2,000 casualties in the battle, but the Bohemian army had simply ceased to exist. Frederick V was then forced into exile.

After the Catholic army had occupied Prague, King Ferdinand I had ordered that all Protestants were to be extinguished from Bohemia. Large trees around cities, towns, and farms throughout Bohemia were covered with tens of thousands of men, women, and children hanging dead by their necks. There were tens of thousands of rapes. Catholic troops interrupted a Bohemian wedding and killed the groom and raped the bride who then disappeared never to be seen again. There were many groups of dead that had been impaled as a display of warning throughout

Bohemia. Over 100,000 of 151,000 farms in Bohemia were destroyed or confiscated by Catholic forces. Only those that were given an opportunity to convert back to Catholicism were spared. Many 3hundreds of thousands fled into Germany where the war soon spread. The population of Bohemia dropped from 3 million to 800,000 during the time between 1620 and 1625. As a result of the defeat at White Mountain, Bohemia spent the next almost 300 years being occupied by Austria or Prussia. Bohemians would not taste freedom again until November 18, 1918, when the new nation of Czechoslovakia was declared at the site of the White Mountain battlefield and confirmed at the Treaty of Versailles in 1919.

Protestants in Denmark, Holland, England, Sweden, and northern Germany as well as Catholics in France were appalled at the genocide of Christians by other Catholic Christians. Transylvania was the next area to be thoroughly sacked with thousands of Protestants being hanged and impaled in retaliation for similar previous attacks on Catholics there. The genocide stirred up further resistance among Protestants in Saxony and in other German states against the Catholic League. Denmark under King Christian IV then championed the Protestant cause in 1625 and declared war on the Catholic League which had been reinforced by the entry of Spain into the war as well. It was the entrance of Denmark and Spain into the conflict that made the Thirty Years War a much wider and thus bloodier war in Europe.

The next 8 years after the defeat at White Mountain were bad years for the Protestants as they were defeated by the Imperialist Austrian Habsburgs, Bavarian, and Spanish forces in Holland, Germany, and Italy. German Protestants were hanged and massacred by the hundreds of thousands as they had been in Bohemia. Catholic France sympathized with the Protestants for political reasons because they feared that the war would make the Spanish and the Austrian Habsburgs too powerful. Despite this, the French did not enter the war to support the

Protestants because they had their own problems with Huguenot rebellions in France from 1620 to 1629. The French proved to be just as brutal in putting down the Huguenot Rebellions as the Catholic League was in dealing with Protestants in Germany with hundreds of thousands of Huguenots dying in the struggle.

In 1624, the Spanish put the fortress city of Breda, Holland under a bloody 11 month siege. Dutch and English relief armies were defeated in an effort to lift the siege. Breda fell in June of 1625, after 10,000 Dutch and English troops died out of a garrison of 14,000. The Spanish lost 4,000 dead during the long siege as well. In November of 1625, a Dutch and English raid on Cadiz, Spain turned into a fiasco that cost them 7,000 dead and 62 ships lost which nearly sent both nations into bankruptcy. On August 27, 1626, King Christian IV lost half of his Danish army in a defeat at the Battle of Lutter as well as a number of other battles into 1629. Catholic forces continued to burn farms, rape women, and to hang Protestants of all ages in areas that they controlled. A new hero for the Protestant cause was desperately needed.

This hero came when King Gustavus Adolphus of Sweden intervened against Poland at the request of German Lutherans who had endured attacks and had thousands massacred by Polish Catholic forces. Adolphus Gustavus landed an army by sea into Poland and proceeded to conquer much of northern Poland, and Livonia (Lithuania and Latvia today) from Polish forces in some very difficult fighting between 1626 and 1629. While in Poland, Gustavus learned how to use cavalry charges to deadly effect from the Poles rather than to just to use cavalry to fire matchlock pistols on the enemy by caracole which was the custom of most nations at this time. The German Protestant princes started pressing Gustavus to become their champion and to attack the Holy Roman Empire's forces in Germany to give some payback for all that the Germans had suffered from the Imperialists. Gustavus started making preparations for the invasion of Catholic held areas of Germany.

From May to August of 1628, 25,000 Imperialist troops of the Holy Roman Empire under Count Albert Wallenstein placed the fortified city of Stralsund, Germany on the Baltic Sea under siege. Stralsund had 20,000 terrified citizens who feared the massacre that would follow should the city's 4,000 militia and the 1,000 German infantry force fail in defending the city. The Austrians dug parallel trenches and created a breach in the city walls with artillery, but were repulsed in bloody fighting in the breach that lasted a week and cost both sides several thousand casualties. A Protestant force of 900 Scots, 600 Swedes, and 1,150 Danes were brought by sea to bolster the defenses of Stralsund in June of 1628. On June 27, Imperial forces created another breach with artillery and assaulted the new breach. The Scottish troops held the breach in desperate fighting with their broad swords that lasted all night. By dawn of June 28, over 500 Scots lay dead in the breach with 300 more wounded which were surrounded by at least twice that many dead Imperialists. The Danes and Swedes then defended the breach all day as Imperialist forces continued to assault until they withdrew because they couldn't get through the mountain of corpses that blocked the opening in the wall. The Danes and Swedes lost another 1,200 men in defending the breach that day. The Imperialists lost over 5,000 casualties in the assaults that lasted an exhausting 24 hours. On July 2, another 1,500 Danes and Scots were brought into Stralsund to hold the city. The Imperialists created a third breach by July 21, but could not assault it due to torrential rains that turned the Imperialist siege works and camp into a marsh. Disease started settling in on the Imperialist army which had been reduced by half during the siege. Wallenstein was forced to lift the siege on August 4. It was the first big victory for the Protestant forces in Germany which helped to restore morale after the previous 8 years of continual defeats.

By 1628, Denmark's army and those of the other Protestant German states had been wrecked with their governments on the verge of collapse from war debts. The Protestant nations appealed to Holland for bailout loans on their debts so that the war could continue. As mentioned in the last chapter, the Dutch government sent a naval expedition under Piet Heyn with 31 ships, 679 canons, and 3,300 Dutch and English sailors, soldiers, and pirates and captured the Spanish treasure fleet which had been making its yearly run from Mexico to Spain laden with treasure from the South American mines. Spain had slipped into bankruptcy in 1627 and desperately needed this gold shipment to straighten out its finances and to continue military operations in the war. Piet Heyn captured the 15 ships of the treasure fleet in Matanzas Bay, Cuba.

The psychological and financial impact for Spain and for its support for the Catholic League was immediate. The Bank of Spain collapsed on the news of the loss of the entire treasure fleet. In addition, Spain could not secure any credit to continue military operations and to catch up soldiers pay which was in arrears all over the European theater. Spanish military operations mostly ceased and its overseas colonies were open to attack for years after this disaster. The Spanish redoubled their mining efforts around the clock in South America for Spain to recover, but had their treasure fleet wrecked in a storm off the Yucatan in1631, and had their entire treasure fleet lost again in a hurricane in the Atlantic in 1632.

Holland on the other hand had captured enough wealth to give the Protestant allies loans to pay their debts and to finance operations well into the 1640's. The Dutch then went on the offensive in 1629 and recaptured several Spanish held cities in Belgium without Spain being able to intervene. The Dutch were also able to capture the colony of Pernambuco, Brazil from the Portuguese and Spanish in 1630 (Portugal and its possessions had been occupied by Spain since the 1580's). The capture of the Spanish treasure fleet and the Protestant victory at Stralsund in 1628 proved to be a turning point for the Protestant forces in the Thirty Years War.

King Gustavus Adolphus invaded Catholic held areas of northern Germany in 1630 with Swedish forces. Gustavus took the total war approach that the Catholic forces had been practicing against Protestant Germans. It is well documented that Swedish forces under Gustavus burned over 18,000 Catholic villages, 1,500 towns, and over 2,000 Castles and fortifications. The Swedish troops and their German mercenaries also raped Catholic women, and hanged tens of thousands of Catholics in revenge for the earlier depredations that had been committed against Protestant Germans and Bohemians.

Both sides believed that God supported their cause over the other side's false faith. Here Gustavus Adolphus calls on God to give him victory over the Catholic forces.

From November of 1630 to May of 1631, the city of Magdeburg was placed under siege by 24,000 Imperialist troops under Count Tilly. On May 20, Magdeburg fell and the Imperialists sought revenge for Swedish atrocities by sacking the city, raping thousands of women, and burning the city to the ground. Over 25,000 inhabitants of Magdeburg were massacred while sparing only 5,000 who were then taken as prisoners to suffer continual torture, rape, and depredations over the months to come. Of these, only 450 inhabitants of Magdeburg survived. Each side in the Thirty Years War felt that they needed to commit atrocities to gain revenge for earlier depredations committed by the other side in a vicious cycle of death and mayhem that seemed to never end.

King Ferdinand II had been counting on the Spanish to loan him money and troops to continue the war in Germany, but the Dutch capture of the Spanish treasure fleet in 1628 meant that no money or troops were coming from Spain for the Holy Roman Empire. Imperialist military operations in Germany in 1629 and 1630 had mostly ceased with many of the Imperialist troops deserting because they had not been paid in over a year. Gustavus had a free hand in Germany to retake previously Catholic held territory. When King Ferdinand II received word of the Swedish intervention into Germany, he panicked and recalled Wallenstein to command the Imperial army after he had been dismissed previously for the defeat at Stralsund. Ferdinand forced banks in the Holy Roman Empire and in Italy to loan him enough money to allow Wallenstein to rebuild an army. Ferdinand loaned Spain enough money to be able to send him elite Spanish tercio infantry of mostly pikemen with supporting musketeers that the Imperialists greatly valued on the battlefield.

In 1631, Wallenstein felt that he had a formidable army to bring against Gustavus and his Swedish and Saxon allied army. Count Tilly was given command of an army of 35,000 Imperialist and Catholic League troops. Gustavus Adolphus with 24,000 Swedish troops and 18,000 Saxons met Count Tilly's army north of Leipzig on Sept. 17, 1631 at the Battle of Breitenfeld.

The Swedish army used at least half of their infantry as musketeers in smaller more maneuverable formations whereas the Imperialists depended on a majority of their infantry organized into huge tercio formations that were 50 or 60 men deep and armed primarily with pikes with some musketeers on the corners of the massive rectangle formations. Gustavus also had 9,000 cavalry that charged instead of using the more common Imperial caracole tactics that used cavalry to ride in formation to within 20 yards of the enemy and to fire their pistols in volleys at the enemy before falling back to reload and then to repeat the same tactic.

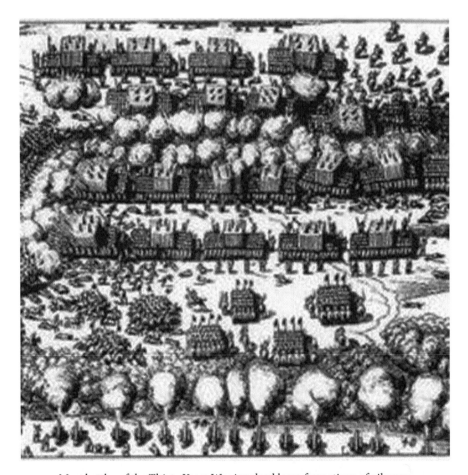

Most battles of the Thirty Years War involved large formations of pikemen supported by musketeers. The Swedes had smaller more maneuverable formations with more musketeers than the Catholic forces used.

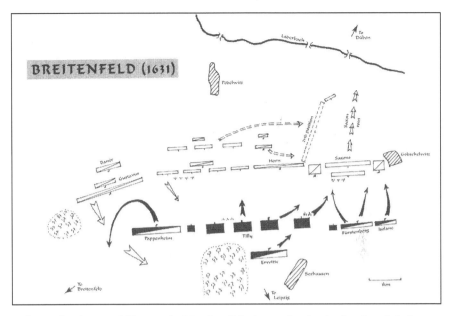

The Battle of Breitenfeld was a decisive Swedish victory despite the fact that their Saxon allies abandoned the battlefield which left their left flank open to Imperialist attack.

Catholic cavalry fire their pistols into a Protestant pike formation which was a maneuver that was called a caracole. Swedish cavalry preferred to charge with swords which brought them victory at the Battle of Breitenfeld. .

Tilly opened the battle by launching an all out attack against the 18,000 Saxons that held the Swedish left wing as Gustavus led a massive cavalry charge against the Imperialist left wing that drove those forces back on the opposite side of the battlefield. The entire Saxon force broke and fled the battlefield as the Imperialist army turned against the Swedish middle. Gustavus' cavalry charge shocked and drove the Imperialist left wing back so that both sides' lines turned almost a full 90 degrees. The Swedes captured most of the Imperialist artillery and turned it on them. It was at this point that the Swedish superiority in fire power took a toll on the Imperialist army as its tercio formations broke apart. Another series of Swedish cavalry attacks then routed the Imperialist army. The Imperialists suffered 7,600 dead, 9,000 captured, and a further 2,400 that deserted after the battle. The Swedes lost 3,500 dead, and the Saxons lost over 2,000 dead in Sweden's decisive victory. Because of the complete lack of medical care almost all wounded in the Thirty Years War were listed as dead because they rarely survived more than a few days before succumbing to their wounds. The victory caused the German states of Hesse, Hanover, and Brandenburg to join the Protestants against the Holy Roman Empire and the Catholic League. Catholic towns and villages continued to be burned with thousands more Catholics being hanged as a result of the Protestant victory at the Battle of Breitenfeld.

In 1632, the Imperialist forces had been rebuilt and fought a number of battles in which they continued to be defeated by the brilliant generalship of Gustavus Adolphus. Wallenstein and his top cavalry commander Count Pappenheim invaded Saxony with an army of 13,000 infantry and 9,000 cavalry in an effort to knock the Saxons out of the war. Gustavus Adolphus brought 13,000 infantry and 6,000 cavalry to confront the Imperialists at the Battle of Lutzen on November 16, 1632.

The battlefield at Lutzen was covered at first by fog into the late morning but then by smoke from gunpowder for much of the rest of the day which made command and control difficult for both sides. The Swedes attacked with cavalry led by Gustavus and threatened to out-flank the Imperialist army's left wing. Pappenheim then led a coun-ter attack with 3,000 Imperialist cavalry that had adopted the Swedish (actually Polish) tactic of charging and drove the Swedish army back, but not before Pappenheim had been mortally wounded. The battle swung back and forth in charges and counter charges. Finally around 1:00 o'clock, both sides committed their cavalry reserves in an effort to reach a decisive conclusion to the battle. Gustavus led 2,000 of his reserve cavalry into some thick smoke against the Imperialist left wing. No one could tell what was going on until a wind drove the smoke away and standing alone and rider less between the two lines was Gustavus Adolfus's horse. There was a shocked quiet pause in the battle.

Finally, the Swedes launched another attack in an effort to locate their commander. After two hours, the Imperialist army retreated, but it proved to only to be a pyrrhic victory because Gustavus Adolphus's body was found on the battlefield. He had become separated and disori-ented in the smoke on the battlefield and accidently rode to within a few yards of some Imperialist musketeers who shot him down with 5 mus-ket balls. Both sides lost around 6,000 dead in the battle. The champion of the Protestant cause was dead and no one was able to fill his shoes. This allowed the Imperialists to rebuild their forces and to regain some of the areas that they had lost in the previous 2 years. Gustavus's death meant that the war would go on to be a 30 year long war as opposed to a 14 or 15 year war.

The Catholic forces over the next two years won a number of victo-ries and regained the initiative against the Protestants. Catholic forces then began taking retribution for the burning of Catholic villages and towns and the hanging of so many people from those areas by the Swedes under Gustavus Adolphus. It was a vicious circle of each side wanting revenge for the other side's depredations against humanity. By the time the war would be over a full 1/3rd of Germany's villages and towns had been destroyed with its population falling from 15 million from before the Thirty Years War began to 10 million by 1648 when the war ended.

In 1634, Swedish forces invaded Bohemia to take revenge on the previous massacres that had happened there over the previous ten years. On August 29, 1634, 21,000 Spanish and Imperialist infantry with 13,000 cavalry met a Swedish army of 16,300 infantry and 9,300 cavalry at the Battle of Nordlingen. The Swedish army launched 15 failed assaults against well defended Imperialist positions. Finally, the Imperial army counter attacked and enveloped the Swedish lines which caused a rout. The Imperial cavalry rode down and massacred thousands of Swedish soldiers in the rout. Over 8,000 Swedish soldiers were killed and over 4,000 were captured as the Imperialists lost only 2,400 men in the battle.

The defeat went down with White Mountain as the worst of the war for the Protestants. Saxony was subsequently invaded and suffered much of the same fate as befell Bohemia and other Protestant areas in Germany under Catholic occupation. Sweden lost its role as the dominant force for the Protestants in Germany. Saxon soldiers were also forced to serve in the Imperialist army. Most of the Protestant kingdoms then made a separate peace with the Holy Roman Empire at the Treaty of Prague in 1635. Despite this, many German partisans attacked supply wagons, killed sentries and hung civilian Catholics in retaliation for the depredations committed against German Protestants. The partisan attacks only caused a vicious cycle of more hanging of Protestants in retaliation by Catholic forces and vigilante civilians which led to more partisan attacks and hangings of Catholics.

France officially entered the war in an alliance with Sweden in 1629 out of fear that the Holy Roman Empire and Spain would dominate the balance of power in Europe and would unite against them. Despite France's entry into the war, the French did not take a leading role in the Protestant cause until 1635 to fill in the void left from

Sweden's defeat. This move caused France to emerge as the dominant political force in Europe after the war's conclusion in 1648. The French first made a move against the Spanish in Belgium to aide their hard pressed Dutch allies who had been fighting Spain since 1568. On May 20, 1636, a French army of 35,000 enveloped and destroyed a Spanish army of 14,000 at the Battle of Les Avins at the cost of just 260 men. This victory gave the Dutch some relief from Spanish military operations for 2 years. In 1638, an army of 22,000 Dutch, Scots and Germans went to capture several Spanish forts near the village of Kallo which protected the approach to Spanish held Antwerp. Over 6,000 Dutch and Scottish assault troops were successful in over running and massacring the garrisons at several forts, but then the Spanish forces counter attacked and recaptured the forts and cut off most of the assault force from returning to their own lines. The Dutch and Scots lost 2,500 dead and another 2,500 captured in the battle. The Spanish lost over 1,100 troops in the battle.

In the meantime, the French cut the Spanish road by which Spain moved troops over land to reinforce operations in Belgium and Holland. In 1639, the Spanish decided to move 20,000 troops in 53 ships to reinforce their army in Belgium. On October 31, 1639, 95 Dutch warships intercepted the Spanish fleet in rough seas at the Battle of the Downs near the English side of the English Channel. The Dutch used 10 fireships to scatter the Spanish fleet and then attacked the isolated ships. One large Spanish galleon named the Santa Teresa dodged three fire ships. A Dutch ship came along side the Santa Teresa to board it when another fire ship struck the Spanish vessel and burst the ship into flames with most of the 1,100 soldiers and sailors on board being burnt alive below deck. The Dutch vessel was also burned along with 100 sailors as most of that ship's crew was able to jump ship and swim to a nearby vessel. In addition to losing the Santa Teresa, Spain lost 15 ships that ran aground with 13 more ships that had been sunk and another 16 that were captured. Over 15,200 Spanish sailors and soldiers died with another 1,800 being captured in the debacle. The Dutch lost just the one ship and 1,000 men in the battle.

This humiliating defeat made it very difficult for the Spanish to reinforce their army in Belgium and opened up the Spanish possessions in the Caribbean, Indonesia, the Philippines, and South America for the Dutch to take a number of lucrative sugar, spice, and coffee producing colonies. In 1640, a Dutch fleet of 41 ships caught a Spanish-Portuguese fleet of warships and transports at the Battle of Pernambuco (Brazil). The Spanish and Portuguese were attempting to take back the colony of Pernambuco from the Dutch. The Dutch sank 11 Spanish and Portuguese ships by using accurate long range gunnery and avoiding Spanish boarding attempts. The Dutch lost 3 ships as the Spanish-Portuguese fleet was turned back. The Dutch held Pernambuco, Brazil until the Portuguese took it back in 1654. In 1639 and 1640, Spain lost a total of 100 ships and 20,000 sailors in other naval disasters. This was the equivalent to Spain having 10 Trafalgar's in just a 2 year period. To make matters worse, Portugal which had been under Spanish control since the1580's rebelled and won independence from Spain in 1640 as well. These Spanish defeats set up the eventual victory and independence for Holland from Spain and helped to cripple the Catholic League's war effort in the Thirty Years War.

In 1642, the Catholic League was in desperate straits and needed to turn the tide of the war. They had one significant army left in Germany made up of 26,000 Imperialists including 1,650 Saxons. Sweden had a manpower shortage and was struggling to put men in the field to fight in Germany. The village of Bygdea in northern Sweden had sent 230 men to serve in the army in Poland and Germany between 1626 and 1639. Of this number, only 10 men made it home alive with 5 of these being crippled. Now Bygdea and other similar villages all over Sweden were asked to provide more men to die in Germany.

Sweden managed to scrape together an army of 15,000 men that was sent to liberate their former ally Saxony which had endured much death and destruction from the Imperialists since 1635. The Swedish army under General Torstensso now found itself very much out numbered and retreated to the old Breitenfeld battlefield in hopes of drawing the Imperialist army into a battle on familiar ground. The Second Battle of Breitenfeld opened with a massive attack by sixteen Imperialist cuirassier regiments to ride around a forest to attack the Swedish left flank, but the Swedes were able to shift enough infantry forces to block the Imperialist cavalry. The center of both lines engaged in some heated artillery and matchlock musket fire that covered the field in smoke. Torstensson then gathered all of his cavalry and sent them on a charge against the Imperialist left wing as was done at the first Battle of Breitenfeld. The Swedish cavalry was completely concealed by smoke and crashed through the unsuspecting first and second lines of the Imperialist infantry and cavalry and then continued to role up the entire line from the rear. The Saxons who had been forced to fight in the Imperialist army switched sides in the middle of the battle which started the Imperialist collapse. Over 15,000 Imperialists were killed or wounded with another 5,000 that were captured. The Swedes lost 4,000 men in the battle which proved to be just as decisive as the first battle at Breitenfeld had been. Saxony was liberated from Imperialist occupation though much of it lay in waste.

The Habsburgs of the Holy Roman Empire requested that the Spanish send an army of 27,000 to advance through the Ardennes Forest and into northern France to bring some pressure off the Imperialists in other sectors. The Spanish army invaded France from the same Ardennes that the Germans used in the two world wars and put the city of Rocroi under siege. A French relief army of 23,000 under the 21 year old Duc d'Enghien (Conde) arrived on May 18, 1643, and both armies set up for battle with their infantry in the center in 2 lines with the cavalry on the wings.

After dawn on May 19, the French center attacked the Spanish, but was driven back. In the meantime, the French cavalry on the right attacked and defeated the Spanish cavalry and attacked the exposed flank of the Spanish infantry. The remaining Spanish cavalry then attacked the French left and drove through their lines in an effort to role up their line. Duc d'Enghien then led an attack with the right cavalry wing which swung around the Spanish right and into the flank of the Spanish cavalry fighting behind their lines. The Spanish cavalry and the Imperial German and Walloon infantry were routed, as the French surrounded the Spanish tercios who fought on for 2 more hours while being blasted at point blank range from artillery and matchlock musket fire before accepting terms for surrender. The Spanish lost 15,000 men in the battle to the French losses of 4,000 casualties with most of the wounded dying over the next days and weeks. The Battle of Rocroi is considered to be the birth place of the French army and was the beginning of the end for the Catholic league in the Thirty Years War.

In 1645, the Dutch captured the city of Hulst from the Spanish in a siege while a Swedish army of 16,000 defeated an Imperialist army of the same size in Bohemia at the Battle of Jankau. At Jankau, the Swedish cavalry supported by new tactics involving mobile artillery defeated and drove off the Imperialist cavalry on both wings. The Swedish army surrounded and decimated the Imperialist infantry without giving any quarter because of the continued atrocities committed by Catholic forces against German Protestants. Over 5,000 Imperialist infantry were killed with another 5,000 who were wounded and captured. Then on August 3, 1645, a French and Saxon army of 16,000 under Vicomte de Turrene and Prince de Conde defeated an Imperialist and Bavarian army of 12,000 in the Second Battle of Nordlingen (Allerheim). The battle turned into a bloody general melee after both sides attacked each other at the same time around 4:00 o'clock along the whole front. The battle ended after nightfall with the Imperialists retreating after each side had lost 5,000 casualties in the battle. These defeats were a real blow to the Catholic league whose members were bankrupt and were in retreat all over Bavaria, Bohemia, Flanders, and Belgium from a war that seemed to never end. The French also began laying waste to large areas of Bavaria in the hopes that total war on this staunch Imperialist ally would help to bring the Catholic League to its knees and an end to the war.

Despite these victories, France who also had its treasury drained by the war was unable to force an end to the conflict in 1646 or 1647. On May 17, 1648, a combined French and Swedish army of 30,000 defeated an Imperialist army of 18,000 at the Battle of Zusmarshausen. The victory allowed a Swedish flying column then to capture Prague in June. The surviving Bohemians then mistakenly celebrated their independence. The final battle of the war was fought on August 20, at the Battle of Lens when a French army of 16,000 which was more than half made up of cavalry defeated a Spanish army of 18,000 that attacked the French line along the whole front. The Spanish were caught in a double envelopment and defeated by a French cavalry counter-attack. The Imperialists had been drained of men and money and could not field anymore armies and sued for a truce.

The Treaty of Westphalia in 1648 brought a final end to the Thirty Years War and the Eighty Years War that had merged with the former war. The treaty stated that each kingdom and principality could decide for themselves what religious affiliation that they would follow without interference by other nations. Calvinism and Lutheranism were to be given legal recognition by all nations in Europe. Protestants and Catholics were redefined as equal under the law and each was to be allowed to practice their religious affiliation even if it was not the religious affiliation of the state that they resided in without the threat of the loss of life and property. The independence of Holland and Switzerland was to be recognized by all parties. France was to receive significant territory in Alsace and Lorraine. Sweden received significant land in the

Baltic and northern Poland and Germany. Bohemia was retained by the Holy Roman Empire. Pope Innocent X condemned the treaty as "null, void, unjust, damnable and reprobate" for all time. France emerged as the big winner in the war in both power and prestige despite still having to fight a war with Spain until the Treaty of the Pyrenees was signed in 1659.

The Thirty Years War was not so unlike World War I in that the war killed off an entire generation of people in Central and northern Europe. Large areas of Germany, Bohemia, and Flanders were laid waste by the war. Of the 8 million people that died from the Thirty Years War over 1.5 million men died from disease or from fighting in the war. Most soldiers of both sides died by the time that they had participated in their third or fourth battle. Few combatants from either side that went on campaign for over a year returned home alive after leaving for war. Atrocities committed in the name of God killed another 2.5 to 3 million people in Germany and Bohemia. Armies from both sides brought famine, bubonic plague, typhus, and dysentery with them that killed another 4 million people wherever the armies had passed through in central Europe. The war did mean that people in Europe could go to the church of their choice without harassment, but it also led to a questioning of organized religion and absolutism that would eventually lead to the Enlightenment, the English Civil War, and the revolutions of the Americas and France.

BIBLIOGRAPHY

Benecke, Gerhard. *Germany in the Thirty Years War.* London, St. Martin's Press, 1978.

Cramer, Kevin. *The Thirty Years War & German Memory in the Nineteenth Century.* Lincoln, University of Nebraska, 2007.

Langer, Herbert. *The Thirty Years War.* Poole, England, Blandford Press, 1980.

Parker, Geoffrey. *The Thirty Years War.* London, Routledge and Kegan Paul Publishing, 1984.

Wedgwood, C.V. *The Thirty Years War.* New York Review Books, 2005.

Wilson, Peter H. *The Thirty Years War: Europe's Tragedy.* Belknap Press, Cambridge, MA. 2009. This massive volume is the best source on this topic.

CHAPTER 12

The Wars for Control of
The African Slave Trade: 1502 – 1850

The wars for control of the Atlantic Slave Trade from Africa to the Americas took place from 1502 to 1850. The Atlantic Slave Trade and the resulting Slave Wars caused the disappearance of at least 25 million Africans from Western and Central Africa. Portugal, Spain, Holland, England, France, Morocco and most African and Arab tribes fought for control of the lucrative slave trade known as "black gold." The Africans taken to the Americas were mostly prisoners of war taken in the vicious Slave Wars. These African slaves were proud warriors that were captured in battle or raids by other African warriors who then sold them to the Europeans. One such African slave, Sengbe Pieh, led a successful slave ship revolt with 56 Africans armed with machetes that they found in the slave hold onboard a Spanish ship (Amistad) in 1839. Sengbe Pieh was returned to West Africa by the United States after a long court case and ordeal only to find that his family, village and tribe (Mende) had been taken away as a result of the Slave Wars. Whole tribes and civilizations ceased to exist in Africa as a result of the slave trade or as Africans referred to it as "the Maafa" which means "holocaust" and "the great disaster" in Swahili.

The big players of the early African slave trade of the 1500's were Portugal, Morocco, and the Songhai Empire of West Africa. Portugal had set up forts for trade in slaves all along the coast of Africa for their colony in Brazil once it was realized that Native Americans were not working out as slaves in the Americas. The Songhai Empire controlled the areas of what is today Mali, Guinea, and Niger and was one of the richest nations in the world from its gold and salt mines and from supplying Africans from other rival nations as slaves to Morocco. The Songhai Empire only traded slaves to Morocco and to other African kingdoms as they resisted Portuguese and Spanish efforts to supply them with slaves from this area. Morocco dominated the Saharan slave trade as a middleman who bought slaves from the Songhai Empire and transported them in a grueling journey across over 1,000 miles of the Sahara Desert that usually killed at least 15-20% of the slaves. Morocco then turned around and sold most of the slaves in the slave markets of the Ottoman Empire for a nice mark up price for all their trouble in getting the slaves to market.

The roots of slavery in the Western Hemisphere began with the discovery of the Americas by Christopher Columbus in 1492 which led to a desire by Spain and Portugal to colonize and to build plantations in the New World run on slave labor. As the Spanish and the Portuguese conquered the Native American civilizations in the early 1500's, they also enslaved the Indians to mine for gold and silver in South America and to work on sugar, rice and indigo (royal blue dye) plantations in the Caribbean islands and in Brazil. Native Americans didn't work out as slaves because they died at an 80%-90% rate within months of captivity from European diseases (mostly smallpox) of which they had no previous contact and no immunity to. Also, when Native Americans ran away from their enslavers, they were virtuously impossible to recapture because they knew the land so much better than the Europeans did. As had been mentioned in an earlier chapter, over 43 million out of 54 million Native Americans from all of the Americas had died in apocalyptic epidemics from diseases brought by the Europeans between 1492 and 1600. Most Indians that had died from European diseases had never laid eyes on a European from whom the diseases had come.

With Native Americans not working out as slaves, the Portuguese and Spanish began looking for replacement slaves from another source in the 1500's. As it so happened, the tribes of Africa had owned slaves taken from rival tribes in wars for thousands of years in Africa. These slaves were then traded to Moroccan and Arab slave traders in West Africa who in turn took them over the Sahara Desert to be traded for trade goods from the days of the Roman Empire to the 1500's. Africans worked out better as slaves because they lived 6 to 7 years longer than Native Americans due to having the same diseases and immunities as the Europeans had. The average length of time that African field slaves lived in captivity in the Americas was still only 7 years on average because of the harsh working conditions on plantations. The high mortality rate of African slaves meant that a constant new supply of slaves was needed in the Americas which led to the Slave Wars that were fought for over 350 years from around the world.

Tuareg warriors fought mostly as elite cavalry and controlled the West African slave trade to sell to whichever European country that would guarantee the best prices for slaves. Any encroachment into the West African slave trade meant war with the Tuaregs.

The Portuguese were the first Europeans to make contact with tribes on the coasts of West and Central Africa in 1502 to trade for slaves that tribes already had taken in their wars with other rival tribes. African chiefs were very open and willing to trade their slaves in return for weapons such as harquebus muskets, crossbows, canons, and horses. The tribes of Gambia started the Slave Wars when they went to war in the early 1500's solely to supply Portugal's voracious need for slaves for their colony in Brazil. These tribal wars for slaves then spread throughout West and Central Africa. The going rate to trade for slaves during the Atlantic slave trade was anywhere from 2 to 20 guns or bags of flour, grain or sugar for a slave and 20 slaves for a horse or canon. Sadly, horses were considered of more value than a man in Africa because horses tended to have a short lifespan in West Africa due to the tropical climate and diseases that made maintaining cavalry there very costly.

In 1578, the 24 year old King Dom Sebastian of Portugal saw his chance to lead a Catholic crusade against Muslim Morocco and to gain control of the lucrative Saharan Slave Trade by answering a call for aide by Sultan Muhammad al-Mutawakki who had been deposed by Abdul Malik al-Mu'tasim. Dom Sebastian's army landed in Morocco with 23,000 armored Portuguese, Dutch, Spanish, and German crusaders and mercenaries. They were joined by 6,000 Moorish allies under Sultan Muhammad al-Mutawakki. The Portuguese army suffered in the heat as they marched to meet the army of Morocco.

The Moroccan army consisted of 70,000 troops which also included 17,000 cavalry and 7,000 elite Janissary Harquebusiers on loan from the Ottoman Empire. The forces met near a village called Qasri al-Kabir. Sultan Abdul Malik al-Mu'tasium formed the Moroccan army between two dry river beds in a large rectangular formation with the cavalry lining the outside of the formation. The Portuguese formed a pike wall supported by musketeers at intervals backed by a second wall of infantry and cavalry.

The Moroccan cavalry started the battle by riding up in mass to within 40 yards of the Portuguese line and firing a devastating volley from their harquebus's before charging and breaking through the first European line. The Portuguese second line counter-attacked and drove back the Moroccan army in fierce hand to hand fighting. Sultan Abdul Malik al-Mu'tasim was able to recover most of the cavalry and the Janissaries and sent them into another desperate attack that enveloped both wings of the disrupted Portuguese army which turned into a vicious hand to hand battle. The Moroccan army's greater numbers took a toll on the Portuguese army before many of them surrendered. Over 15,000 Portuguese, Dutch, Spanish, and German troops were captured with another 8,000 dead that littered the battlefield. The Moroccan army also took heavy casualties in the vicious fighting in the battle. All three kings died in the battle as well (known as the Battle of the Three Kings). Before Abdul Malik al-Mu'tasim died, he named his brother Ahmad as successor as the Sultan of Morocco. A weakened Portugal went bankrupt paying the ransoms for the thousands of Portuguese prisoners (many were nobles) to be returned. Spain was able to take advantage of the situation to occupy and to rule the Portuguese Empire from 1581 to 1640 as a result of this devastating defeat.

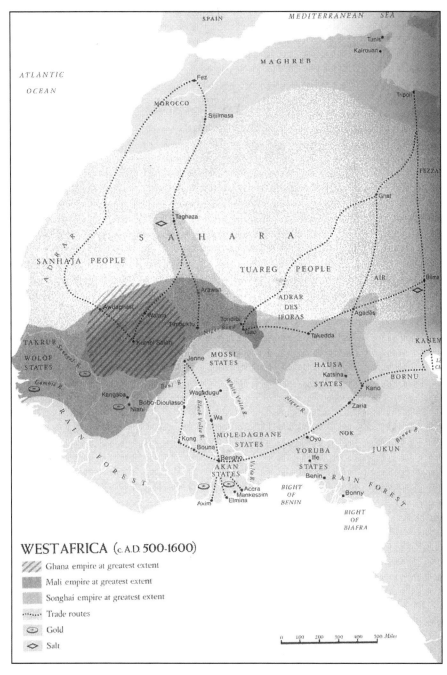

WEST AFRICA (c. A.D. 500-1600)

- Ghana empire at greatest extent
- Mali empire at greatest extent
- Songhai empire at greatest extent
- Trade routes
- Gold
- Salt

West Africa had been one of the most powerful and wealthy areas in the world between 500 and 1600, but the Slave Wars weakened and caused the demise of West African kingdoms.

Portuguese Conquistadors operated Portugal's slave colonies in Angola and Brazil somewhat under Spain's authority, but pocketed most of the profits themselves during this time from 1581 to 1640. The Portuguese colony of Angola was created solely for the purpose of supplying slaves primarily for the colony of Brazil. As a result, most slaves taken to Brazil came from Angola and the Kongo (Zaire or the Congo today) and most slaves from West Africa went to supply Spanish Latin America, the West Indies (Caribbean), and to what is today the southern United States. Starting in the 1600's, during the Trans-Atlantic slave trade, over 39% of all slaves came from Angola or the Kongo, and 59% of all slaves came from West Africa with another 2% that came from Mozambique and Madagascar. The Portuguese Conquistadors and benefactors of the colonies of Angola and Brazil had a system in place to continue to operate independently of Portugal or Spain for that matter and were mostly left alone to do it.

After Portugal's defeat in 1578, Morocco's Sultan Ahmad al-Mansur wanted to gain complete control of the Saharan slave trade and the famed gold mines and wealth of the Songhai Empire. In 1591, the Sultan sent 10,000 infantry, 4,000 harquebusiers with artillery, and 3,000 cavalry under Judar Pasha in a 1,000 mile journey over the Saharan Desert to attack the Songhai Empire in what is today Mali. The journey took an arduous five months to complete with over 3,500 men and 500 horses dying in the desert from thirst and raids by Tuareg warriors in the service of the Songhai Empire. Once the Moroccan army had escaped the Sahara, they were met along the Niger River near the village of Tondibi by 32,000 Songhai infantry armed with spears, swords, and shields in a solid line and 18,000 Songhai cavalry in chain mail armor and armed with javelins and spears that backed the rear and wings of the line. In front of the middle of the Songhai positions were 5,000 cattle densely packed into a fenced holding area. The Moroccan army formed for battle with 4,000 harquebusiers and the artillery in the middle and 2,500 cavalry on the wings and rear with another 7,000 infantry armed with spears, swords, and shields also in reserve.

Moroccan warriors charge after firing a devastating volley with their harquebus's at the Battle of Tondibi in 1591.

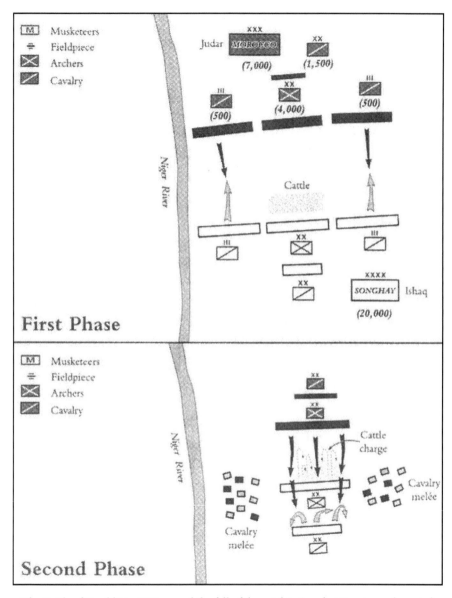

The Battle of Tondibi in 1591 caused the fall of the mighty Songhai Empire and created a power vacuum that caused smaller nations to ally themselves to European powers in the slave trade to obtain guns and goods to defend themselves. Morocco did not have the resources or manpower to take advantage of their victory at Tondibi.

The battle opened with a heated cavalry charge and melee by both side's cavalry wings. The Moroccan cavalry were holding their own, but started to give some ground due to the huge advantage in numbers that the Songhai cavalry had. The Songhai then drove their 5,000 cattle toward the Moroccan harquebusiers to absorb their artillery and gun fire in the middle of the line followed closely by most of their infantry who were going to close with the Moroccans once the cattle had passed through their lines. The Moroccan harquebusiers opened fire with all their guns and artillery when the cattle were within 50 yards from their line which killed over a 1,000 cattle, but caused the other 4,000 or so cattle to stampede over the Songhai infantry. Thousands of Songhai infantry were killed or wounded in the stampede as they ran away in panic back toward their own lines. The Moroccan harquebusiers threw down their guns, drew their swords, and charged forward with their reserve infantry as they slaughtered thousands more of the Songhai warriors. The Songhai cavalry fled the field in panic. The Moroccan victory caused the complete collapse of the Songhai Empire.

All was not well with the Moroccans despite the great victory because it was discovered that the famed Songhai gold mines had run out of gold in 1590. The collapse of the Songhai Empire meant that there was no one really in control of West Africa and the tiny Moroccan army couldn't maintain control of such a huge area. Then the Tuaregs and other tribes who didn't want to be cut out of the slave trade began a bloody insurgency that killed hundreds of Moroccans on a weekly basis. Despite the victory at the Battle of Tondibi, Judar Pasha had to return to Morocco with only 4,000 men left and little to show for toppling the Songhai Empire after recrossing the Sahara Desert. Morocco returned to their role as middlemen in the Saharan slave trade, but the fall of the Songhai Empire opened up West Africa to participation with the Europeans in the Trans-Atlantic Slave Trade which would eventually lead to the disappearance of millions of people from Africa. The Mali Empire eventually replaced the Songhai Empire and became major participants in both the Saharan and the Trans-Atlantic Slave Trades.

As African tribes traded for European weapons and horses, wars became more deadly and frenzied as all tribes became involved raiding and attacking each other to get more slaves to trade for weapons in an African arms race. A Danish factor named Romer worked in Africa as a commodities trader in slaves to the highest European bidders. Romer was told by an African ruler in 1745 near Ghana, "You are the cause of our troubles. Your merchandise causes us to fight each other and to sell people. Once there were many thousands of families here, but now you can scarcely count 100 persons here." The same factor was also told by an Akan tribal elder that the killing of women and children was seen as necessary by most tribes so that potential enemies would not rise up in retaliation in later years. Families were torn apart while women were often repeatedly raped and abducted by the invading African armies, then raped again at African and European holding forts on the African coasts, then raped again by sailors on the slave ships, and lastly on the plantations by overseers and owners in the Americas. Many women tried to commit suicide by jumping into the Atlantic Ocean on the slave ships to try to end the torment that they repeatedly endured.

Whole African tribes traveled hundreds of miles into the interior of Africa to escape the slave catchers. African chiefs that participated in the slave trade simply sent their warriors to go deeper into Africa to maintain a constant supply of humans to sell to the Europeans at the coast.

Slave catching tribes increasingly traded for horses for cavalry to follow fleeing tribes deeper into the African interior. The going rate to trade for horses was to trade 20 slaves for one horse. .

The Portuguese and the other European nations established trading forts on the coasts of Africa in the 1500's and 1600's to trade for slaves. The Europeans didn't often venture into the interior of Africa (except in the Kongo and Angola) to trade for slaves because they often got sick and died from mosquito born diseases such as malaria and yellow fever until the 1800's when a Quinine cure was discovered. Europeans could never have maintained forts on the African coasts nor have traded for slaves had they not had permission to do so from African kingdoms who could have and sometimes did destroy the European forts and trade on the coast at will.

England replaced Spain as the top world naval power in the world by defeating the Spanish Armada in 1588 when they attempted to invade the British Isles. England then became the dominant power in the Trans-Atlantic Slave Trade out of West Africa until they abolished the trade in 1807. The Triangular Trade began in the early 1600's with ships from Europe taking guns and other goods to Africa as the first leg of the trade. Then these goods would be traded for African slaves that would be chained and packed into the bottom holds of slave ships under horrible living conditions and taken to Brazil, the West Indies, and to what would be the southern United States. Slaves were often kept in chains while laying in their own filth and other's filth in very hot, humid, and cramped conditions that killed 2.5 million of the 12.5 million slaves loaded onto these slave ships. The third part of the Triangular Trade was to take slave produced crops and goods to be sold in Europe. Most everyone involved with the slave trade except for the slaves and the Africans killed in the Slave Wars got rich as a result of the slave trade.

It is a myth that Europeans attacked African villages themselves to capture slaves. It was the Africans who did 99.9% of the raiding and capturing of other rival Africans to trade to the Europeans as slaves at their coastal forts. Only occasionally would Europeans raid a village if their slave ships were not full, but if they raided the wrong villages then trade could be cut off with that tribe or kingdom. The Kingdom of Benin cut off trade with the Europeans for this reason because some of their villages had been attacked and raided by crews from some slave ships in the 1700's. Often, the Europeans would work two rival African tribes or kingdoms against each other unbeknown to the other which would effectively destroy both tribes. European troops sometimes fought with African allies against rival tribes who had other English, Dutch, French, or Portuguese allies who fought with them as well for control of the slave trade, but the actual capturing of slaves was what the African allies did.

Warfare in West and Central Africa of the Atlantic Slave Trade period was not so different from warfare in North America at this time with groups of 20 to 200 warriors ambushing similar sized groups of warriors and people on trails or villages in the forests for captives to sell into slavery. Because so much of West and Central Africa was covered in dense forest and bush country, a smaller African force often could hold off a much larger force by simply blocking a key trail that was difficult to outflank. Battles were fought by formations of infantry armed with spears, swords, clubs, and shields with a separate arm of archers who formed behind the infantry. Having muskets and artillery didn't necessarily have an impact on the battlefield unless the men using these firearms had training on how to operate in disciplined units. Africans with firearms preferred to fight as irregular infantry in ambush mode similar to the tactics of the Native Americans in the French and Indian Wars. Any forces of European infantry or Africans trained to fight in disciplined formations with muskets and artillery tended to dominate the battlefields of Africa. Cavalry had a difficult time maneuvering in the forests and bush country of West and Central Africa and weren't as decisive on the battlefield there.

In the Sahel region just south of the Sahara Desert and in the savannah grasslands, cavalry armed with lances, javelins, swords, shields, helmets, and chain mail armor dominated these regions as they hunted for villages and people to enslave. The fierce Tuareg tribe located in what is today Mali and Mauritania fought as mercenaries on horses and camels that hunted slaves for whomever would pay them well for their services. Europeans or West African empires wanting slaves from these regions had to get the Tuareg's support and help to have any success in obtaining slaves.

The difficulty of traveling in and controlling the dense forests and bush country of West and Central Africa meant that controlling rivers and coasts where the slave forts and slave ships were located was very important. Africans used large canoes that could hold 2 to 4 warriors abreast and as many as 180 total warriors in boats that were from 20 to 40 yards long. Muskets, bows, and small swivel canon if available would be fired from the boats in skirmishing until boarding would be attempted in hand to hand fighting. There were times that these African river fleets overwhelmed and captured unwanted ships from rival European nations. Several Portuguese ships were captured in this way when they had tried to expand their slave trading operations into the Kingdom of Kongo in the 1500's and 1600's. If a European ship was well armed with canon and prepared they rarely were boarded by unwanted African enemies.

Many of the wars around the world between Holland, Portugal, Spain, and England in the sixteenth through the 18th centuries were wholly or at least in part fought over who would dominate the slave trade. The Dutch-Portuguese War from 1620 to 1655 was fought over who would control the slave trade in Senegal, Gambia, and Brazil. Holland had taken over Senegal and Gambia in 1620. In 1630, Holland landed an army on the coast of Brazil at Pernambuco to establish a fort and base to take over the slave colony of Brazil from Portugal. In 1640, 41 Dutch ships intercepted an invasion fleet of 91 Portuguese and Spanish ships and transports at the Battle of Pernambuco. The Dutch dominated a four day sea battle with long range artillery followed by aggressive boarding tactics which cost the Portuguese and Spanish fleet 11 ships at the cost of 2 Dutch ships lost. In 1649, a land force of 2,500 Portuguese soldiers with colonist militia, Native Americans and musket armed slave militia all from Brazil defeated 3,500 Dutch troops at the Battle of Guararapes near Pernambuco. The Portuguese and militia forces fired at the Dutch pike and musket line from the cover of the jungle before a vicious attack led by the slave militia killed and wounded over 1,045 Dutch troops. The Portuguese lost just 245 troops in the battle. The Battle of Guararapes permanently ejected the Dutch from Brazil and returned the war for control of the slave trade to Africa for these nations.

Portugal reemerged as a sovereign nation with its own empire to maintain after the overthrow of Spain in 1640. Jesuit missionaries had been in Angola and the Kongo since the early 1500's had converted these nations to Catholic Christianity including the ruling family of the Kongo who took Portuguese Christian names. The Kongo Civil War from 1665 to 1709 was a war where Portugal supported factions that wanted to overthrow the Kingdom of Kongo. The Portuguese wanted to take over and to add the Kongo to their colony in Angola to provide a much larger pool of African slaves to send to Brazil whose slaves were dying at as faster rate than they could be replaced. Holland also wanted to control the slave trade in the Kingdom of the Kongo and supported King Antonio I against Portugal. The Kongo Civil War started when factions from Mbwila appealed to both King Antonio of Kongo and to Portugal for aide in gaining control of this area.

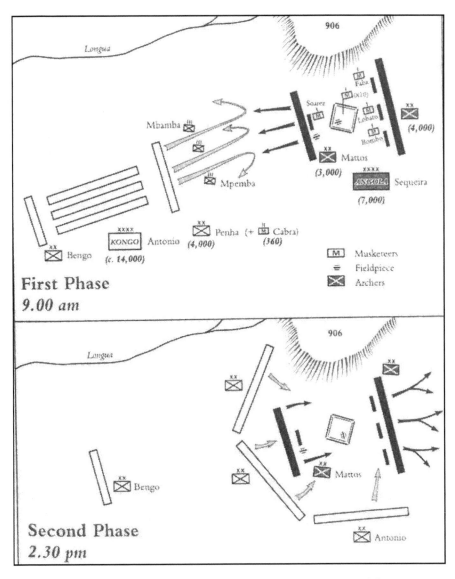

The Battle of Mbwilla in 1665 was a Portuguese victory over a much larger
army of Kongo whose primary weapons were bows and spears.

In 1665, the Kongo army attacked the Portuguese army at the Battle
of Mbwila. The Kongolese army consisted of 15,000 archers, 5,000 heavy

infantry armed with shields and swords and 380 Dutch musketeers and 29 Portuguese mercenaries. Waiting for them was a Portuguese army of 450 Conquistadors and 15,000 Brazilian colonists, Native Americans, and slave militia with African auxiliaries.

The Portuguese Conquistadors and the better trained militia troops formed a tight diamond formation in the middle of the battlefield. The lesser disciplined Brazilian colonists, Native Americans, slave militia and African auxiliaries formed lines in the front and rear of the diamond formation. The Army of the Kongo opened the battle with their 15,000 archers firing clouds of arrows into the unarmored Brazilian militia units and their African auxiliaries which caused them to retreat after suffering heavy casualties. The Portuguese diamond formation had 1,000 troops armed with muskets, pikes, and armor which held as they were repeatedly assaulted by the army of the Kongo's heavy infantry. The fighting around the diamond formation was vicious with over 5,000 of the Kongo's army and 500 Portuguese being killed and wounded in the battle before the Kongolese retreated. King Antonio and 495 nobles and title holders from the Kingdom of Kongo also died in the battle which gave Portugal temporary control of the Kongo.

Hundreds of thousands of people in the Kingdom of the Kongo were then taken captive to be taken to Brazil as slaves by Angolan soldiers and slave catchers. Kongo insurgents aided by the Dutch ambushed and killed hundreds of Portuguese Conquistadors and thousands of Angolan soldiers and slave catchers to regain control of the Kongo by 1670.

In June of 1670, over 10,000 heavy infantry and archers from the Kongo tribes of Soyo and Ngoyo attacked 400 Portuguese Conquistadors with 1,000 Angolan troops and militia armed with muskets at the Battle of the Mbidizi River. Hundreds of attacking Soyo and Ngoyo heavy infantry were killed by musket fire and grapeshot from four artillery pieces that the Portuguese had fired. The forces of Soyo and Ngoyo fell back to their mountain sanctuary to regroup where several hundred muskets with four artillery pieces that had been brought by Dutch mercenaries was waiting for them.

The Portuguese Conquistadors, and the Angolan troops and militia pursued the Soyo and Ngoyo to their mountain sanctuary several days later where they were ambushed as they were climbing some very dense and steep jungle trails. Hundreds of Portuguese and Angolan troops were hit initially by Kongo musket and artillery fire from concealed jungle positions followed by a ferocious attack from the Kongolese heavy infantry. Portuguese organized resistance collapsed along the trail as most of their force was overwhelmed and massacred in the jungle. Over a hundred Portuguese Conquistadors escaped the ambush and drowned as they tried to cross a fast moving river and were swept over some treacherous waterfalls. The few Portuguese survivors surrendered and were then given to the Dutch mercenaries as slaves. Portuguese power was permanently broken in the Kingdom of the Kongo after this.

The Portuguese did continue to send Angolans into the Kongo on slave raiding missions which was aided by fighting between rival forces in the Kongo that continued until 1709. The Portuguese took over 1 million people from the Kingdom of the Kongo to Brazil as slaves during the Atlantic Slave Trade period. Dutch troops and advisors were also ejected from the Kingdom of Kongo once it was realized that they were only interested in dominating the taking of slaves from the Kongo.

The Komenda War from 1694 to 1700 was a war that the Dutch West India Company stirred up with the Equafo Kingdom that caused a civil war that pulled in England as well over who would control the slave trade in West Africa. England and Holland fought against each other in Africa for control of the slave trade despite being allied in the War of the Grand Alliance in Europe at this time. Ten African kingdoms were pulled into the Komenda War on one side or the other and were mostly destroyed as a result. Many battles had forces of several hundred

Dutch and English fighting in the center of the battle lines against each other with thousands of African allies (some trained and armed with muskets) fighting on the wings. At times, land had to be cleared at the request of English and Dutch officers to have pitched battles. Most of the fighting in the war involved Africans raiding other rival African villages while killing and capturing everyone from those villages to be sold into slavery by whomever they were allied to. Hundreds of thousands of Africans were killed or sold into slavery as a result of the Komenda War. England and Holland agreed to cease hostilities in West Africa in 1700. The Africans continued the war until 1704.

In 1702, during the War of the Spanish Succession, England and Holland allied together to check the power of France and Spain from European domination and partially for control of the lucrative West African slave trade. The West Africans were very confused because multitudes of Africans had died or were sold off as slaves supporting either England or Holland and then they decide to share the slave trade so that they could fight France. As always, the real losers in the Slave Wars were the Africans regardless of which European power that they had supported.

In 1708, again as part of the War of the Spanish Succession, the French helped one side as the English and Dutch forces helped another in the Whydah Civil War (upper Benin) to get control of the slave trade in this area. A number of bloody and inconclusive battles were fought between French forces and the Anglo-Dutch army as factions of Whydah warriors armed with muskets and spears fought on both sides. By the time the War of the Spanish Succession ended in 1713, the entire Whydah nation had been killed off or taken away into slavery by the English, Dutch and French slave traders.

Portugal had sold its' slave trading rights to Gambia and Senegal to the British in 1588. Holland then took over the British trading forts there in 1621. France captured Gambia and Senegal from the Dutch in 1677 and built several forts from which slaves would be transferred to slave ships going to the French West Indies. In 1758, during the Seven Years War, Britain decided to take over the slave trade in French Senegal and Gambia and landed 200 Royal Marines at the mouth of the Senegal River to attack Fort Louis. As the British marines were landing, the Royal Navy was sinking and chasing off 7 French gunboats and sloops while also firing on Fort Louis. African auxiliaries in the service of the French ambushed and killed several Royal Marines working their way to attack the weaker walls of Fort Louis from the landward side. After recovering from the ambush, the Royal Marines forced the African auxiliaries to retreat with a volley and a bayonet charge. The French forces then surrendered when they realized that they were surrounded and cut off. The British captured huge amounts of trade goods and enough slaves to fill several slave ships from the French at Fort Louis. The British also captured a French island fort at Goree also off the coast of Senegal. A British attempt by 700 Royal Marines to capture a French Fort and trading station further down the Gambia River failed when the Fort put up a stout defense followed by an African auxiliary attack on the British flanks that caused 60 casualties.

The British also attacked and took over the French West Indies islands of Martinique, Guadalupe, St.Lucia, and Dominica in very fierce fighting during the Seven Years War. The Treaty of Versailles returned Goree and Martinique to France in 1763.

The French regained control of the coast of Gambia and Senegal in 1779 during the American Revolution. The French chose to divert large numbers of naval and land forces originally slated for North America in 1779 in order to completely recapture Gambia and Senegal which was of a higher priority to the French because of the value of the slave trade. France kept the area of Senegal, but had to give back all of Gambia except for the one slave fort on the Gambia River that had never been taken according to the Treaty of Paris in 1783 which ended the American

Revolution. Over 3 million of the eventual 12 million slaves to come out of Africa to the Americas came out of or through Gambia and Senegal to mostly the Caribbean Islands or to the American South by French, British, Dutch, Portuguese, and American slave ships.

Of 173 African tribes and kingdoms that existed in West and Central Africa in 1502, only 68 still existed in 1850. The kingdoms of Ashanti, Benin, Dahomey, Oyo, and the Kongo emerged as the dominant powers in Africa because of the Slave Wars mostly because they had obtained the most muskets and training in how to operate disciplined units in battle. Generally, these kingdoms used disciplined musket volleys followed by a charge to close with their enemies in fierce hand to hand fighting with spears and swords as their battle tactics. These tribes killed and captured millions of Africans during the slave trade for whichever European nation supplied them with goods and guns.

Great Britain and the United States, after being pressured by Christian missionaries, abolished the Atlantic Slave Trade in 1807. Britain did not emancipate its' 700,000 slaves in the West Indies until 1833 though and the U.S. emancipated its' 4 million slaves between 1863 and 1865. From 1807 to 1860, Britain's West African Squadron seized approximately 1,600 slave ships and freed over 150,000 slaves on these ships. Holland also abolished the slave trade in 1814 and France followed suit in 1818.

France only had slaves on Martinique in 1818 because they had lost their richest colony in Haiti, when 300,000 slaves rebelled and killed over 60,000 French troops and civilians between 1794 and 1804 to win independence which is covered in detail in a later chapter. The Haitian slave revolt leader, Toussaint L'Ouverture, mentioned that captured prisoners of war from Africa who were sent to Haiti as slaves had a major role in leading and organizing the slave forces against the French. The Haitians also had slave units that were disciplined in European tactics and could fight the French in open field combat that aided their cause.

Not all African kingdoms were happy to see the slave trade abolished. The Kingdom of Ashanti (Ghana) was very rich and powerful because of their participation with the Europeans in capturing and selling slaves. The Ashanti attacked some British posts in 1807 in anger over the British announcement that they were abolishing the slave trade. In 1811, during the Ga-Fante War the Ashanti warriors breached an English fort and a Dutch fort (over rumors that the Dutch were soon going to abolish the slave trade too) with artillery and massacred the garrisons inside in an effort to force Britain to reestablish the slave trade. From 1814 to 1816, the Ashanti fought to access the West African coast at Fante to establish their own slave trading forts to supply the Portuguese with slaves for plantations in Brazil. The Ashanti were so frustrated with Britain's efforts to stop them from selling slaves from their forts in Fante that it led to the First Anglo-Ashanti War in 1823. Over 1,490 British troops with 11,000 African auxiliaries were attacked by 10,000 Ashanti warriors at their camp at the Battle of Nsamankow. The Ashanti believed that the African auxiliaries would not stand and fight for long and would abandon the British when attacked. At the Battle of Nsamankow, the British and the Ashanti forces were separated by a mile long 60 foot wide stream in a gully as they fired volleys of musket fire at each other for 2 hours which killed and wounded hundreds on both sides. When the British ran out of ammunition, the Ashanti assaulted across the stream and up the embankment to attack the British camp with spears, swords, and shields. The African auxiliaries abandoned the British camp in panic. The British troops fought desperately in groups after their line was outflanked until being overwhelmed with all but 20 men being massacred in the battle. The Ashanti were defeated by better prepared British forces in 1827 and 1831 and had to cease their slave trading activities after this. Brazil abolished the slave trade from Africa in 1850 which ended the Trans-Atlantic Slave Trade and the subsequent wars for it's' control. Brazil didn't emancipate its slaves until 1888 though.

The Slave Wars gave way then to the Scramble for Africa and the wars for the European conquest of Africa. It has been estimated that out of the 25 million Africans that disappeared out of Africa during the slave trade that over 13 million Africans died in the Slave Wars.

Many slave ships traveling from Africa to the America's had bloody slave revolts. It is estimated that over 4,000 out of more than 40,000 slave ship voyages to the America's had slave revolts onboard.

SLAVESHIP REBELLIONS

Africans did not go willingly into captivity and historians have documented over 383 slave ship rebellions from ship logs during the entire period of the Trans-Atlantic Slave Trade. Historians also believe that there were over 3,000 undocumented slave ship rebellions out of the over 30,000 slave ship voyages to have taken slaves to the Americas. Of these, only 23 slave ship rebellions were successful in commandeering the ships which the Africans knew very little about. In 16 of the 23 successful slave ship rebellions, the slaves were killed or recaptured and returned to slavery by European warships that attacked the stranded ships. The fiercely proud West African warriors started most of the slave ship rebellions as opposed to slaves from Angola and the Kongo who went mostly to Brazil in shorter journeys. Often, it was young African women who were almost always raped by the slave ship crews and who frequently stayed in the officer's cabins that gave intelligence to the other slaves or provided diversions to make the shipboard rebellions possible. The majority of these slave ship rebellions took place before 1800. After 1800, slave ships mostly carried women and children to avoid the slave rebellions that captured African warriors frequently started. Also, African boys raised as slaves were easier to control than defiant former African warriors.

In 1750, a rebellion broke out on the French slave ship named the *Levant*. The slaves rebelled when they were brought on deck to jump and dance for exercise. The slaves noticed that the French had let their guard down as they played cards. The slaves grabbed weapons that were left lying around the deck by the card players and also used their chains as blunt force instruments to overcome the French crew in vicious hand to hand fighting. Half of the French crew was killed while the other half occupied the Levant behind barricades above and below deck. The surviving slaves barricaded the other half of the ship in a tenuous stand-off. A bloody five day battle for control of the ship commenced back and forth over both side's barricades on all four decks. The decks on the *Levant* became a scene out of Hell from the many mutilated white and black bodies of the dead whose blood dripped down into the lower decks. On the 4th day of battle there was a gunpowder accident on the 3rd deck as a number of slaves and crew fought for control of the last barrel of gunpowder when a pistol shot detonated the barrel killing everyone on that deck while causing an irreparable leak in the hull. On the 5th day of battle, the last few slaves surrendered to the last 9 surviving crew members from the *Levant*. The crew and the last few slaves were rescued by a passing Dutch ship before the *Levant* sank.

In 1773, Captain Stephen Deane's slave ship, the *Black Banff,* needed to bring aboard around 10 free blacks to augment his crew of 70 to handle the 230 slaves that he planned on taking to be sold in South Carolina from West Africa. The free blacks then helped the slaves by unchaining them and giving them carpenter tools which were then used to get into the ammunition room. A below deck battle ensued with the American crew. As the Africans were being overcome they set the ammunition room on fire and blew up the ship with only one man surviving to tell the story.

Only seven slave ship rebellions such as the slave ship *Jolly Bachelor* in 1742, the *Industry* in 1772, the *Amistad* in 1839, and the *Regina Coeli* in 1858 ended with the slaves being returned to Africa. In 1742, the *Jolly Bachelor* was boarding slaves onto the ship near the shore on the Sierra Leone River as the crew began arguing over which women they were going to rape and who was getting them. The slaves took advantage of the turmoil on board the ship and began beating and killing the crew with their chains. Africans from the villages that the slaves were taken from came and followed the ship in canoes from a distance and then swarmed the ship, killed most of the the crew and set the slaves free.

In 1772, on the London based ship called the *Industry,* a slave woman whom the captain of the ship had been keeping in his cabin snuck out at night when the captain was sleeping with the keys to unchain the men below. The slaves then killed all but 2 crewmen and ran the ship ashore in Sierra Leone.

In 1858, slaves were being boarded onto the illegal French slave ship, *Regina Coeli,* on the coast of Senegal. The captured warriors told each other in their own languages that they needed to rebel while the crew were busy chaining slaves in the bottom of the ship or they would be condemned forever to slavery. The slaves then used their chains as weapons to beat many of the crew to death and then took their weapons to finish off the rest of the French except for 2 crew members on the ship. A British ship then helped to guide the Regina Coeli to Liberia which was under U.S. protection (since 1821) for former slaves who wanted to return to Africa where the slaves were returned to freedom. If rebellions failed or weren't seen as possible by the Africans, many would try to jump into the sea to commit suicide. Slave ships often had nets around the sides to prevent mass suicide by the slaves, but there were still a large number of documented and undocumented cases of mass suicides that still took place during the Trans-Atlantic Slave Trade.

BIBLIOGRAPHY

Alan, Lloyd. *The Drums of Kumasi.* Panther Press, London, 1964.

Anderson, Fred. *Crucible of War.* Borzoi Books, NY. 2000.

American Heritage, *History of Africa.* American Heritage Publishing, 1971.

Birmingham, David. *Portugal and Africa.* Ohio University Press, Athens, 1999.

Eltis, David. *The Rise of African Slavery in the Americas.* Cambridge University Press, NY. 2000. (Most information from the side bar article came from this book).

Fowler, William M. *Empires at War.* Walker & Company, New York, 2005.

Rogerson, Barnaby. *The Last Crusaders*. Overlook Press, New York, 2009.

Grant, R.G. *Battle*. DK Publishing, New York, 2005. p. 140-141.

Grant, R.G. *Battle at Sea*. DK Publishing, New York, 2008.

Kohn, George Childs. *Dictionary of Wars*. Checkmark Books, NY. 2007.

Thornton, John K. *Warfare in Atlantic Africa 1500-1800*. Routledge Printing, UK, 2003. (This is the most important book on this time period).

Wilks, Ivor. *Asante in the Nineteenth Century*. Cambridge University Press, London: 1975.

CHAPTER 13

African Slave Revolts in The Caribbean and South America: 1605 – 1790

For slaves who made it to the Americas to be slaves on plantations, life was hard, short and rife with indignation. Masters and
overseers used brutality to stamp out the defiant look of hate that the
former African warriors gave them. Public whippings, hot iron brand-
ings, decapitating of limbs, castration and the selling off of children
and spouses were common punishments for even minor infringements
to the many rules to force slave compliance with the wishes of their
European masters. Many proud African warriors couldn't endure the
constant humiliation and rose up in violent rebellions against their
white masters particularly in the Caribbean and in South America.

African slaves began arriving in Brazil in the 1530's when it became
clear that the native Brazilian Indians were dying off at an 80-85%
rate from European diseases within a few months of captivity. In 1605,
African slaves in Brazil began running away from the brutal conditions
on Portuguese plantations to the interior and formed a community called
Quilombo dos Palmares. From 1630 to 1654, the Dutch and Portuguese
fought for control of the lucrative Portuguese colony at Pernambuco,
Brazil. The fighting between the Dutch and Portuguese and the burning

of plantations allowed many slaves to run away when there were few or no overseers to force them to stay. Quilombo dos Palmares grew to between 20,000 and 30,000 runaway slaves by the 1630's. This situation became intolerable for the Portuguese with the high expense of bringing in slaves from Africa. In the 1680's, the Portuguese sent three expeditions of between 2000-3000 soldiers to try to recapture these slaves, but these expeditions were ambushed and defeated in the dense jungle interior of Brazil before they could ever reach the slave settlements. The slaves would fire well aimed harquebus musket volleys from concealed positions at river crossings with simultaneous attacks on the Portuguese flanks by crazed Africans armed with machetes. In all three expeditions, the Portuguese columns disintegrated in panic and were routed while leaving behind most of the wounded to be hacked to death by former slaves that wanted to let their former owners to know what else machetes could be used for other than harvesting crops.

In 1694, the Portuguese sent their best general in Brazil, Domingos Jorge Velho with 5,000 Portuguese troops and 2,000 Native American Brazilians to cover the flanks and to scout ahead to warn of possible slave ambushes. The ambushes that had given victories to the Africans before were detected and counter ambushed from behind by the Brazilian Indians. The African stockade fortifications that surrounded Quilombo de Palmares were each put under siege and breached by canon fire and assaulted by disciplined Portuguese infantry at bayonet point where the Africans fought desperately before being overcome. Several hundred Portuguese were killed in one fort when the Africans threw a torch in the gun powder magazine that blew everyone up when it was clear the fort would fall. Many panicked Africans fled into the jungle to try to escape from the colony, but Brazilian Indians were waiting to kill or capture them for the Portuguese. In 1695, the Portuguese finally entered Quilombo dos Palmares and found that thousands had committed suicide by either eating poisonous plants or had hung themselves from trees in the town and from the surrounding jungle rather than to submit themselves or their families to the degradations of slavery again.

The Conquistadors in Panama had many problems with slave rebellions and mass communities of maroons (runaway slaves) that were established in the jungle covered mountains from the 1500's until independence from Spain was established in the early 1800's. The runaway slaves formed guerrilla bands called cimarron's that attacked Spanish plantations and freed more Africans to join them in the mountains. The Conquistadors attacked and massacred the Africans at a few of these maroon communities, but at times were ambushed themselves and massacred in conjunction with the Kuna and Guaymi Native American tribes in Panama.

The Akwamu became a great African power in the late 1600's in what is today Ghana. In 1693, the Akwamu attacked and overwhelmed a Danish slave trading fort called Osu Castle that was near their capital on the coast. This gave the Akwamu control of the slave trade by cutting out the Danish middlemen. The Danes never forgot how they were ousted out of Ghana and saw their chance to regain control when the Akwamu Kingdom broke out in civil war in the 1720's. With Danish muskets and aide, the Akwamu rebels defeated and captured the Akwamu Kings June and Bolombo and half the tribe. The captured Akwamu kings and thousands of the tribe's people were then sold by the rebels to the Danes to be slaves in the Caribbean. In 1734, the remaining Akwamu in Ghana were defeated by the Akyem with guns and aide by their former Danish allies who then also brought these prisoners of war to be slaves to the West Indies as well.

By 1718, Denmark had established the islands of St.John and Curacao as colonies and needed slaves to work the sugar plantations on these islands. The Danes then took the Akwamu slaves taken from their civil war to these islands in the late 1720's to work their plantations. Keeping the Akwamu slaves together would prove to be a fatal mistake that the Danes would come to regret. In 1733, the island of St.John had 1,087 Akwamu slaves including their kings, June and Bolombo to work the island's sugar plantations under the control of only 200 Danish settlers and six Danish soldiers.

The year 1733 was a difficult year on St.John with drought and crop failure followed by a severe hurricane. This created an unstable situation that caused the slaves on the Suhm estate to leave and to form a maroon community around the Coral Bay region. King June who worked at the Sodtmann plantation began organizing a rebellion with the help of King Bolombo and Prince Aquashie in other parts of the island. On Nov.23, 1733, slaves entered the Danish fort at Coral Bay carrying wood as was their nightly custom, when they pulled out hidden knives and machetes and killed 5 Danish soldiers and 15 settler militiamen. One Danish soldier escaped and alerted the Danish officials at St.Thomas about the slave rebellion. The slave rebellion rapidly spread throughout St.John with over a hundred Danish settlers being killed by the Akwamu. The surviving settlers then made their way to the Durloe plantation which was located on a hill. The Akwamu then attacked the plantation and killed a number of settlers before being repulsed by disciplined militia musket volleys as the Danish fought for their very lives. The surviving Danes at the Durloe plantation then made their way down to some boats and escaped to St.Thomas in fear that they could not resist another determined Akwamu attack.

The Akwamu temporarily had complete control of St.John as their new kingdom until April 23, 1734, when the alarmed French sent several hundred troops from Martinique to put the rebellion down in fear that the rebellion might spread to other islands. The French troops landed and moved inland in a square formation. The Akwamu repeatedly attacked the French square, but were decimated by disciplined musket volley fire. The Akwamu kept attacking even when they knew they were defeated because they preferred death to life as a slave. Most of the last remaining Akwamu then killed their own women and children before committing suicide. The rebellion really shook the West Indies and caused a crackdown of security measures on all of the European controlled islands. In 1795, the Akwamu again rebelled on Curacao, but this time the Danish and the fearful British garrisons from nearby islands reacted decisively to put the slave revolt down after just a few days of death and mayhem.

The Seven Years War from 1756 to 1763 was partially fought in the Caribbean and created opportunities for slave rebellions while the European forces were preoccupied fighting each other all over the world. In 1759, there was an unsuccessful slave revolt against the French on Saint Domingue (Haiti) when an attempt to poison a number of plantation owners was discovered. With British troops busy fighting the French in Canada, a very serious slave revolt called Tacky's War or Rebellion broke out in Jamaica. The slave uprising took place in May, June, and July of 1760 and put fear into the entire slave holding colonies of the Americas. A slave named, Tacky had been a chief of the Fanti and Kormantse tribes in Africa and had been captured in battle in Africa and brought to Jamaica in the late 1750's. Jamaica had a history of small slave revolts between 1655 and 1739 which resulted in a Maroon community that lived in the interior of the island. When Tacky realized that there were no British troops in Jamaica because of Britain's many commitments during the Seven Years War, he began organizing a revolt among his own tribesmen on the island.

For over a week in May of 1760, Tacky's Rebellion swept a large area of Jamaica with all whites including women and children on many plantations being massacred by machete wielding Africans desperate to be free before the British authorities in other areas of the island knew anything about the uprising. In early June, the Jamaican colonists gathered together a large militia force of over 1,000 white troops allied with a runaway maroon force of over 500 Africans living in the mountains.

The maroons agreed to help the British if their community would be recognized as free for helping to put down the revolt.

A battle was fought near one of the rebel slave held plantations. The militia formed a firing line in a clearing on the plantation as the Maroon force worked secretly in the forests to envelope both wings of the African rebel force of close to 1,000 warrior slaves who formed opposite of the colonist line. The Africans began a ferocious charge with machetes at the militia line. Over 200 panicked militia fired too early before the Africans were even 100 yards away and then fled in terror. Militia officers cursed at and warned the remaining militia troops to hold their fire until the African rebels were only 60 yards away and to stand their ground or they'd all be massacred that day. At 60 yards, the 800 remaining militia made a disciplined volley that killed and wounded hundreds of the Africans and stopped their attack cold. Tacky began frantically trying to rally his men when the maroon allies attacked on both flanks from the forests as the militia kept firing their muskets. The African rebels broke in a rout and Tacky was killed by a maroon sharpshooter. The surviving Africans held out in the mountains until the last survivors committed suicide in July of 1760 when British regulars from Canada finally arrived too late in Jamaica to put the rebellion down.

In Guyana and Suriname (on the northern coast of South America), the slave populations had exploded to over ten times the number of Dutch colonists and soldiers that were stationed there by 1760. The Dutch greatly feared their slaves after learning of Tacky's War and became very brutal in the use of torture such as slow dismemberment and the use of hot iron hooks to slowly remove ribs until the slave had died a gruesome death to keep the slaves fearful of disobedience toward their masters. In 1762, 36 slaves revolted as a response to the brutal tortures used by the Dutch in Berbice, Guyana. As the Dutch were torturing a slave, the African onlookers attacked the Dutch and killed them with their own hot iron hooks and with chains. A small Dutch force of around 20 militiamen was then ambushed and massacred outside of Berbice in the tropical forest. A stronger Dutch militia force of 100 men was then sent and put down the rebellion. These troops were able to get the slaves to surrender by threatening torture on their families that they took hostage in Berbice. The rebel slaves were put to death by the same hot iron hook torture that they had protested.

Slave hatred and anger continued until a larger more organized rebellion broke out on February 23, 1763. A slave named Coffey or Cuffy led a revolt of most of the 3,833 slaves in and around Berbice who attacked and killed many of the 346 Dutch whites living there on plantations including women and children. The African rebels also burned buildings and sugar cane fields. The Dutch survivors of the revolt fled to Fort Nassau and to war ships on the Berbice River. On March 3, some survivors took refuge in a large brick house at the Peerboom Plantation. Over 500 slaves under Coffey fought the Dutch inside the house all night while burning down the roof. In the morning, Coffey offered to allow the Dutch to leave on their boats down the Berbice River. All the whites then attempted to leave and were then killed except for a few women and children who were taken captive. Coffey forced the beautiful young wife of one of the dead plantation owners to be his wife. Coffey then declared himself governor of Berbice as a free African state, but it was at this point when he lost control of the rebels that they began fighting each other over captured plantations and homes.

The Dutch abandoned Fort Nassau on March 8 and traveled upriver to Fort Andries at the mouth of the Berbice River to regroup. Some Dutch troops with three English warships arrived from Suriname to help put down the revolt. The three English warships with 150 Dutch troops established a fortified position at Dageraad about 10 miles up the Berbice River from Fort Andries. An African force of 2,000 attacked the fortified position, but retreated after 58 of their men were cut down by grapeshot fired from the English ships. The woman that Coffey had forced to be his wife was able to escape in the confusion of the retreat by swimming out to one of the British ships. A civil war broke out among the rebel slaves caused by African tribal rivalries that went back hundreds of years and resentment between field slaves and household slaves. Coffey's forces were defeated by another African chief named Atta. Coffey then committed suicide after the defeat.

In December of 1763, the Dutch had brought over 2,000 regular troops from Holland to get back control of the colony. The Dutch then sent out two reconnaissance forces of over 100 men each which were ambushed and massacred at Wikki Creek as they tried to cross in different places. The Dutch allied themselves to Native American tribes in Guyana who were also fighting with the Africans. By April of 1764, the Dutch army moved inland with the help of Indians who foiled ambushes and covered their flanks. The Africans were decisively defeated by disciplined Dutch troops combined with Indian flank and rear attacks on the rebels. Hundreds of Africans were tortured and executed for their part in the rebellion. Unexpectedly in 1765 for the Dutch, another slave rebellion spread to Suriname where eventually 26,000 slaves would flee to form an inland maroon community that attacked the Dutch settlements and troops in guerilla attacks. The Africans successfully resisted Dutch efforts to destroy their maroon community until another civil war based on old African tribal rivalries led to a Dutch victory in 1793. The fire of slave revolt then spread to French Domingue (Haiti).

BIBLIOGRAPHY

Burnard, Trevor. *Mastery, Tyranny, and Desire: Slaves in the Anglo-Jamaican World*. Chapel Hill, NC: University of North Carolina Press, 2004.

Edison, Carneiro. *Quilombo dos Palmares*. Sao Paulo Publishing, 1947.

R. Kent. "Palmares: An African State in Brazil." *Journal of African History*. 1971.

Rodriguez, Junius. *Encyclopedia of Slave Resistance and Rebellion*. Westport, CT. 2006.

St. John's Slave Revolt of 1733. History Channel Documentary, 2007.

"St. John Slave Rebellion." *St. John Off the Beaten Track*. Sombrero Publishing Co. 2000.

www.guyana.org – "The Berbice and Suriname Slave Rebellions."

CHAPTER 14

Blood in the Fields:
The Haitian Slave Revolution 1791 to 1803

The Haitian Revolution of 1791 to 1803 was the only slave revolt that successfully defeated a European power and resulted in an independent nation of former slaves. Saint Domingue (Haiti) was France's greatest money making colony that produced 60% of the world's sugar, 40% of the world's coffee, and 80% of the world's Indigo (a royal blue dye that only the rich could afford). Life was so bad for the slaves of Saint Domingue that from 40,000 to 70,000 of them died a year from the harsh working conditions on over 3,000 mostly sugar plantations. The French brought anywhere from 30,000 to 100,000 slaves a year from Africa to keep up the slave population on Saint Domingue.

The roots of the Haitian Revolution of 1791 go back to the French and American siege against the British at Savannah, Georgia during the American Revolution in 1779. The French sent 4,000 troops to join 2,000 American troops from Georgia and South Carolina to capture Savannah from the British. The American Southerners were shocked and offended to see that the French had brought 545 black troops from Haiti in an elite unit called the Chasseurs-Volontaires de Saint-Domingue. The Chasseurs de Domingue was among the first French troops to land near

Savannah and won a couple of skirmishes against British Loyalists and Regulars who wanted to prevent the French from landing their whole army. These free black troops fought well in a disciplined unit in their immaculate white and blue uniforms. The Chasseurs de Domingue came to admire the American cause of freedom despite the fact that freedom did not extend to the slaves of the American South. The Chasseurs lost 25 men in the disastrous French and American attack on October 8, 1779, that caused close to 1,000 casualties during the siege of Savannah. The Chasseurs then successfully resisted attacks by the British and Loyalists as they covered the French and American retreat from Savannah. They were the last unit to embark on the French ships heading back to Haiti.

The Chasseurs de Domingue was an elite French unit made up of former slaves and slaves from Haiti (Saint Domingue) who were released by their owners to serve in the American Revolution. The unit participated heroically in battles near Savannah, GA., Charleston, SC., and Pensacola, Florida. Members of this unit led the Haitian forces during the slave revolt from 1791 until 1803.

The French allowed a company of 60 Chasseurs to return to Charleston with the American Patriots because they believed so much in the American cause for liberty. The site of a company of black soldiers marching in precision in Charleston, SC. caused much protest in the city from the white plantation owners who lived there. The company was then asked to dig and man some trenches outside the city where they fought valiantly before being captured by the British in 1780 at the Siege of Charleston. The company then chose to fight in the British army rather than to be returned to slavery in Jamaica. The company had become disillusioned with the American cause once they realized that liberty did not extend to slaves.

The rest of the Chasseurs de Domingue took part in the taking of a British redoubt in a bayonet charge at the successful joint Spanish and French Siege of Pensacola, FL. in May of 1780. The members of this unit such as Henri Christophe would later lead the Haitian Revolution as officers in the slave army against France after being further inspired by the events of the French Revolution of 1789.

In 1775, the slave population of Haiti was over 300,000, but by 1789, the slave population had risen to 500,000 from an extra 200,000 Africans taken as prisoners of war by tribes allied to the French in West Africa. The white French population of Haiti remained at 40,000 during this time. These 200,000 new slaves saw themselves as warriors from proud tribes and were looking for an opportunity to overthrow the French and to form a new African nation in Haiti. The French Revolution in 1789 led an educated free man of color named Vincent Oge to lead a revolt of free blacks against the French in early 1791 when his appeals for equal rights for all free people of color was ignored by the French National Assembly in Paris. Voodoo priests encouraged Oge and the slaves to revolt as well. Oge then led a brief rebellion in the Le Cap Francois area of Haiti before being captured and tortured by French troops in a violent crackdown on the rebels. On August 21, 1791, a group of runaway slaves that had been recent arrivals to Saint Domingue as prisoners of war led a more widespread revolt that involved 100,000 slaves who burned more than 300 plantations in the northern third of the colony. Over 4,000 French men, women and children were tortured, killed and mutilated during this initial stage of the revolt.

France dispatched 6,000 troops from France in March of 1792 to add to the 17,000 French troops already stationed on the island to try to stop the rebellion in their wealthiest colony. The French troops who tried to venture into this rebellious northern third were ambushed and attacked constantly from all sides and at times massacred by machete and axe armed slaves. The slave rebellion then spread into the rest of Saint Domingue against other French as a civil war broke out between those that had been slaves against the free blacks and the mixed mulattos who had been treated much better by their French masters. The civil war among the slaves was also fought between the more recent African arrivals based on ancient tribal rivalries from their wars in Africa. The French just didn't have the manpower available to subdue hundreds of thousands of rebellious slaves.

In March of 1793, France declared war on Britain while the white French planters made agreements with the British to take sovereignty of the colony over if they would just put down the slave revolt. The British sent over 25,000 troops to put down this revolt and to claim control of the world's wealthiest colony. The British soon found that they were having many men from small garrisons or supply convoys being massacred by the African rebels as well. The British could only control the cities on the coast, but were at a great disadvantage in the surrounding tropical jungles where the Haitians had the advantage of guerilla warfare. Then disease such as yellow fever began taking a toll on British forces as well.

Guerilla warfare by Haitian slaves wore the French, Spanish, and British armies down until they dared not to leave the major cities and fortifications of the island of Hispaniola.

In the summer of 1793, an educated free black man named Toussaint L'Ouverture, rose rapidly through the ranks of the slave army to lead his own organized black army against the French forces in Saint Domingue. Toussaint L'Ouverture was born at Breda Plantation, but had been the grandson of an African chief of the area of Gaou-Guinou. His grandfather had been captured with thousands of other warriors from his tribe and sold to the French and taken to Haiti. Toussaint gained favor with his owners and became an educated slave in charge of administrative duties in running a number of plantations.

Toussaint L'Overture was the Washington and Lincoln of the Haitian slave rebellion. His death in a French prison in 1803 left a leadership void for the only republic to be formed by slaves to have overthrown their white masters.

Toussaint earned freedom for his services to the French by 1779 and soon owned his own plantation and a number of slaves. One day shortly after gaining freedom, Toussaint was reading a book on a public bench on the main street of Haut de Cap in a nice new cream colored suit that he had just bought. He was spotted by a poor French farmer and beaten up which left blood stains all over his suit. Toussaint continued to wear the bloodstained suit right up until 1793 when he killed the Frenchman who had beaten him and then joined the slave revolt. Many former soldiers from the Chasseurs de Domingue served as officers that trained Toussaint's army to fight in the disciplined European style while maintaining a large force of militia and irregulars (cultivators armed with machetes and axes). Toussaint also formed an elite force of 600 cavalry called the Honor Guard made up of the best horses and horsemen in Saint Domingue. The Honor Guard included Africans who had served as cavalry in West Africa as well as French, Spanish, British and American mercenaries who had served in cavalry forces from their respective countries. In June of 1793, the Haitian Honor Guard charged out of a forest and killed and captured a surprised French column of 1,150 infantry. The French were reduced to just 3,500 troops left on the island due to disease and guerrilla warfare as Toussaint's army grew to 15,000 disciplined troops. Most of the other African forces on the island were undisciplined rabbles that often fought against each other because of grudges or old tribal rivalries.

Toussaint decided to ally himself to an invading Spanish force from the Spanish colony of Santo Domingo on the western part of the island (Dominican Republic) to resist the British who were now the greater threat. The Spanish forces and Toussaint's organized infantry and cavalry forces successfully defeated the British and the French forces separately which drove them back to the coastal cities. In April of 1794, Toussaint became aware that Spain intended to keep Saint Domingue as a colony of Spain and intended to re-establish slavery as it still existed in Santo Domingo. In fact, some Haitian African leaders such as Jean-Francois and Biassou had been selling former slaves from opposing African tribes in Saint Domingue to the Spanish as they had done in Africa. Toussaint was determined to put a stop to this and first began by attacking and massacring small Spanish garrisons and supply convoys. The Spanish army's advance stalled and began pulling back which left the Haitian interior under the control of Toussaint's African army. Then the French allied themselves to Toussaint on May 6, 1794 in return for recognition of emancipation of slavery on Saint Domingue which was also confirmed by the French National Convention in Paris as well. Toussaint first defeated the other 2 African armies under Jean-Francois and Biassou who were still helping the Spanish. The British and Spanish decided to join forces at this point to try to jointly gain control of the colony.

The Battle of Croix des Bouquets in 1794 pitted the French and Haitians in a temporary alliance to defeat the British and Spanish army in an 18th century version of "the enemy of my enemy is my friend." The English and Spanish thought they could take advantage of the chaos of the rebellion to seize the world's most lucrative colony. The Haitians and French later resumed their war which lasted until 1803.

On June 23, 1794, French forces aided by Toussaint's well disciplined African army defeated a joint British and Spanish army at the Battle of Croix de Bouquets. The British with 3,000 infantry and the Spanish with 4,000 infantry occupied four hill redoubts (earthworks forts) with the British controlling two forward parallel hill redoubts while the Spanish held two redoubts on both outer flanks of the British redoubts. The French with 3,000 infantry assaulted the left British redoubt in column formation as Toussaint with 5,000 disciplined African infantry and his Honor Guard cavalry assaulted the right British redoubt also in column formation. The remaining 10,000 militia and irregulars of Toussaint's army attacked the Spanish redoubts. Toussaint's forces overran the right British redoubt after a fierce hand to hand battle while the left British redoubt facing the French eventually retreated after the Spanish redoubts were completely overrun and mostly massacred by the African militia and irregulars. The British lost over 1,500 casualties and retreated with most of their troops from the left forward redoubt because of the preoc-cupation of the African militia in the massacres at the Spanish redoubts.

The Spanish quit the war as a result of this defeat and had to give Santo Domingo (Dominican Republic) over to Toussaint as part of the free nation of former slaves that he was building. There was occasional fighting with Spanish settlers and militias to continue until 1802, but Spain was never able to support these settlers or reassert any control over Santo Domingo again. The British stayed only in coastal cities racked by yellow fever and attempted a few failed offensives until they evacuated Haiti in 1798 with only 5,000 out of their original force of 25,000 troops that they arrived with in 1793 left alive. It is estimated that over 24,000 mostly French whites and over 100,000 blacks (mostly from the civil wars between themselves) had died in this early phase of the Haitian Revolution. Toussaint let the French believe that they had gained both Saint Domingue and Santo Domingo, but in truth they had gained nothing.

The slave revolt on Saint Domingue was first taken out on French slave owners and their families who were mostly massacred in a very brutal fashion.

Thousands of French troops and civilians were hung by their former slaves
in revenge for years of degradations committed against them.

Saint Domingue and Santo Domingo broke out in civil wars again with unprecedented violence. Many atrocities were committed by factions of tribal Africans brought to Haiti in the 1780's against blacks born in Haiti, and Mulattos (the children and grandchildren of white masters and overseers with their slave women). Most of the remaining 16,000 French whites in Saint Domingue supported Toussaint who protected their rights and property as much as he was able in the areas he controlled. By 1801, Toussaint had regained control of both Saint Domingue and Santo Domingo and issued a constitution as governor-general of a free nation while giving only lip service of submission to France and First Consul Napoleon Bonaparte.

In 1801, the British wanted Napoleon to regain control of Saint Domingue and Santo Domingo because of their fear that slave insurrections that had raged there since 1791 would spread in the Caribbean. The British promised no opposition from their navy and open trade with the colony if Napoleon could regain control of the island. Napoleon was determined to regain control and to re-establish slavery to provide funds for his planned conquest of Europe and to build a massive fleet to invade Britain with. Napoleon also wanted to use Saint Domingue and the Louisiana Territory as bases to invade the southern United States and to take over the rest of the West Indies.

On January 20, 1802, Napoleon sent 41 ships of the line and 21 frigates to take a French army of 35,000 troops to retake Saint Domingue and Santo Domingo. Included in the expedition were 21,175 veteran French troops from Napoleon's victories in Italy and at the Battle of Marengo (1800) to go under his brother in law, General Emmanuel Charles Leclerc. General Donation Rochambeau served as 2nd in command whose father helped win the Battle of Yorktown (1781) in the American Revolution. The French troops went to Saint Domingue with an unrealistic intention to loot for riches, but few knew that they would not survive the ordeal they were about to embark upon.

Toussaint prepared to meet the French with 13 demi-brigades of 1,500 infantry trained in European warfare and uniformed in a mixture of blood stained French, British, and Spanish uniforms that had been captured or mostly taken off of dead enemies from the previous ten years of fighting. A number of these demi-brigades had the look of buccaneer pirates because they mixed and matched different articles of uniforms and weapons from different nations and wore bandanas on their heads if they didn't have enemy hats to wear. Toussaint's Honor Guard had been increased to 5,500 cavalry and elite infantry and wore the best of the French uniforms that were available. Toussaint's top two commanders were Jean-Jacques Dessalines and Henry Christophe. This gave Toussaint a trained regular army of 25,000 troops and 100,000 militia and irregulars armed with machetes and axes to meet Napoleon's army with. Toussaint's main disadvantage was that he had to spread his army fairly thin to cover both Saint Domingue and Santo Domingo. The greatest weapon that Toussaint possessed though was yellow fever and time which had decimated the European forces in the previous fighting of the 1790's. Toussaint's strategy involved fortifying key crossroads and mountain passes of the interior of Haiti while fighting a delaying slash and burn action at the coastal cities.

African rebels on Hispaniola wore a mix of various field clothing and a mix of various French, British, and Spanish uniforms taken from enemy corpses. The sight of the blood stained assortment of uniforms on the former slaves had a terrifying effect on the Europeans. Some Haitian units resembled pirates with bandanas on their heads and a motley assortment of captured weapons.

General Henry Christophe who had fought with the Chasseurs de Domingue in the American Revolution held the island's largest port at Le Cap Francois and Fort Liberte with three demi- brigades of 4,800 Haitians. On February 4, 1802, the French assaulted Fort Liberte with 4,000 troops in an amphibious assault from large row boats. The first two waves of French troops were killed in their boats by accurate canon fire or were decimated in the surf by grapeshot and musket fire. Finally, the third wave of French troops was able to get a foothold below the walls of the fort when the Haitians ran low on ammunition. The French scaled the walls with ladders and fought a vicious hand to hand battle all night until they had captured the fort by morning. The Haitians then fell back on Le Cap Francois as the French landed 8,000 more men to take the city. General Henri Christophe fought a delaying action from a series of entrenchments and redoubts that his forces would retreat to for two more days as his troops massacred several thousand French whites in Le Cap Francois. Leclerc's forces entered the city in horror on February 6, 1802, to see the city and its' provisions burned and the muti-lated French corpses in the streets of men, women, and children. Both sides had lost over 2,000 casualties in the battle.

Toussaint wanted a similar defense at Port-au-Prince, but Dessalines was too slow in organizing its' defenses and the French captured the city intact with the Haitians falling back to the mountains. The Haitians then began massacring most of the remaining 16,000 white French civil-ians of Saint Domingue. Only at Port-au-Prince and a few plantations were the French able to rescue the French civilians. The French then began their own war of extermination against the Africans because they now knew that the blacks would never willingly go back to slavery again. Leclerc wrote to Napoleon that all of the blacks of Saint Domingue and Santo Domingo would have to be killed and new slaves from Africa and possibly from a possible future invasion of the southern United States would have to resupply the colony with new submissive slaves.

Toussaint fell back to some entrenchments and an arms depot in a valley between two mountains called Ravine a Couleuvre. Toussaint had 3,000 troops of his Honor Guard and another demi-brigade of 1,500 infantry with 10,000 armed cultivators to defend the pass with. Rochambeau marched on Ravine a Couleuvre with 8,000 French troops to take Toussaint's arms depot.

The French assaulted the Haitian trenches all night on February 22, 1802. Toussaint's Honor Guard and regulars bravely defended their trenches with musket fire and grapeshot as the machete and axe wield-ing cultivators would counter attack the French when their attacks on the trenches stalled. By morning, the French had taken Ravine a Couleuvre at great cost, but Toussaint counter attacked with a reserve force of 1,000 of his Honor Guard cavalry and retook the lost ground in the early morning fog of February 23. The battle was really a defeat for both sides. Rochambeau reported to Leclerc that he had lost 600 dead and 3,500 wounded in the battle. Many of the wounded French would die in the days and weeks ahead from gaping wounds from machetes, axes, swords, and grapeshot. Toussaint couldn't claim victory either with over 4,000 of his own casualties which wrecked part of his Honor Guard and an entire demi-brigade. Most of the remaining cultivators deserted after the battle. Toussaint fell back to Gonaives with 1,500 exhausted and wounded Haitian troops where he entered a local cathedral and tore down the cross and proclaimed to God that he would no longer be a Christian because Jesus had betrayed him.

To make matters worse, on February 25, one of Toussaint's best trained and uniformed units, the 9th demi-brigade, defected to the French after Leclerc announced to them that the French had come to Saint Domingue to end slavery and not to re-enslave them. Toussaint was trying to find the unit and didn't know about the defection until March 2 when Toussaint met the French at the Battle of Plaisance. Toussaint had joined up with Christophe's forces with over 5,000 Haitian regulars and another 5,000 militia and cultivators against 7,000 French troops on an open plain. The Haitians were holding their own by answering French musket volleys with volleys of their own when in the midst of the battlefield came the 9th demi-brigade in column formation right at the center of Toussaint's line. A dismayed Toussaint rode out between his army and to the front of the 9th and cried out, "Soldiers of the Ninth, do you dare fire on your brother?" At these words the 9th tried to come over to Toussaint as others fell to their knees in shame as the French army fired on them and then killed most of the unit in a cavalry and bayonet charge. Toussaint made it back to his own lines, but couldn't get a counter attack organized to save his 9th demi-brigade from their awful fate. Toussaint was so discouraged and broken hearted that he ordered a retreat from the battlefield.

Dessalines then stationed 300 infantry and 600 cavalry of the Honor Guard at an abandoned 100 by 100 yard fort built by the British on a hill called La Crete a Pierrot above the town of Petite Riviere. The French mistakenly believed that a large cache of gold was inside the fort and wanted it captured. On March 4, over 2,000 French troops were out-raged to see that every white man, woman, and child in Petite Riviere was butchered and lying in the streets. Over 500 grenadiers were coaxed into charging some Haitian skirmishers who fired on them and then ran and jumped into some trenches below the fort's walls. Grapeshot was fired from the fort at pointblank range and mowed most of the grenadiers down. As the surviving French were retreating down the hill, the Honor Guard cavalry came out from a concealed position in some nearby woods and cut down most of the rest of the grenadiers. The French lost 400 dead including 2 generals in the attack.

The French became obsessed with the idea that there was gold at Fort La Crete a Pierrot and sent close to 10,000 more troops under Rochambeau on March 11 to take the fort as Toussaint brought the fort's garrison up to 1,200 infantry with a second smaller earthworks fort outside the main fort. General Boudet wanted to get to the nonex-istent gold before Rochambeau's arrival and sent his grenadiers again at the fort's canon and again were decimated by canon fire followed by another devastating Honor Guard charge that killed and wounded hundreds more of the French including General Boudet. Then a second attack was launched from Petite Riviere against a different side of the fort. The Haitian garrison scrambled to move the fort's 12 canons to the side of the fort where the attack was coming from and managed to fire grapeshot at point blank range which killed and wounded hundreds of more French troops. Rochambeau was disgusted to see 800 French dead and wounded around the Haitian fort when he arrived. The failed attacks were repeated on March 12 with again hundreds of French being killed or wounded followed by a counter attack by the Honor Guard cavalry with several hundred cultivators armed with machetes and axes. At night, the French were shocked to hear that the Haitians were singing the "The Marseillaise" with great revolutionary fervor. The French brought in mortars that made life in the forts difficult and caused casualties in the packed enclosures .

On March 22, the French lost 300 men in an assault that overwhelmed the 200 Haitian defenders of the smaller earthworks fort in vicious hand to hand fighting. On March 24, over 800 Haitians broke out of Fort La Crete a Pierrot through French lines to safety. The siege cost the French 2,000 dead while the Haitians lost 400 dead in the battle. Once the French had entered the fort, they learned from some wounded Haitians that there never was any gold in the fort. All the French sacrifice and efforts at the fort had really accomplished nothing.

On March 29, Toussaint and Christophe took over 3,000 regulars that they could round up from various units with several thousand militia and cultivators and circled behind the French army to attack the 400 French troops and 1,200 French sailors defending Le Cap Francois. The 2nd Battle of Le Cap Francois was a bloody all night street to street battle that was fought in the ruins of this once great city. The French lost 500 casualties before they retreated to their ships in the harbor. Leclerc the next day took all the French troops he could muster and retook the city as Toussaint and Christophe retreated. On April 1, 1802, Leclerc sent Napoleon a letter stating that he only had 7,000 effectives left because of losses to battle and to yellow fever which was running rampant through the French army. Most of the veterans of the glorious Battle of Marengo were now dead. Napoleon then sent over 30,000 more troops including over 8,000 elite troops from the famed Polish Legion to die in Saint Domingue as well.

Napoleon sent 7,000 elite Polish troops to subdue the rebel slaves in 1802. Few were alive in 1803 except around 1,000 defectors who mostly settled in the United States after the war.

The proud army that Toussaint had built was also wrecked and the war turned into a guerilla insurgency with the over 100,000 militia and cultivators becoming much more important to the Haitian cause. It was at this point that Dessalines and Christophe were convinced from secret correspondence from Leclerc that Napoleon was freeing the slaves of Saint Domingue and switched sides. They then convinced Toussaint to surrender and to come to a secret meeting on June 7 where he was seized and taken to France where he died in a jail cell a year later. Napoleon would later say that taking Toussaint L'Ouverture prisoner was a great mistake and that he should have ruled Saint Domingue and made his conquests in the West through this noble black statesman and general.

The loss of Toussaint was a tragedy for Haiti. They had lost their George Washington and Abraham Lincoln all in one and Haiti didn't have anyone of his ability to lead the young nation of former slaves that brilliantly broke away from France.

When the lower and mid level soldiers that were left of Toussaint's army realized that their leader had been betrayed, they rose up again with a vengeance by late June of 1802 against the French and against those blacks that had gone over to the enemy. Dessalines and Christophe realized their mistake and came back to lead the insurgency against the French again. The new troops that Napoleon sent to Saint Domingue started coming down with yellow fever at an alarming rate almost as soon as they got off the ships in the late summer and fall of 1802. Over 10,000 French and Polish troops died of yellow fever within two months of arriving on the island.

On November 2, 1802, Leclerc died of yellow fever and General Rochambeau continued his genocidal policies. On April 27, 1803, the French officially announced that slavery was to be reintroduced to the island. The French massacred thousands of blacks all over the island in a reign of terror. The French brought in 600 slave catching dogs from Cuba that proved unpredictable and killed and ate a French drummer boy and several soldiers that had disappeared into the jungle chasing some black insurgents in their first battle. The dogs killed several thousand blacks before they were mostly all eventually killed as well. Both sides hanged hundreds of combatants and civilians from trees all around the island. One of the Polish brigades was so disgusted by the senseless slaughter that they switched sides to the insurgents. It got where the French couldn't leave their fortification without getting their men ambushed and massacred. There were hundreds of small scale battles and ambushes in the jungles around the French fortified positions at this time.

The British realized that Napoleon was making plans to invade the British Isles and blockaded Saint Domingue and Santo Domingo and provided the insurgents with muskets and uniforms for a new army of 18,000 that was led by Dessalines and Christophe. On June 26, 1803, Rochambeau pulled his last 5,900 troops on the island into Le Cap Francois. Over 2,000 of these troops and 72 artillery pieces were to defend a series of redoubts and blockhouses that surrounded Fort Vertieres and the approach to Le Cap Francois.

Henri Christophe had fought in the Chasseurs de St.Domingue in the American Revolution and became the leader of the Haitian Revolution and of Haiti after Toussaint's capture and death. This picture was of a re-enactor for a BBC documentary.

On October 7, 1803, Dessalines and Christophe brought their army of 18,000 to assault the redoubts and Fort Vertieres in a night attack. All night the Haitians came on in human wave assaults against the redoubts. The French initially mowed down 1,200 Haitians with grapeshot and underground mines that were buried in front of the redoubts filled with gunpowder and explosives that were detonated with time fuses. Despite this initial success, the black troops kept coming without let up. One by one the redoubts fell in vicious close quarters fighting. Then the artillery from the redoubts was turned on Fort Vertieres by the Haitians and a lucky shot blew up the powder magazine and all the remaining French troops in the fort. Once Rochambeau realized that the fort had fallen, he sent word to the blockading British fleet to take him and his remaining 3,900 troops as their prisoners on the morning of October 8 before they'd all be massacred by the Haitians. The French lost 20 generals and close to 60,000 men dead and the Haitians lost 80,000 dead in the campaign of 1802 and 1803 of the Haitian Revolution. In addition, the Haitian Revolution had eliminated the French population of 40,000, and more than 200,000 civilian Haitians from the island from its pre war population of more than 500,000.

On January 1, 1804, Dessalines declared a free republic of Haiti and then ordered all of the remaining whites on the island to be put to death. Thousands of mostly white Spanish and French refuges in Santo Domingo were massacred. Only some Americans, British, and the Poles were spared. Haiti has been in perpetual civil war off and on for the last 200+ years in which they had over 200 presidents and dictators assassinated in the often troubled nation. The Haitian Revolution still inspires many because it was a real blow to the institution of slavery. The Haitian Revolution also may have saved the United States from a possible Napoleonic invasion and led to the Louisiana Purchase that added so much land to this nation and also financed much of Napoleon's conquest of Europe between 1804 and 1809.

BIBLIOGRAPHY

Bell, Madison Smart. *Toussaint Louverture*. Pantheon Books, NY. 2007. (This was one of my best sources on this topic).

Dubois, Laurent. *Avengers of the New World: The Story of the Haitian Revolution*. Cambridge, Mass.: Belknap Press of Harvard University. 2005.

Greggus, John. *Haitian Revolutionary Studies*. University of South Carolina Press, 2002.

James, C.L.R. *The Black Jacobins: Toussaint L'Ouverture and the San Domingo Revolution.* Vintage Press, 2nd Edition, 1989.

Ott, Thomas. *The Haitian Revolution.* University of Tennessee Press, 1973.

Parkinson, Wenda. *The Gilded African: Toussaint L'Ouverture*. London: Quarter Books, 1980.

External Links

"Egalite for All: Toussaint Louverture and the Haitian Revolution." Noland Walker. *PBS Documentary*, 2009.

For the French free colored participation in the Siege of Savannah:

- "Chasseurs Volontaires" monument, by Jason Mastin, located in Franklin Square, Savannah, Ga.

- Savannah Battlefield Park at Springhill Redoubt, Savannah, Ga.

CHAPTER 15

A Settlement Dark and Bloody:
The Cherokee Wars: 1654 – 1865

The Cherokee nation (eastern Tennessee, southern Kentucky, western North Carolina and Virginia, and northern South Carolina and Georgia in the US) had been a warlike nation through much of its history. The Cherokees always needed and sought war with other Indian nations or with colonists as a way to prove and to maintain their warrior skills in battle and to be considered a full fledged Cherokee warrior. The Cherokee nation's first conflict with the colonists took place in 1654, when over 500 Jamestown Militiamen with between 600-700 Pamuncky Indians attacked the Cherokee town of Rechaherians in Virginia in an effort to capture Indian slaves. The Cherokees held off the Jamestown Militia and the Pamuncky warriors from their traditional round stockade fort until warriors from other towns attacked and drove off the Pamuncky who then abandoned their English allies. The vulnerable Jamestown Militia then lost over 100 men in a running battle before they could get back to Jamestown several days later.

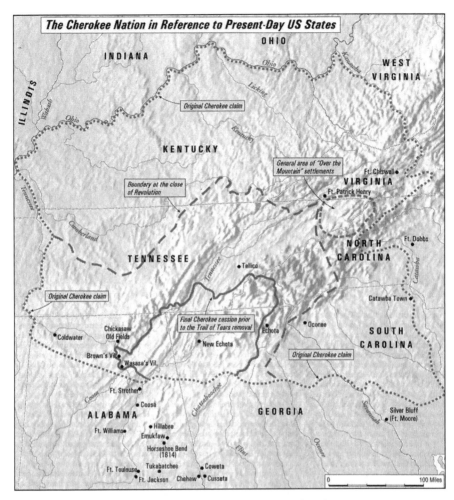

The Cherokee Nation in Reference to Present-Day US States

Map of the Cherokee nation and area of conflict.

In 1711, Tuscarora Indians killed hundreds of English, German, and Dutch settlers along the Roanoke River in Virginia because the lands that they had settled were hunting grounds that belonged to the Tuscarora. In 1712, 600 Virginia and North Carolina Militia with 360 Cherokees attacked the round Tuscarora fort at Narhantes along the Neuse River killing over 300 Indians and capturing 100 women and children to be sold as slaves. The Cherokees were told by the governors of North Carolina and Virginia that they could occupy and absorb the lands of the Tuscarora in North Carolina in return for forcing their removal. In 1713, 1,000 Cherokee and Catawba Indians massacred over 1,000 Tuscarora Indians at their settlement at Fort Neoheroka. By 1715, most of the surviving Tuscarora had migrated to New York to become part of the Six Nations of the Iroquois. This war and alliance with the settlers caused the Cherokees and the Catawba Indians to enter into a bloody 30 year war with the Iroquois's Six Nations which eventually ended in a stalemate in 1745.

In 1715, the Cherokee, Catawba, Creek, and Yamasee Indians killed hundreds of English settlers and had burned all of their settlements in South Carolina except for Charlestown (Charleston). The Yamasee War started because hundreds of Indians were being enslaved to work on plantations in South Carolina. Quite a number of Indians had their wives and daughters kidnapped to be forced to become brides (Cherokee women were particularly desired for their beauty) for the large population of English bachelors in South Carolina. The colony of South Carolina was on the verge of being destroyed with only Charlestown remaining with around 2,000 terrified settlers who had taken refuge there.

The Cherokees and Creeks who had been traditional enemies for hundreds of years were starting to have tensions between them. At the same time, the English settlers opened negotiations with the Cherokees to see if they would switch sides or else they would face annihilation. The Cherokees said that they would switch sides if all the remaining Cherokee slaves and women were returned, and if the English would trade guns and gunpowder with them to use against the Iroquois and the Creeks. They also let it be known that in the future if the English settlers wanted a Cherokee wife that they had to come up to Cherokee territory as a guest and they had to get to know a girl and her family and if everyone agreed then the settler could have a wife. The English agreed to all of the Cherokee terms for the alliance to take place. The Cherokees with their Catawba allies then descended on the Creek and the Yamasee Indians with a vengeance and by 1717 had completely defeated them thus saving the South Carolina colony from destruction. South Carolina and the Cherokees then enjoyed very good relations with a lucrative trade of deer skins in exchange for guns and gunpowder which benefited both partners. Hundreds of South Carolina settlers traveled to the Cherokee nation to take wives during this time as well. The Cherokees also traded for the return of runaway slaves (Africans) that were trying to reach sanctuary with the Seminoles in Florida.

The decision to switch sides and to attack the Creek Indians in the Yamasee War caused a war between the Cherokee and Creek nations that lasted from 1715 until 1755. There was constant raiding and many small battles during this period of war between these powerful rivals. The Battle of Taliwa in 1755 was an unusual all Indian pitched battle in northern Georgia that decided the outcome of this war. In the Battle of Taliwa, over 1,000 Muskogee Creek warriors met a force of 500 Cherokee warriors out in a clearing when both sides traded musket fire followed by a Creek attack. The fighting was vicious hand to hand fighting with tomahawks, clubs, and knives when the Creek numbers drove the Cherokees back into the forest. The Cherokees fell back about a mile when they regrouped and counter attacked the Creeks who believed they had won the battle and were spread out around the forest battlefield looking for dead or wounded Cherokees to scalp as trophies. The Cherokee counter attack was vicious and was able to overcome the Creeks in small groups so that they retook the lost battlefield in triumph. The Cherokees had close to 200 dead and wounded to the Creek losses of more than 400 dead and wounded which made this the bloodiest known Indian versus Indian battle in US history. The Creeks sued for peace with the Cherokees and agreed to never set foot in northern Georgia again.

The English began bringing in Africans to replace Indians as slaves because Indians tended to die from smallpox within a few months to a few years into captivity, and they were difficult to catch when they ran away because they knew the land so well. Enslaving Indians also led to wars such as the Yamasee War. Africans had the same diseases as whites and lived longer than Indians in captivity plus they didn't know the Americas when they ran away and didn't really have anywhere to go. Africans could go for refuge in Florida to the Seminoles who took in African slaves as members of the tribe, but there were hundreds of miles of swamps, marshes, alligators, snakes, and Indians to deal with to get there.

Relations between the Cherokees and the English changed in 1758 when 700 Cherokee warriors had been recruited by Gen. John Forbes to aide the British and colonist army marching against the French at Fort Duquesne near present day Pittsburgh. In 1755, at the beginning of the French and Indian War (1754-1763) the British had lost more than a 1,000 men in an ambush by 637 Indians and 254 French and Canadians when they previously tried to march on Fort Duquesne. Gen. John Forbes was determined to use the Cherokee Indians to spearhead the British force and to prevent another disastrous ambush.

The Cherokees as well as the colonists from day one were treated in a condescending and disrespectful manner by Forbes and the British officers. Forbes was angry whenever "the savages" as he referred to them as would attempt to come into the British camp to socialize and to trade deer meat for bread and sugar with their allies. Forbes also didn't like the Cherokee Chief; Little Carpenter's input into strategy and tactics for the campaign and had him temporarily arrested for sedition and desertion when the chief had left for a few days on a scouting mission without permission. After three weeks of this, the 700 Cherokees had enough and abandoned Forbes taking with them the muskets and powder that the British had provided them with. The British force went on to capture Fort

Duquesne from the French because the French allied Indians had there numbers greatly reduced from a smallpox epidemic during the previous winter of 1758.

The Cherokee, Catawba, Iroquois, Huron, and Ottawa warriors all looked terrifyingly similar with their red and black war paint and partially shaved heads. This similarity in appearance to Indian enemies caused Cherokee warriors to be mistaken for Huron and Ottawa Indians and to be attacked by allied British and American colonists which led to the first Cherokee War in 1759.

As the Cherokees traveled back through Virginia and North Carolina, they found themselves being ambushed and hunted by local militias. The Virginia and North Carolina Militias couldn't distinguish between their Cherokee allies and the French allied Huron and Ottawa Indians who looked terrifying with their hair partially shaved and their faces painted in red and black. Over 30 Cherokees were killed before they reached their villages. Then the Cherokees discovered that hunters from the Long Cane settlements in South Carolina had taken advantage of the Cherokee warrior's absence and had been poaching the Cherokee game which threatened their food supply and the number of skins that they had for trading. In 1759, the enraged Cherokees raided the South Carolina frontier massacring over 30 settlers in reprisal.

South Carolina countered by stopping all trade and embargoing all gunpowder shipments to the Cherokees. A delegation of chiefs then traveled to Charleston to negotiate an end to hostilities and a return to peaceful relations and trade. Governor William Lyttleton then took the 22 chiefs as hostages until the Cherokees gave up those warriors that had killed the 30 settlers on the frontier. The hostages were then taken to Fort Prince George in upper South Carolina by 1,300 militiamen with three tons of gunpowder to be given to the Cherokees in exchange for their handing over of the guilty warriors. Not long after arriving, the militia was being decimated by smallpox at Fort Prince George and went back to Charleston leaving the hostages and gunpowder with the garrison.

The Cherokees saw this taking of their chiefs as hostages as a declaration of war and they then put Fort Prince George and Fort Loudoun in Tennessee under siege. At Fort Prince George, the commanding officer and a small group of men were ambushed and killed when they ventured out of the fort because it seemed that the Cherokees had left. The 22 chiefs in the fort were then massacred in reprisal by the garrison. The Cherokees then attacked and burned the backwoods settlements from Virginia to Georgia and massacred over 100 settlers and traders. The frontier was rolled back to within 75 miles of Charleston in South Carolina as several hundred panicked families fled for their lives.

Cherokee warriors ambushed and defeated British Highlander troops in their first invasion of Cherokee lands in 1760 at the First Battle of Echoe.

In April of 1760, 1,300 Scottish Highlanders from the British 1st and 77th Regiments arrived in Charleston under the command of Colonel Archibald Montgomery. The Highlanders were drafted in large numbers by the British government and sent to America for fear that they might rebel again like the rebellion that ended in the Scottish defeat at the Battle of Culloden in 1746. On June 1, 1760, with the addition of 300 SC. Rangers and 50 Catawba Indians, the British force started burning down the Cherokee Lower Towns in the Carolinas with over 100 Cherokees being killed in skirmishes. As the British came near to the town of Echoe, 1,000 Cherokees ambushed the column from front and back. The lead force of 100 Highlanders was wiped out as the Cherokees opened with a devastating musket volley and then charged out splitting skulls and scalping with tomahawks, clubs and knives. Most of the unprotected pack horses and mules carrying the supplies at the rear were shot and killed also. The Highlanders and Rangers in between hunkered down paralyzed with fear. The loss of the pack horses and mules meant that the column could go no further because they didn't have a way to carry their supplies and ammunition. After the ambush, Montgomery ordered the rest of the supplies to be destroyed and his force to march back to Charleston where he declared victory and then loaded his troops onto ships and returned to New York.

On August 5, the garrison of 200 at Fort Loudoun had run out of supplies and was told by the Cherokees that they could leave if they would surrender the fort and its canon and gunpowder supply. The garrison buried the canon and gunpowder and then proceeded under Cherokee escort three miles to camp at Ball Play Creek. When the Cherokees found the buried gunpowder and canon, they attacked at dawn on August 6 with 700 warriors. The Cherokees launched a volley of arrows (because they were almost out of gunpowder) and then rushed the camp killing 22 men and 3 women. A number of the garrison had Cherokee wives and these women came running with the warriors and claimed their husbands so that they wouldn't be killed. The husbands were allowed to go with their wives (many men also had another wife in Charleston). The others were taken as hostages with some being tortured and burned in the Cherokee fires.

The Cherokees believed that they had won the war and agreed to a six month truce with South Carolina. The Cherokees sent emissaries to the French at Fort Toulouse in Alabama asking for an alliance in case hostilities were renewed. The French had considered sending 10,000 troops to link up with the Cherokees and to occupy the Carolinas in 1759 as a response to the British buildup on the St. Lawrence River. The loss of Quebec to the British in 1759 put the French in no position to ally with the Cherokees, but the French did send the Cherokees some gunpowder and food supplies with their best wishes. The winter of 1761 was particularly bitter in Cherokee country with shortages of food and infectious disease which killed many.

When the British high command found out that Montgomery in fact had been defeated by the Cherokees, they sent back the 1st Highlanders and the 17th and 22nd Regiments to Charleston under Colonel James Grant. On June 7, 1,400 British Regulars with 1,400 Colonial Provincials and Rangers, 100 Mohawks and Catawba's, and 600 pack animals headed back toward Echoe. On June 10, 1,000 Cherokee warriors ambushed the British at the exact same location as their earlier ambush. The Cherokees killed and wounded 52 British regulars in the initial volley and ferocious attack with tomahawks and knives. This time the Rangers, Mohawks, and Catawba's came in from the Cherokee flanks in the forest and killed over 100 Cherokees in vicious hand to hand fighting. While this was going on, half of the Cherokee force was trying to kill off the pack animals at the rear of the column in order to cripple the British like they had in the previous engagement. This time the pack animals were well defended by the Provincials. Over 60 pack animals, 11 Provincials and 20 Cherokees were killed or wounded in the battle at the rear of the column. After six more hours of musket fire exchange, the Cherokees retreated, but most damaging of all was that they had expended all of their gunpowder in the battle.

The British went on to burn down the Cherokee settlements in North Carolina and Tennessee so that three out of every five Cherokees were homeless. Only the homes and property of the Cherokee women living with their white husbands were spared. The Cherokees skirmished with bows, but couldn't really do anything to hinder the British column. At the same time the Cherokees were under pressure from the Cherokee-Chickasaw War that lasted from 1758 to 1769. Finally in August of 1761, the Cherokees sued for peace. The Cherokees had to agree to give up their lands and hunting grounds in South Carolina and part of North Carolina in the peace treaty that followed.

In September of 1773, Daniel Boone and around 50 emigrants made their first attempt to establish a settlement in Kentucky. The party made their way into Cherokee territory in southern Kentucky. A small group of frontiersmen went to gather supplies when they were attacked by a war party of Cherokees and Shawnee. Several of the party were killed and captured. Daniel Boone's eldest son James and Henry Russell were then tortured and burned in a brutal manner at night where the party could hear, but couldn't do anything to stop the killings. Dunmore's War between Virginia and the Shawnee came out of this atrocity in which Virginia won on October 10, 1774 at the Battle of Point Pleasant. The Shawnee had to give land in northern Kentucky to Virginia, but the Cherokees were left alone despite their involvement in the killings.

On March 17, 1775, the Cherokee nation sold 20,000,000 acres of land in Kentucky and Tennessee for 2,000 pounds sterling silver and 8,000 pounds of gunpowder to the Transylvania Land Company. Many Cherokees opposed the sale of so much of their land. One was Chief Dragging Canoe who ominously told buyers from North Carolina, "You have bought a fair land, but there is a cloud hanging over it; you will find its settlement dark and bloody." In early 1776, the Cherokees received thousands of muskets and huge quantities of gunpowder from Great Britain in an alliance against the American Patriots in the American Revolution. The Cherokees wanted to use the war as a way to get back all of their lost lands. The British would continue to supply muskets and gunpowder to the Cherokees well after the American Revolution into 1794.

In 1776, 4,000 Cherokees descended on the Upstate of South Carolina and the frontiers of Virginia and Kentucky burning settlements and killing hundreds of settlers in a war of extermination. A number of forts were put under siege, but the Cherokees abandoned these after a few weeks. The Southern colonies then put together a force of 4,000 militia troops that invaded the Cherokee nation and burned and pillaged over

50 settlements. Over 3,000 Cherokee men, women, and children and 300 American Militia were killed in this bitter hate filled invasion by the Southern colonies. All of the Cherokees except the Chickamauga Cherokees under Dragging Canoe in Northern Georgia and Southern Tennessee signed peace treaties in 1777. The Chickamauga Cherokees refused to sign the treaty and continued burning settlements and killing on the frontiers in Georgia, South Carolina, and Tennessee. In 1778-1779, the Chickamauga Cherokees aided the British in capturing Savannah and Augusta, Georgia. A number of runaway slaves and loyalists joined the Chickamauga's in their raids and attacks in the South.

Chickamauga Cherokees ambush a wood cutting party at Fort Nashborough in 1781. The Indians charged the gate before it could be closed and killed and wounded over 100 Tennessee militiamen and colonists before being repulsed.

In 1779 and 1780, Col. John Sevier led the Tennessee Militia in raids deep into Chickamauga territory around Lookout Mountain, Tennessee and northern Georgia burning villages and food stores as well as taking female hostages. In reprisal, several hundred Chickamauga Cherokee warriors led by Dragging Canoe attacked Fort Nashborough (Nashville, Tennessee) on April 2, 1781. The garrison at Fort Nashborough was cutting wood outside the fort with the gates wide open. The Chickamauga ambushed and killed the wood cutters and then rushed the gate before it could be shut. Half of the garrison of over 200 was killed or wounded in desperate hand to hand fighting inside the fort before the Chickamauga Cherokees were repulsed with heavy casualties as well. In 1782, Sevier again led Tennessee Militia in another attack into Chickamauga territory. Dragging Canoe with advance warning evacuated all of the Chickamauga Cherokees and relocated on more defendable islands along the rapids of the Tennessee River Gorge. After the American Revolution, the Chickamauga Cherokees refused to cease hostilities and continued raiding on the frontier.

In 1785, the Chickamauga Cherokees joined the Western Confederacy of Indian tribes led by the Shawnee in Kentucky and Ohio to protect their lands on the frontier from settler encroachment from the fledgling United States. Thousands of settlers began abandoning the frontier in fear for their lives. In 1786, Dragging Canoe led Chickamauga war parties against settlements in eastern Tennessee and Kentucky. In reprisal, John Sevier led Tennessee Militia in a raid on the over mountain settlements which were friendly and had not been involved in the frontier raids since 1776. This led many Cherokees in the over mountain settlements to unofficially join the Chickamauga Cherokees in their war with the white settlements on the frontier.

In May of 1788, there was outrage on the frontier when a war party of 40 Cherokees from Chilhowie (30 miles north of Chattanooga, TN.) massacred two prominent families on the Little River and on the White

Creek in Tennessee. In June, John Sevier led 100 militiamen to Chilhowie and raised a flag of truce. Four area Cherokee Chiefs who did not support the war came and were led into a cabin where they were killed with a tomahawk by John Kirk, who was the only survivor of the previous month's massacre. Now the entire Cherokee nation became involved in the war in outrage at the killing of these chiefs who had previously called for restraint.

In August, 500 Virginia Militia were ambushed and routed by Dragging Canoe's warriors on Lookout Mountain, TN. while trying to find the Chickamauga's Tennessee River Gorge settlements. The Virginians split up into small groups as they tried to make their way out of the ambush. Only about half of the Virginians made their way back to Virginia. Most of the captured Virginians were tortured and burned to death in the Cherokee fires.

In October of 1788, Dragging Canoe sent out 3,000 Cherokee warriors to destroy the frontier settlements from North Carolina all the way north to Kentucky. Several hundred warriors attacked Gillespie's Station Fort along the Holston River in Tennessee. Many settlers were captured or killed in the fields around the fort. The fort was stormed after the settlers defending it ran out of gunpowder. More than 200 settlers were brutally killed with tomahawks and scalped. Only 28 women and children were spared as captives and were sent to various Cherokee settlements. The women were forced to become wives to Cherokee warriors and the children were adopted to replace dead Cherokee family members. The same group of Cherokees was then repulsed when they went on to attack Houston's Station and White's fort also in Tennessee.

In retaliation, Sevier led Tennessee Militia in destroying most of the Valley Towns and over mountain settlements before being routed in an ambush by 400 Cherokees. In January of 1789, Sevier returned with more militiamen, cavalry and several grasshopper canons and surrounded the same band of Cherokee in camp at the Flint River. The militiamen fired their muskets and canon and then charged the Cherokee camp led by the cavalry. A bloody hand to hand battle ensued with tomahawks, knives, musket ends, and fists. Over 150 Cherokees and around 100 Tennesseans were killed or wounded before the Cherokees broke out of the trap and fled in all directions. The Valley Towns and the over mountain settlements quit the war and sued for peace after the Battle of the Flint River. The Treaty of Holston wasn't signed until July of 1791. The treaty required these settlements to set aside more land for white settlement and that white captives and wives had to be returned. Most of the white women and the adopted white children had adapted to Cherokee life and refused to go back and chose to stay with their Cherokee families instead. Because the white families of these captives were mostly dead, there was little protest that this provision of the treaty was not adhered to.

In 1789, a party of Shawnee with a young warrior named Tecumseh joined Dragging Canoe and the Chickamauga Cherokees in their raids and battles on the frontier. Dragging Canoe became a father figure and mentor to Tecumseh whose own father had died in the American Revolution in fighting in Kentucky. Tecumseh would later go on to lead another Confederacy of Indians (including 47 Cherokees) against the United States in Tecumseh's War from 1810 to 1811 and in the War of 1812 in which he died at the Battle of the Thames in 1813. Tecumseh had claimed that Dragging Canoe was one of the most influential people in his life.

In September of 1791, Dragging Canoe sent over 100 Chickamauga warriors under his brother, Badger, to join up with other Western Confederacy allied tribes in Ohio. The Indian warriors faced a force of 1,120 United States army troops and militia with several artillery pieces, including 200 camp followers under Arthur St.Clair. At dawn on November 4, 1791, 1,000 Western Confederacy warriors surrounded the U.S. camp near the Wabash River and waited for the troops to stack their muskets and to sit down to eat breakfast. Once this was done, the Indian warriors screamed a blood curdling battle cry and rushed the camp and overran the militia who took off running into the woods and across a stream without trying to collect their muskets. The Cherokees and over 200 other Indians were waiting across the creek and shot and hacked to death several hundred panicked militiamen with tomahawks. In the meantime, the U.S. Regulars formed a firing line in the middle of the camp and fired a volley which drove back the Indians.

The Regulars then fixed bayonets and charged as the Indians retreated into the woods. Other Indians slipped behind the soldiers into the camp and began killing and scalping the camp followers. The Regulars became separated from each other and disorganized in the forest when the Indians encircled the exhausted troops and began massacring them. Small groups of men made their way back to camp under cover of the artillery until Indian marksmen killed all the men manning the canons. Several bayonet charges were attempted with the Indians falling back and then counter attacking and killing most of the scattered attackers with tomahawks. The Indians couldn't miss when they fired their muskets into the terrified packed mob of U.S. troops and camp followers. Finally, all order broke down and an attempt to break out was made as the soldiers were hunted down for three miles to Fort Jefferson. Only 24 soldiers made it to the fort unscathed with another 24 wounded. For several days, the screams could be heard at the fort from the captured soldiers and camp followers being tortured and burned in the Indian fires at the battlefield site. The Battle of the Wabash was the worst defeat to Indians in United States history with 632 soldiers and all 200 of the camp followers killed and 264 wounded at a loss of just 61 Indian casualties. Most of the 264 wounded ended up tortured and burned in the Indian celebration fires.

In early 1792, Dragging Canoe was actively trying to recruit more Cherokees, Chickasaw, and Choctaw Indians to join the war when he died mysteriously on March 1 after dancing the ghost dance all night. The ghost dance was believed by the Cherokee to allow contact with dead warriors and later the Sioux (1890 Wounded Knee) believed that the dance could resurrect dead warriors for a final battle.

On September 30, 1792, the Cherokees lost a number of key leaders and warriors in a failed attack at the Buchanan's Station Fort near Nashville, TN. Another war party of 60 warriors near Nashville ambushed and killed 6 militia scouts when they in turn were ambushed by the Tennessee Militia which was not too far behind the scouts losing 13 dead. The Chickamauga Cherokees continued raids on the frontier with increased brutality toward every white man, woman and child on the frontier that they could find, but they were taking higher casualties. In late 1793, John Sevier and a large force of Tennessee Militia soundly defeated a large group of Chickamauga warriors returning from frontier raids at the Battle of Etowah in what is today Cartersville, Georgia. In early 1793, a Cherokee diplomatic party headed for Knoxville to work out an end to the war when they were killed at Coyatee by militia seeking revenge for previous raids. In retaliation, 1,000 Cherokees massacred all the settlers at Cavett's Station in a particularly brutal manner. In 1794, U.S. Regulars found and destroyed the Cherokee town of Nickajack on the Tennessee River Gorge and massacred its inhabitants. The other Tennessee River Gorge settlements evacuated before the U.S. troops could reach their villages. The Chickamauga now no longer had a safe refuge to fall back on and had become increasingly weary of the war.

The desperate Chickamauga Cherokees sent over 100 warriors to join their Western Confederacy allies in Ohio again in an effort to end this bloody war in a decisive battle against the United States. On August 20, 1794, 1,500 Western Confederacy Indians set up an ambush in a large clearing of trees that had been knocked down by a tornado. A lead party of 200 Kentucky Militia cavalry was ambushed with more than

100 casualties. The 3,000 U.S. troops under General "Mad" Anthony Wayne were now alerted to the Indian ambush and came up and attacked and outflanked the Indians causing a decisive victory at the Battle of Fallen Timbers. It was all over for the Western Confederacy and the Cherokees after this defeat. On November 7, 1794, the Treaty of Tellico Blockhouse finally ended the long and brutal 2nd Cherokee War. Surprisingly, the Cherokees didn't have to cede more land other than what was already agreed to at the Holston Treaty. Most surprising of all was that the Chickamauga Cherokees lost very little land despite being the ones who did a majority of the raiding and killing in the war.

In 1814, 600 Cherokee warriors joined Andrew Jackson's 3,000 mostly Georgia and Tennessee Militias to attack the British allied Creek Indians. At the Battle of Horseshoe Bend on March 27, 1814, 600 Cherokees with militia cavalry attacked across the rear of the Creek fortifications at the Horseshoe Bend River which caused panic from the Creeks facing Jackson's militia to their front behind eight foot tall stockade walls. Hundreds of Creeks were killed by the Cherokees as they tried to flee across the Horseshoe Bend River (the Creeks lost 857 out of 1,000 men, the Cherokees lost 70 men, and the militias lost 206 men).

In 1817, Cherokee Cavalry and scouts fought for Jackson again in the 1st Seminole War and helped him to kill and capture several hundred runaway slaves at the Negro Fort on the Apalachicola River. After the powder magazine blew up Negro Fort and 250 defenders from a lucky artillery shot, the Cherokees and Creeks served as a catching force that killed and captured several hundred former slaves and Seminoles who tried to flee. President Andrew Jackson later repaid the Cherokee's loyalty to him by ordering the removal of all, but the North Carolina Cherokees in 1831 to a reservation in Oklahoma. From 1831 to 1833, 4,000 out of around 16,000 Cherokees died on the Trail of Tears to the Oklahoma Indian Territory.

In 1834, most of the Cherokees bolted their mostly barren reservation in Oklahoma for Texas with the permission of the Mexican government. In 1836, the Texans won independence from Mexico and ordered the Cherokees to go back to Oklahoma. On July 15 and 16, 1839, 500 Texans defeated 700 Cherokees at the Battle of Neches (the Cherokees had over 100 casualties to the Texans 34) in what was the 3rd Cherokee War. The Cherokees fled to Arkansas with most eventually being forced back to their god forsaken Oklahoma reservation. Some Cherokees had already migrated to form a settlement in Arkansas in 1817 and had taken land from the Osage tribe in the Cherokee-Osage War from 1817-1823.

During the Civil War, the eastern Cherokees from North Carolina fought in the Thomas Legion for the Confederacy. In February 1864, about half of the legion was captured and switched sides to the Union army where many were present at Lee's surrender at Appomattox Courthouse in April of 1865. The rest of the Thomas Legion held out as guerrillas in western North Carolina until their final surrender to Union forces on May 10, 1865.

The Oklahoma Cherokees fought for both sides with most joining the Confederate 1st Indian Brigade and the Cherokee Mounted Rifles of the Trans-Mississippi Army of the South. On Dec.9, 1861, the Battle of Bird Creek near Tulsa, Oklahoma was fought between 1,300 Cherokees of the 1st Indian Brigade and 500 Union Cherokees under John Ross. The Confederate Cherokees in a four hour engagement caused 412 Union Cherokee casualties at a cost of just 52 for themselves. After the battle, many of the surviving Cherokees on both sides quit the war in disgust that the Cherokees were killing each other for the whites.

Cherokee soldiers tended to wear a mixture of Confederate and Union uniforms and weapons in the American Civil War. The Cherokees fought for both sides with the Confederate Cherokees being noted for scalping the dead as their calling card.

By the end of December 1861, the Confederates had driven 9,000 pro-Union Indians out of Oklahoma and into Kansas as refugees. At the Battle of Pea Ridge (Arkansas) on March 6-8, 1862, 800 Confederate Cherokees ambushed and scalped 41 soldiers from the 1st Iowa and captured an artillery battery when they unknowingly advanced into the Cherokee's hidden positions in some tall grass and a patch of trees. Union artillery was brought up and forced the Cherokees from their positions before they recovered to cover the retreat of the Confederate army.

On July 3, 1862, the Cherokee Mounted Rifles switched to the Union side for the remainder of the war. Many Cherokees who fought for the Confederacy switched sides during the war because they felt that they were treated in a disrespectful and condescending way by their Confederate allies. Chief Stand Watie (slave holder and plantation owner) and 200-300 pro-Confederate Cherokees served the rest of the war as irregular cavalry raiding into Kansas and pro-Union parts of Oklahoma. In September of 1864, Stand Watie's irregular cavalry captured a Union wagon train loaded down with a million dollars worth of wagon's, mules, supplies, and Union pay chests. Stand Watie's cavalry became the last Confederate force to surrender to Union forces on June 25, 1865. Stand Watie and his remaining warriors were released from Union captivity after taking the oath of loyalty to the United States in September of 1865. The Cherokee Indians never fought another battle as a distinct and separate force.

BIBLIOGRAPHY

Alderman, Pat. *Dragging Canoe: Cherokee-Chickamauga War Chief.* (Johnson City: Overmountain Press, 1978).

Anderson, Fred. *Crucible of War.* (Vintage Books USA: 2001).

Conley, Robert. *The Cherokee Nation: A History.* (University of New Mexico Press, Albuquerque, 2005).

McLynn, Frank. *1759.* (Glove Press: New York, 2004).

Mooney, James. *Historical Sketch of the Cherokee.* (Aldine Publishing: Chicago, 1975).

Raymond, Evans E. "The Last Battles of the American Revolution." *Journal of Cherokee Studies,* Vol. V, No.1, pp. 30-40. (Cherokee: Museum of the Cherokee Indians, 1980).

Pickens, T. Boone, *Boone: A Biography.* (Houghton Mifflin Harcourt: 2008 reprint from 1989).

Sugden, John. *Tecumseh.* (Henry Holt and Company: New York, 1997).

CHAPTER 16

God's Chinese Son: The Taiping Rebellion 1851 – 1871

While the United States was involved in the American Civil War that caused over a million casualties between both sides in the early 1860's, an even bloodier and more destructive civil war called the Taiping Rebellion was being fought in China. One of the most destructive and bloody wars in history was started by the misunderstanding of a poorly translated gospel tract given out by an American missionary to a man named Hong Xiuquan in Canton, China in 1836. The Taiping Rebellion which was fought from 1851 to 1871 was the 3rd bloodiest war in history with over 30 million deaths (World War II had more than 61 million deaths and the An Lushan Rebellion from 755 until 763 had 36 million deaths are the 1st and 2nd bloodiest wars in history, with World War I being 4th with more than 20 million deaths). There were literally hundreds of battles around China during the Taiping Rebellion, but the decisive battles of the war were around the almost continuous Sieges of Nanjing which was the Taiping Rebels capital from 1853 to 1864.

The Qing (Manchus) took over China in 1644 from the Ming Dynasty. The Qing were hated among many Chinese as the very barbarians that (like the Mongols before them) the Great Wall was supposed to, but failed to keep out of China. In the 19th century, China had become a corrupt, weak and backward nation. It was estimated that perhaps as many as 1/3rd of all Chinese were addicted to opium that was supplied illegally by Britain. Opium was previously only available to emperors and the very rich of China. The total defeat of the Qing armies in the Opium War (1839-1842) against Great Britain showed the people of China just how weak the Qing had become. China was a tinderbox for a rebellion that just needed a charismatic leader to lead it.

Hong Xiuquan had been born to poor parents near Guangzhou in 1814 who at age 15 could no longer afford their bright son's education. Nevertheless, Hong studied for the very difficult Confucian exams (only 1% of those that took the exams passed). Passing the exams meant a life as a government official where one could obtain wealth and status that normally would be out of the question for a commoner. It was excepted practice that a government official would skim off the taxes of the people to make oneself wealthy in Qing China.

In 1836, Hong Xiuquan failed the exams and walked around the city of Canton totally dejected. An American Baptist missionary named Reverend Edwin Stevens handed him some gospel tracts in Chinese. Unknown to Stevens, the tracts were translated with some errors from a Chinese convert that had claimed he could translate well from English to Chinese. Hong took the tracts home, but did not read them at that time. Hong retook the Confucian exams four more times, but failed. This was partly due to not having the money to properly bribe an official to pass him. Hong was very upset at his failure and at the corruption of the Qing officials. He went home in 1837 and became very sick from being so depressed at his failures to pass the exams. While Hong was sick, he had a number of mystical visions in which he saw Confucius being chastised, an old man in a heavenly setting saying that men in China were being punished for worshipping demons, and an angel that carried him to Heaven where he was commissioned by the old man in a dragon robe to purge China of the demons with a sword and a magic seal. Hong wasn't sure what the visions meant and spent the next seven years as a village school teacher.

In 1844, Hong's cousin, Feng Yunshan found the gospel tracts and encouraged Hong to read them. When Hong finished reading the tracts he had come to the conclusion that the tracts were a message from Heaven to him personally and the man in his earlier visions was Jesus Christ. Hong believed that the tracts revealed that he was Jesus's brother and the third member of the Holy Trinity with God (Hong taught that he replaced the Holy Spirit as a member of the Trinity). He believed that God wanted him to rid China of Confucianism and of the Qing in order to usher in the Taiping Heavenly Kingdom. In this quasi-Christian cult, Hong was to be worshipped along with God the Father, and Jesus Christ, the eldest of God's two sons.

Hong Xiuquan's first converts were his cousins Feng Yunshan and Hong Rengan and other members of his family. They began preaching their new religion in the Guangzhou area and began destroying Confucian, Buddhist and other traditional Chinese religious idols. Persecution forced the new cult to go to an area 300 miles west where they won thousands of fanatical converts among the Hakka population of western China. The Hakka people would be one of Hong Xiuquan's most recruited and loyal ethnic groups that fought for the Taiping rebel armies.

In 1847, Hong Xiuquan went to study with the American Baptist missionary, Reverend Issachar Roberts for 2 months in Guangzhou as Feng Yunshan recruited thousands of followers to the new religion. This is the only teaching that Hong Xiuquan ever received on Christianity. After two months of study, Reverend Roberts did not realize that Hong believed that he was God's second son after Jesus Christ. Rev. Roberts was using the same poorly translated tracts that Hong had received earlier and wasn't aware of the mistakes in these books until Hong had started the Taiping Rebellion in 1851. Hong was baptized by Rev. Roberts before leaving to teach his followers about his version of what he had learned in Guangzhou.

By 1850, Hong Xiuquan had more than over 10,000 converts that increasingly defied local Qing officials. The Taiping Rebellion began when the rebels were about to be attacked by Qing forces in early January of 1851 at their stronghold at Jintian. The larger Taiping forces armed with mostly farm tools worked their way around the Qing forces as they approached Jintian and attacked them from behind. The Qing forces were massacred and their commanders were beheaded in the Taiping's first battle. In March of 1851, Hong Xiuquan dressed in the yellow robes of a Chinese emperor and announced the founding of the Heavenly Kingdom of Transcendent Peace (the Taiping or "God worshippers") that he claimed was replacing the corrupt Qing Dynasty. Hong started giving out a long list of edicts that he claimed came from his daily conversations with Jesus Christ through a man named Xiao Chaogui who served as Jesus' mouthpiece. Most Taiping followers obeyed the edicts with great zeal and devotion. Those that were found guilty of disobeying any edicts were given from 100 to 1,000 blows with a cane as divine punishment.

The Taiping Rebels maintained an army of more than 500,000 troops
recruited mostly in the western provinces of China whose
religious zeal almost toppled the Qing Dynasty.

The Taiping army and camp followers then burnt their homes and
base to show that there was no turning back and proceeded to fight their
way out of a ring of Qing defenses that were meant to hem them in to
the Jintian and Wuxuan areas. The Taiping forces then took the city of
Yongan which was then besieged by Qing forces. It is in a battle outside of Yongan that Xiao Chaogui was wounded and ceased to give the
daily edicts as the voice of Jesus Christ to Hong. The Taiping then set
Yongan on fire and set off explosions to confuse the Qing army as their
40,000 troops and camp followers broke out successfully. The Taiping
rearguard of 2,000 troops held off the Qing so that the others could
escape and were all killed. As the 46,000 man Qing army gave chase to

overtake the rebels, they were led into a pass where the Taiping troops had laid mines and explosives to bring down thousands of large rocks and boulders that were kept in bundles and in cages on the sides of the pass onto the Qing forces. As the Qing forces rushed into the pass, the explosives and the mines were detonated which let loose an avalanche of heavy rocks that crushed and killed over 5,000 Qing troops and blocked the pass as the Taiping army escaped.

The Taiping forces next put the city of Guilin under siege, but they did not have enough artillery or explosives to breach the massive walls of the city so they decided to lift the siege and to move on after a month there. The Taiping were able to gather over 400 ships at Guilin to be able to move 15,000 troops by river while the other 25,000 troops and camp followers followed a little behind along the river bank. There goal was to capture cities along the Yangtze River before taking the southern Chinese capital of Nanjing. The Taiping rebels were in a rage after seeing Feng Yunshan mortally wounded while assaulting the city of Quanzhou. Taiping forces then blew the gate open to the city and massacred all of the inhabitants.

On June 10, 1852, the Taiping river fleet was moving along the Xiang River to get to the Yangtze River when they were ambushed at Suoyi Ford. The Chinese Militia forces under a brilliant commander named Jiang Zhongyuan had blocked the 100 yard wide river at the ford with logs that had been driven into the riverbed across the entire span of the river. Over 300 ships of the Taiping fleet were carried into the log barrier and into each other by the fast moving currents as Qing forces fired canons and matchlock muskets at point blank range. Many of the Taiping boats holding gunpowder exploded which caused the whole jammed up fleet to catch fire. Over 10,000 of the best and most fanatical Taiping troops died at Suoyi Ford.

The remaining 30,000 Taiping troops and camp followers abandoned their remaining ships and headed overland toward the Yangtze River.

After the defeat, the Taiping army recovered and then captured most cities that they encountered along the Yangtze River as they marched toward Nanjing. The Taiping rebels recruited a huge army from people that despised the Qing Dynasty so that their numbers grew daily.

The key to controlling China was in controlling the rivers where most travel and commerce took place. There were hundreds of river battles between the Taiping and Qing river fleets.

The Taiping army became well disciplined and armed themselves with military equipment that they captured from defeated Qing forces. The Taiping and the Qing forces used primarily 17th century tactics with pikemen mixed in at intervals with units that fired old matchlock muskets in their battle lines. Archers were used extensively by Qing forces, but also on occasion by the Taiping army. Most troops charged and fought hand to hand with broad swords at some point after they had fired their muskets. Qing government troops were organized into Banner armies that were often rarely paid, poorly trained, and were very unmotivated to fight against the fanatical Taiping army. Both sides also used earthworks fortifications fronted by trenches when they set up camps around cities in all directions when they were conducting sieges. Both sides also used mining extensively to breach fortified city walls or camps before an assault that would lead to the massacre of everyone inside.

In July of 1852, Hong Xiuquan ordered that any city that refused to convert as his followers when given the chance would be massacred. Millions of Chinese were massacred by the Taiping troops after their Qing commanders had refused the offer to convert. Whole cities also agreed to convert to the Taiping version of Christianity with some converting out of fear and some out of a sincere desire to follow the new religion. There was a real backlash against traditional Confucian, Buddhist, and traditional beliefs in China at this time that greatly aided Taiping recruiting efforts.

The only bust of Hong Xiuquan who believed he was the brother of Jesus Christ and God's only Chinese son. The Taiping Rebellion that he started caused more than 30 million deaths in China.

The massive Taiping army grew to over a half a million men with over a half million camp followers that destroyed and consumed everything in their way as they marched down the Yangtze River toward Nanjing. The Taiping forces had momentum and just could not be defeated by the much weaker Qing armies and had taken control of a large area in southern China. Finally, in March of 1853 the Taiping army reached Nanjing and began digging siege lines and tunnels to create breaches in sections of the over 40 foot tall walls of the city that was seen as impregnable by Qing officials. One reason that Nanjing was seen as impregnable by Qing officials was that the city's walls were over 25 miles in circumference around the city. Nanjing was defended by 60,000 Qing soldiers and had over 60,000 men, women, and children still living in the city after more than 800,000 Chinese had fled the city before the arrival of the Taiping army. The Qing officials were surprised that the Taiping army was actually large enough to have surrounded and cutoff the entire city.

Taiping miners started the siege by digging several tunnels toward the northwest bastion of Nanjing which was seen as the weakest part of the city's walls. Each tunnel was dug by the Taiping miners with another tunnel that was 15 to 20 feet below the upper tunnel. After the tunnels had reached under the walls of Nanjing's northwest bastion, they were filled with gunpowder and timed fuses so that the upper mines would explode 10 minutes before the lower ones would explode to catch the Qing soldiers as they scrambled to defend the breach made by the first explosion.

On March 19, 1853, the first mine explosions brought down the northwest bastion along with a large section of the surrounding walls. Several thousand Qing troops rushed to defend the breach who met 100 hand picked Taiping soldiers that had not received the word to wait for a second explosion before making their attack. The second explosion killed all from both sides that had rushed into the breach and cleared a lot of the ruble that was left from the 1st explosion into the crater created by the second explosion. The Taiping forces then poured into the city and began massacring both Qing soldiers and civilians in the streets and houses of Nanjing. Over 10,000 veteran Qing soldiers died trying to defend the city as another 50,000 Qing troops fell back (many with their families) into the citadel in the interior of the city. The Taiping troops began massacring the population of the city, but were shocked to see that thousands of Chinese families were committing suicide together by either slashing their throats with knives or hanging themselves. The Chinese were taught from over two thousand years of bad experiences with their northern Mongol neighbors that it was preferable to commit suicide (especially for women) or to kill one's own family themselves rather than to endure the humiliation of rape, torture, or enslavement. Chinese females were taught that it was the pinnacle of virtue to choose suicide over capture. Taiping soldiers were forbidden to rape or abuse anyone under penalty of death from their officers, but they were encouraged to kill the populations of cities that did not submit to them. Over 30,000 Chinese civilians outside the citadel in Nanjing had either been killed or had committed suicide.

On March 20, the Taiping sent hundreds of troops under fire to pile up gunpowder bags and explosives up against the citadel's gates. When Taiping soldiers with their bags of gunpowder or explosives fell from matchlock or canon fire, others immediately ran out and carried the powder and explosives to their places. Finally, fuses were lit and the gates to the citadel were blown in. The Taiping troops rushed into the citadel and began slaughtering the Qing who had lost all discipline and had become a panic stricken mob. Thousands of Qing soldiers rushed to where their families were to slay them with swords before they then slit their own throats. Qing soldiers were seen each stabbing or shooting each other at the same time in mutual suicide for fear of the Taiping soldiers. The citadel caught on fire and many were also burned to death.

All 50,000 Qing troops along with another 30,000 of their family members died. The Taiping forces lost 10,000 men in the siege.

The Qing army used mostly bows, spears, pikes, swords, shields, and antiquated firelock muskets and artillery at the time of the American Civil War. The Qing were able to obtain more up to date muskets by 1864 during the final stages of the Siege of Nanjing.

On March 29, 1853, Hong Xiuquan was carried into Nanjing dressed in the yellow robe of a Chinese emperor and behind him also dressed in yellow on horseback were his 32 wives. Hong and his wives then resided in the emperor's palace and never left again. The war was then turned over to his subordinate generals (called kings). The next day on March 30, a Qing army of 44,000 troops arrived and built a fortified camp outside of Nanjing and began a very porous siege. Soon another Qing army of 80,000 set up another fortified camp outside the city walls, but Nanjing was so big in circumference that the Qing could not cut the city off without a lot more men. The Qing armies outside of Nanjing for the most part did not venture outside of their fortified camps out of fear of the huge Taiping army of 80,000 regulars and 460,000 militia troops.

In October, all 80,000 regulars of the Taiping army marched out of Nanjing and right past the two fortified Qing camps and headed north to capture Beijing and to overthrow the emperor in what was called the "great northern expedition." The great northern expedition ran into a lot of opposition in the north and suffered from the cold. The Taiping army made it to within 30 miles of Beijing before falling back to the city of Lianzhen where they were trapped and placed under siege for 8 months by Qing forces and their mercenary Mongol cavalry. In 1854, the Qing forces diverted a river to flood the Taiping forces in Lianzhen where over half of their army died. The rest of the Taiping forces in the city had no other option but to surrender in March of 1855 to the Qing army. The Taiping prisoners were then all beheaded.

In 1855, Taiping forces began digging mines and siege trenches against the Qing camps at Nanjing. On June 1, 1856, Taiping forces detonated a mine against a third fortified camp outside of Nanjing that blew a large breach in the earthwork fortifications. Over 100,000 Taiping soldiers swarmed through the breach and massacred the entire garrison of 7,800 Qing troops. In August, the Taiping forces detonated several mines that breached the main Qing camp fortifications followed by an overwhelming charge by several hundred thousand Taiping troops that killed 44,000 Qing troops and sent another 36,000 retreating north in disarray.

The victory was short lived though because Xiao Chaogui, who had been the voice of Jesus to Hong Xiuquan before he had been wounded in 1851, started giving the daily messages again. The messages this time were very critical of Hong Xiuquan and had caused a rift among Taiping forces in Nanjing. Over 20,000 Taiping residents and troops including six of the "seven brothers" who had helped to lead the rebellion up to this point felt their loyalty was to be toward Xiao Chaogui and not to Hong Xiuquan. Hong wasn't having this and ordered Xiao Chaogui and all 20,000 of his followers to be killed. Also, six of the seven brothers were killed as well. In addition, over 100,000 Taiping troops and two of Hong's top generals were killed by Qing forces in another setback at the Battle of Tianjing in October of 1856.

With many of Hong's trusted leaders of the Taiping movement dead, very little was attempted in 1857. In March of 1858, a formidable Qing army of 200,000 troops under a general named Zhang Guoliang renewed the siege of the Taiping capital by digging new trench parallels and fortifying camps outside of Nanjing. Still this larger army could not cut off Nanjing completely from Taiping troops and supplies coming and going. Hong Xiuquan's trusted cousin, Hong Rengan, who had spent time as a Christian missionary in Canton had made his way to Nanjing with much difficulty and was placed as second in command of all Taiping affairs as the Shield King. By 1859, the Qing army had built 45 miles of siege trenches with two main camps in the north and south of the city and over 100 smaller fortified camps that blocked access to Nanjing in all, but one route from the north.

Hong Rengan then decided on a bold attack on the main Qing supply base at Hangzhou over 150 miles away to bring relief to Nanjing. The attack on Hangzhou would then draw off Qing forces as three Taiping armies would be recalled from other areas of central China to converge on Nanjing to destroy the Qing camps with their remaining forces. The cities of Suzhou and Hankow would also be seized to completely split the Qing Empire in two along the Yangtze River Valley.

On February 10, 1860, Li Xiucheng known as the Loyal King led 6,000 hand picked troops disguised in captured Qing uniforms out of Nanjing and all the way to Hangzhou without any opposition or even questions from other Qing forces and commanders along the way. The Qing commander at Hangzhou was suspicious though and locked the gates to the city as the Taiping troops attacked through the front gate after sappers had blasted it open with explosives. Over 200 Taiping troops were then cut down by musket and grapeshot fire as they were trapped in a killing zone between the blown open front gate and the fortified second gate which blocked the way into the city. The Taiping sappers then began digging a mine tunnel under the adjacent wall over the next several weeks. Surprisingly, no Qing forces made any attempt to relieve Hangzhou.

On March 19, the mine was detonated which brought down a large section of the city wall followed by a charge by Taiping troops into the city. The Taiping troops found the Qing militia and the residents of Hangzhou fighting each other as the Qing troops were trying to loot homes as a raging fire broke out. Thousands of women began committing suicide by slitting their own throats, jumping into fires, drowning in wells, taking poison or by hanging to spare themselves the rapes that they felt were sure to come. The Qing commander with his regulars fell back to the citadel. Li Xiucheng decided to abandon the siege of the citadel after six more days when he received word that over 50,000 Qing troops were on their way to relieve Hangzhou from Nanjing. The Qing forces also looted the city after they arrived and found the Taiping gone and no semblance of any government in the mostly burned out city.

By early April of 1860, over 100,000 Taiping troops attacked and overran the southern Qing camp outside of Nanjing from all sides. Panic gripped the Qing army as thousands drowned in the Yangtze River in a futile effort to escape. Over 80,000 Qing troops were either drowned or were cut down by Taiping forces. The Qing commander, Zhang Guoliang committed suicide by over dosing on opium. Again, the siege of Nanjing was relieved and the Taiping capital was saved. By June 2, Suzhou and Hankow had also been taken by Taiping forces.

Qing troops in the later stages of the Taiping Rebellion were better armed
under the warlord system. Mongols were used to conduct genocide
on areas believed to be sympathetic to the Taiping rebels.

1: Taiping wang
2: Taiping spearman
3: Taiping musketeer

The Taiping rebels fought with pikes, spears, swords, and firelock and smoothbore muskets. Their tactics in battle often resembled 17th century European warfare.

Taiping forces also made an unsuccessful attempt with 70,000 troops to take Shanghai in the false belief that the British and French who had extensive commercial interests there would support them given the somewhat common Christian views of the Europeans to themselves. The British and French came to realize that the Taiping movement was a quasi-Christian cult and used their troops along with the European-American lead Chinese force called the Ever Victorious Army to aide the Qing army in repelling the attacks on Shanghai in 1861 and 1862 despite the fact that Britain and France had been at war with the Qing the previous year. In that war which was fought in October of 1860, Imperial Qing forces had been defeated by British and French forces near Beijing. The British and French forces proceeded to burn the emperor's summer palace in what is known as the 2nd Opium War or the Arrow War. Despite this embarrassing setback, the Qing were happy to receive help in defending Shanghai from the British and French forces.

A Qing warlord general named Zeng Guofan, had success fighting the Taiping in Hunan province and in the taking of Anqing in a methodical 8 month siege in 1861 by raising troops that were paid and supplied by him personally. Thus the loyalty of his troops was personally to himself and not to the emperor. In return, Zeng Guofan received an allowance from the emperor for each soldier who served in his army. Zeng Guofan was placed in charge of the effort to capture Nanjing by Emperor Xianfeng with the authority to raise as many troops as he could to fight the Taiping rebels under the warlord system. Other Qing warlords were similarly empowered to raise personal armies loyal to themselves instead of rebuilding the failed Imperial Banner armies. This temporary solution to China's inability to defend itself helped to set the stage for large scale corruption where warlords inflated their numbers in order to pocket much of the money at government expense with armies that were loyal to their warlords and not to the emperor. Though this system helped in bringing about a formidable resistance to the Taiping rebels, it set the stage for the Revolution of 1912 that saw the overthrow of the emperor's power and the beginning of civil wars between warlords and then the Communists and the Nationalists that would last until 1949 in China.

In 1853, Hong Xiuquan had sent his former Baptist teacher Issachar Roberts an invitation to come see him in Nanjing to discuss Christian doctrine. Rev. Roberts had desperately tried to get to Nanjing to correct Hong Xiuquan on his doctrinal mistakes that had led to such a destructive and bloody war, but could not get through the various forces to the Taiping capital until 1861. Hong at first was very happy to see Rev. Roberts until he was told by Roberts about some of the errors in the gospel materials that Hong had received in its translations from English to Chinese. Roberts went on tell Hong Xiuquan that he could not be the brother of Jesus Christ and about some other Taiping errors in doctrine. Hong was polite to Rev. Roberts, but never saw him again and seemed very disturbed by what Roberts had to say to him. Hong Xuiquan then announced that he was withdrawing from earthly affairs and no longer held court or made decisions regarding the war. Roberts was forbidden to teach anything other than Taiping Christianity and eventually left after a few months in Nanjing feeling upset that he had completely failed in his mission to correct his former student.

In 1861, Emperor Xianfeng died shortly after a comet and an alignment of 5 planets had appeared in the sky which was seen to be a frightening omen of things to come all over China. Emperor Tongzhi succeeded Xianfeng who continued the warlord system and placed General Zeng Guofan in charge of all military operations. General Zeng Guofan began a very brutal campaign of genocide against villages and cities that were known to support the Taiping forces for up to a hundred miles around Nanjing in all directions. Cities, villages, and food stores that could be used by the Taiping forces were confiscated or were burned by roving bands of mercenary Mongol cavalry who were fighting for the

Qing. The Mongols were particularly good at genocide considering that they had killed over 25 million Chinese during the 74 years it took them to conquer China in the thirteenth century. The problem with using the Mongols as executioners was that they didn't always know or care that they were also killing and taking food from people that supported the emperor as well. Qing troops often stripped villages and cities of food that were supporters of the government without much thought of the famine that this would cause among the emperor's subjects. By the middle of 1862, much of the area around Nanjing for hundreds of miles was a wasteland where millions had been slain or had died from famine. Rice fields had grown over with weeds. Whole villages and cities from supporters of both sides in the Taiping Rebellion were found with nothing, but the dead. Not even small animals such as rats could be found because they had been eaten already. Zeng Guofan had ordered his troops to send away the tens of thousands of starving people that begged them daily for food saying that the people were to feed the army not the other way around. Starving Taiping troops from garrisons outside of Nanjing would surrender to Qing forces in the hope that they would be fed only to be executed because General Zeng didn't feel he had the extra food to feed prisoners. Over one and a half million refuges crammed into Shanghai, but Cholera and other diseases followed them and caused hundreds of thousands of deaths there.

Zeng Guofan then made plans for three Qing armies to converge on Nanjing by first taking control of the outer cities and fortifications that the Taiping had been using as a buffer to protect Nanjing. In May of 1862, 30,000 Qing troops began rebuilding their siege works and fortified camps around parts of Nanjing. Zeng had his troops to dig trenches at the base of a strategic hill named Yuhuatai where a Taiping stone fort overlooked Nanjing. The Qing troops dug their trenches to within 40 yards of the stone fort. The Taiping garrison attacked and occupied the front trenches on more than a dozen occasions followed by Qing counter attacks that retook the front trenches in front of the stone fort. The front Qing trenches and the area between the fort was covered with piles of bodies from the vicious back and forth trench warfare. Over 100,000 Taiping troops in Nanjing fought to eliminate the main Qing camp. Battles were fought throughout October and November of 1862 while Taiping sappers dug a mine under the trenches and earthworks of the main Qing camp. The Qing sappers dug tunnels to intercept the Taiping mines followed by vicious underground battles. A couple of the Taiping mines reached the Qing camp and blew breaches in the trenches and earthworks followed by a massive Taiping assault. The Qing had anticipated this move and had fallen back to secondary trenches and earthworks to repulse the attack. On November 26, the fighting stopped around the stone fort and the Qing camp because both sides were exhausted and had taken heavy casualties of over 12,000 Qing and 27,000 Taiping troops lost in the battle. The Shield King (Hong Rengan) realized that Zeng Guofan was a fighter and would not retreat as other Qing commanders had done when faced with heavy resistance.

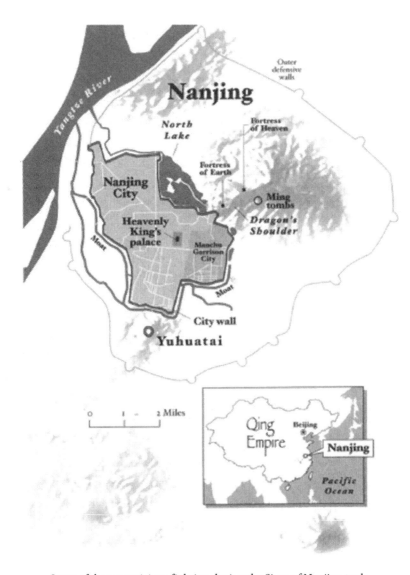

Some of the most vicious fighting during the Siege of Nanjing took
place around the outer fort of Yuhuatai, the Fortress of Heaven,
and the Fortress of Earth on the Dragon's Shoulder.

After months of inactivity, the stone fort on Yuhuatai was taken on June 13, 1863 in a secret night time attack. The garrison of 6,000 Taiping troops who had put up such a heroic defense had let their guard down and were massacred with very few losses for the Qing troops. Zeng Guofan had a strategic hill to bombard the city from with a large battery of 100 artillery pieces. As the battery began firing into the city from this hill, a large cry almost in unison could be heard in Nanjing, but after a few days the people continued to go about their business just a little more carefully.

Nanjing's main supply source was Suzhou, so Zeng Guofan concentrated on taking this key city in 1863. Qing forces and the foreign trained Ever Victorious Army (led by Charles "Chinese" Gordon) had many difficulties in taking the well fortified city of Suzhou. Every mine that was dug toward Suzhou's walls by Qing forces was destroyed by Taiping counter miners with explosives in underground battles. The mines locations were given away by the dead grass on top that gradually moved toward the city's walls. In October and November, tens of thousands of Qing troops died in futile assaults against Suzhou's walls. The Qing were on the verge of abandoning the siege when a Taiping commander and his contingent of troops entered into secret negotiations to surrender the city if the inhabitants and the troops would be spared. The plot was discovered on December 4 before the prearranged time for the gates to be opened to the Qing army. Fighting between the Taiping factions broke out in the city. At some point the gates were opened and followed by a charge into the city by the Qing troops that massacred the entire Taiping garrison and over 100,000 people in Suzhou. The wealthier people in Suzhou, who were actually pro-Qing government supporters were massacred also so that the Qing troops could loot their homes.

While Nanjing's supply base was under siege, Zeng Guofan had brought close to 500,000 Qing troops to build 45 miles of earthworks fortifications and trenches to completely cut off Nanjing by October of

1863. The Qing troops were ordered to extend the scorched earth policy and genocide of Taiping sympathizers for hundreds of square miles around Nanjing. It was said that no people, no animals, not even a blade of grass could be found alive. Millions of pro-Qing supporters died of starvation and disease so that Nanjing would be starved into submission. The plan worked too well because Zeng also had problems bringing in enough food to feed his half a million troops that were besieging Nanjing.

In December, large groups of women and children were sent out of Nanjing so that there would be fewer mouths to feed inside the city. The women were mostly all raped and given to the troops as "wives." Hong Rengan dressed in the uniform of a Qing officer and escaped to try to organize a relief army to rescue the Taiping capital. There were still several hundred thousand Taiping troops in the western provinces, but these forces felt little enthusiasm to relieve Nanjing because they feared their own homes and provinces would be laid waste by Qing forces if they tried to save Nanjing.

In February of 1864, Qing troops captured a castle called the Fortress of Earth on another strategic hill outside of Nanjing called the Dragon's Shoulder. A mine blew a breach in the castle followed by a continuous battle that lasted for several days and nights for possession of the breach until the Taiping garrison ran out of men. Over 6,000 Taiping and 20,000 Qing troops died in the battle for control of the Fortress of Earth. Batteries of over 200 Qing artillery pieces firing from both captured hills could not penetrate Nanjing's 50 foot thick walls so Zeng ordered over 100 mines to be dug to blast breaches in the city walls for a final assault. One problem in mining against Nanjing was that the city's 30 yard wide and 20 yard deep moat proved to be a huge and difficult obstacle to mine under. Fierce underground battles commenced as Taiping miners dug counter mines to intercept the Qing mines under the moat. The first few Qing mines were dug directly under the moat.

Taiping miners with wick lit grenades intercepted the Qing mines. The fighting and the explosives caused the moat waters to flood both the Qing and Taiping mines drowning men from both sides.

Zeng then ordered the mines to be dug at least 30 yards below the moat. The Taiping still managed to find most of the Qing mines from the ventilation holes that had to be drilled up to the surface for men to be able to breathe. Mine battles continued with vicious fighting with muskets, pistols, grenades, spears, torches, and swords in the darkness over 50 or 60 yards below the surface. Both sides used incendiaries from lit clay pots that burned men alive and ignited gases that brought down the mines onto all who were in them. The Taiping also drowned many Qing troops with diverted sewage that drowned everyone caught in the mines. The Qing sometimes allowed the Taiping miners to break into their mines while they pumped in poisonous gases that killed them by the hundreds as well. Over 4,000 Qing and 3,000 Taiping miners died in the bitter suicidal underground battles below Nanjing's moat and walls. The Taiping were successful in finding and destroying 70 Qing mines. Yet, there were 30 mines that were successful in reaching under Nanjing's walls in July of 1864 behind the Fortress of Earth where there was no moat and it was harder to detect where the mines were located.

In the meantime, in late May, Zeng Guofan knew that his forces with very little food could not last much longer and the siege needed to be brought to a successful conclusion or be abandoned. In Nanjing, nothing was left to eat for anyone. Hong Xuiquan had been in his own world in his palace and increasingly showed signs of insanity. Commanders went to Hong Xuiquan to ask him what they were to do with no food in the city not even for him. Hong said that they would all eat manna from heaven that would be mixed with the morning dew. Hong said that he would eat of the manna first and for his servants to gather it for him. Hong was handed a bowl of weeds that he ate. On June 1, 1864, Hong Xuiquan died from having eaten some

The epic Siege of Nanjing lasted from 1853 until 1864 and was the most decisive event that brought down the Taiping rebels. Over 13,000 Qing and Taiping troops died in grim underground battles in mining tunnels that both sides used extensively during the siege.

poison ivy and vines mixed in his daily bowl of weeds. His body was laid out in a dirty ragged looking yellow robe in the palace attended by his wives in anticipation of his resurrection. The smell in the palace became so unbearable from Hong's decomposing body that most of his wives left to stay in the city by the middle of June.

On July 19, 1864, at noon, thirty mines packed with 200 tons of gunpowder and explosives were detonated which brought down around 70 yards of Nanjing's walls. The blast was so massive that it killed 400 Qing vanguard troops because their trench had been too close to one of the exploding mines. Again, a loud cry came up from the city as Taiping reserves put up a desperate fight in the breach and in the streets nearby until resistance turned into panic. The Qing army came rampaging through the city killing, looting, and raping everyone they could find (the 1st Rape of Nanjing). In the chaos, a massive fire broke out that burned and killed thousands on both sides. Thousands of Qing troops became trapped in narrow alleyways and were burned alive. It is estimated that over 80,000 Taiping soldiers and inhabitants and over 20,000 Qing troops died in the street fighting, the massacres, and from the raging fires that consumed Nanjing in the final assault. Hong Xuiquan's heir escaped disguised in a Qing uniform, but was captured and executed a few weeks later.

Hong Rengan was trying to get back to Nanjing after failing to organize a relief army when he was captured. On November 23, 1864, Hong Rengan was executed after being the only captured Taiping leader to refuse to recant that Hong Xuiquan was really not the brother of Jesus Christ and God's only Chinese son. Several hundred thousand Taiping followers held out in the western provinces until their lands were also laid waste between 1868 and 1871 by more than a million Qing soldiers while waiting for the second coming of Jesus Christ and Hong Xuiquan.

BIBLIOGRAPHY

Cummings, Joseph. *The War Chronicles: From Flintlocks to Machine Guns.* Quayside Publishers, Beverly, MA, 2009.

Jen Yu-wen. *The Taiping Revolutionary Movement.* New Haven, Connecticut, Yale University Press, 1973.

Platt, Stephen, *Autumn In The Heavenly Kingdom: China, The West, and the Epic Story of the Taiping Rebellion.* Alfred A. Knopf, New York, 2012.

Reilly, Thomas H. *The Taiping Heavenly Kingdom: Rebellion and the Blasphemy of Empire.* Seattle: University of Washington Press, 2004.

Spence, Jonathan. *God's Chinese Son.* Harper Collins Publishers, London, 1996.

Yu, Maochun. "The Taiping Rebellion." In *A Military History of China,* ed. David Graff and Robin Higham. Boulder, Colorado: Westview, 2002.

Wu, James T.K. "The Impact of the Taiping Rebellion Upon Manchu Fiscal System." *Pacific Historical Review 19, no. 3,* 1950: Pages 265-275.

Research done at the Museum of the Taiping Rebellion in Nanjing, China in 2005.

CHAPTER 17

The French Conquest of Indo-China: 1857 – 1884

In 1975, the U.S. embassy in South Vietnam was evacuated as that country fell to communist North Vietnam after the failure of Vietnamization that was supposed to have ended the Vietnam War with an honorable outcome for the United States. This event would have never happened had France not sent Catholic missionaries to Annam and Cochinchina (Vietnam) in the 1600's to convert the Vietnamese to Christianity. The persecution of French missionaries in the 1800's then gave Napoleon III the excuse that he needed to send troops for France to claim Indochina (Vietnam, Cambodia, and Laos) at first as a protectorate and then later as a colony. It was the defeat of France in 1954 that caused French Indochina to be split up into Cambodia, Laos, Communist North Vietnam, and Democratic South Vietnam that set the stage for the eventual entry of the United States into the Vietnam War.

In 1627, France had sent Jesuit missionaries to join Portuguese missionaries in converting the Vietnamese and Cambodians to Catholicism.

By 1664, the French Jesuits had completely taken over control of missions in Indo-China. French missionaries did most of the early exploring and mapping of Indo-China in the 1600's and 1700's. In 1799, the French priest, Pigneau de Be'haine led an army of mercenaries to help Nguyen Anh take the throne as emperor of Annam. Pigneau did this in the false belief that Nguyen Anh would show the French favor to gain influence and to possibly begin the role of protectorate over Annam. Instead, Nguyen Anh was suspicious that the French missionary presence and aide had more sinister motives. Between 1825 and 1842, the persecution of French missionaries increased with seven priests being tortured to death. The French then sent a fleet to rescue a number of missionaries and to maintain a permanent presence in Indo-China in 1843.

In 1844, a Jesuit priest known as Father Lefebure plotted to replace the Vietnamese emperor, Thieu Tri, for an emperor more receptive to Christianity. The plot was foiled and Lefebure was imprisoned at the protests of the French government. Thieu Tri finally released Lefebure in early March of 1847 in fear of some military retaliation by the French government. Unaware of the priest's release, the French fleet then attacked the Vietnamese port of Tourane. Within 70 minutes, the French sank 3 Vietnamese vessels, destroyed the harbor forts and killed hundreds of local inhabitants in the bombardment. The fleet then put out to sea without concern for the fate of the other French missionaries or the Vietnamese Christians that were tortured and killed as a consequence of this attack. Nor did the French inquire about the fate of Lefebure who had escaped to Singapore.

In 1847, Tu Duc succeeded Thieu Tri as emperor of Annam and Cochinchina. Tu Duc had a bitter hatred for the French missionaries and their Vietnamese converts and embarked on a fierce campaign to eliminate Christianity from Vietnam. Vietnamese Catholics were to be branded with the word "ta doo" (infidel) on their left cheek and all of their property was to be confiscated by the state. French priests were to be drowned and Vietnamese priests were to be sawed in half lengthwise. In 1851 and 1852, two prominent priests were put to death and missionaries all over Asia called for action by the French government.

Napoleon III came to power in a coup d'état with the support of the church in 1852. Thus he could not escape a commitment to missionary goals in Asia. He also had his own ambitions to gain expansionist glory as his illustrious uncle had. Napoleon III was reluctant to act at first for fear of reprisals against missionaries in interior areas of Indochina, but finally, in 1856 he endorsed a plan to capture the city of Tourane from Annam. Napoleon III had mistakenly believed that the French would be welcomed as liberators from an oppressive emperor.

In 1858, a force of 2,500 French Foreign Legionnaires and 500 Spanish troops began their conquest of Indochina by landing to occupy Tourane to use as a base for future operations. The French Legionnaires and the Spanish troops found that the Vietnamese troops would not fight them in pitched battles, but withdrew into the jungle and set ambushes on small groups of French troops who left Tourane to scout or patrol around the city. Many French troops suffered crippling wounds from covered pits with sharpened bamboo stakes covered in dung that impaled feet and often caused death from gangrene infection. These guerrilla tactics would haunt the French and then the Americans for over a hundred years and proved to be very difficult to counter. The French also wilted in the searing sun and in the torrential monsoon rains, outfitted in their heavy sweat or rain soaked uniforms. After 6 months of occupation, the French army was losing hundreds of men to ambushes, cholera, malaria, dysentery and gangrene infections. Napoleon III's glorious expedition was turning into a disaster.

Unable to make any progress in Tourane, the French looked to Saigon in southern Cochinchina to make some progress. Saigon was an important trading center in a town of over 2,000 inhabitants which was protected by a strong citadel. On February 16, 1859, a flotilla of French warships began exchanging canon fire with the Vietnamese citadel and eventually blasted a small breach in the northeast wall. Two companies of French marines and sailors landed and charged the citadel breach which was widened by explosives laid under fire by some accompanying sapper troops. The column then scrambled up the ruble in the breech and into the citadel with bayonets. The Vietnamese fought briefly, but then melted into Saigon and into the surrounding jungle. Though the French and Spanish troops controlled Saigon they could not venture outside the town without losing men to ambush or from sharpened bamboo pits. The French commander Admiral de Genouilly left 1,000 French troops to garrison Saigon and then returned to Tourane where he found that the garrison had lost several hundred more men from tropical diseases. De Genouilly decided to abandon Tourane and took the remainder of his troops to join a British invasion of northern China in the Second Opium War.

The French and Spanish assault on Saigon in 1859.

In 1859 and 1860, Emperor Tu Duc sent a Vietnamese army of 12,000 to begin digging trench lines toward French positions and the citadel at Saigon. The siege turned Saigon into a hellhole for the French forces left there. Both sides sortied to disrupt the other sides' entrenchments. On December 7, 1860, over 1,000 screaming sword, pike and halberd wielding Vietnamese troops sortied against French entrenchments near the Khai Tuong Pagoda and decapitated one of the Foreign Legion commanders and caused over 100 casualties in a desperate action that was eventually repulsed by French bayonets.

The Siege of Saigon had lasted for over a year when Vice Admiral Leonard Charner brought 3,000 French marines and naval infantry with 270 Spanish troops to Saigon in January of 1861 to relieve the siege. The Vietnamese had been reinforced to close to 30,000 troops and had built over 10 miles of entrenchments and redoubts with thousands of sharpened bamboo pits and ditches around the French fortifications at Saigon. The center piece of the Vietnamese defenses was the Ky Hoa fort complex that consisted of 5 fortifications with connecting walls fronted by redoubts that sat close to a mile outside of the French fortifications at Saigon. On February 24, 1861, a French column supported by gunboats on the Saigon River assaulted and took a redoubt at bayonet point in front of the Ky Hoa forts at the cost of 6 dead and 20 wounded. Many of the French wounded had been pierced through the feet by dung covered bamboo stakes and were in great agony. The Vietnamese launched a counter attack to retake the redoubt with several thousand troops and a number of war elephants with swivel guns on their top castles. French rifle fire with army and gunboat artillery killed and wounded hundreds of Vietnamese and most of the elephants before they turned back.

On February 25, the French brought up artillery next to the redoubt to support an attack on the Ky Hoa forts by 1,200 marines supported by 600 more French and Spanish troops. The Vietnamese fire was heavy especially just under the forts earthen walls with the French taking heavy casualties. After a half hour, the French managed to mount the fort's ramparts with grenades, grappling hooks, and the only 3 ladders to have made it intact to the walls. The Vietnamese fought viciously, but were no real match for the larger stronger French troops with their 19 inch bayonets. After the Vietnamese fell back, the French started taking heavy casualties from Vietnamese artillery from another fort called the Mandarin Fort which sat 100 yards back in the middle of the Ky Hoa fort system. The French troops had no cover from the artillery fire and had no choice but to charge the Mandarin Fort as well. Many French troops were shot and dismembered in a hurricane of bullets, canon balls, and grapeshot as they tried to bring up grappling hooks, ladders and sappers to find a way in to the fort.

The French reserve was then brought up through the maelstrom and breached the main gate to the Mandarin Fort with axes and hatchets. The French troops then charged through the gate and killed over 300 Vietnamese troops inside the fort before the entire Vietnamese army broke and retreated from their entrenchments around Saigon. The assault on the Mandarin Fort cost the French another 225 casualties. Emperor Tu Duc's power was broken as the French then occupied all 6 provinces of Cochinchina (southern Vietnam). In 1862, a treaty was signed with Napoleon III that made France a protectorate of Vietnam in return for allowing Tu Duc to remain as a puppet ruler. Spain decided to end their involvement in Cochinchina because the region seemed to be a "cesspool of blood and mud to swallow men" and France seemed to have more in mind than just saving missionaries.

The French and Vietnamese experienced peace for the next 10 years as the French explored and mapped Indochina. In 1870, Napoleon III was defeated and removed from power during the Franco-Prussian War. The loss was so humiliating that France sought to regain its nationalistic pride and respect by extending its power into Africa and especially Indochina since the French had no French colonies in Asia.

In 1873, a French merchant by the name of Jean Dupuis began a daring enterprise to open the Red River to French trade without the knowledge of the French government. Dupuis hired a mercenary force of 200 armed Europeans, Filipinos, and Chinese to open trade in northern Vietnam. Dupuis and his mercenaries began by assaulting Hanoi and raising the French flag over part of the city which was against the treaty that had been signed between Napoleon III and Tu Duc. Dupuis appealed to the French military in Saigon for reinforcements because he and his small force of mercenaries were in an untenable position in Hanoi with thousands of Vietnamese troops gathering near the Hanoi citadel. Several hundred French troops were sent under Francis Garnier who stormed the Hanoi citadel as the Vietnamese forces fled. Then Garnier went on to conquer the area from Hanoi to the Gulf of Tonkin against Emperor Tu Duc's protests.

The French attacks had set the whole Tonkin area into chaos. The Taiping Rebellion which convulsed China from 1851 to 1871 and cost 30 million lives before being put down by Chinese government forces drove thousands of Taiping insurgents into Vietnam where they joined a powerful Chinese bandit-pirate army called the Black Flags. The Black Flags proceeded to plunder defenseless villages and to commit piracy along the Tonkin and in the rivers of northern Vietnam in the 1860's and 1870's. Tu Duc appealed to China for help which sent an army that simply deserted and joined the Black Flags who had the real power along the Chinese and Vietnamese border areas. Tu Duc then appealed to the Black Flags for help ejecting the French from Hanoi.

On December 21, 1873, several thousand Black Flag troops brought up canon that blasted open the front gate to the Hanoi citadel. Dupuis and his mercenaries were all massacred and beheaded by the Black Flag forces. Garnier arrived in Hanoi and impetuously counter-attacked to retake the citadel with just 50 French infantry who were all cut down and beheaded outside the citadel. The Black Flags then pickled the heads of Garnier and the dead French infantry in jars filled with brine to be displayed in Tu Duc's palace. The remainder of the French troops outside of Hanoi then withdrew from the Tonkin. Tu Duc launched a campaign of retaliation against Vietnamese Catholics that slaughtered thousands of believers as well as having killed some European missionaries as well. In France, there were outcries for retribution for the deaths of Garnier's men and the dead missionaries and Vietnamese Catholics.

The French army and Foreign Legion were busy quelling Bedouin rebellions in Algiers and other African hot spots and could not respond to these provocations for 10 years. In 1883, a French captain named Henri Riviere was sent with 600 French troops to retake Hanoi and the Tonkin area. Riviere took the city of Hongay and then proceeded toward Hanoi through a hot, dense jungle trail. At Tu Duc's request, several thousand Black Flag troops had set an ambush in the jungle. The French troops came into an area of the jungle trail of 8 foot tall elephant grass where there were hundreds of concealed sharpened bamboo pits that a number of the lead group had impaled their feet on after they stepped into the pits. The screams of agony of those whose feet were pierced stopped the column cold. Suddenly, musket fire through the elephant grass dropped a over a hundred of the unsuspecting French troops followed by a charge of screaming Black flag troops armed with swords, pikes, and halberds. The French troops gathered into small groups and fought desperately killing many Black Flag troops before being overwhelmed and cut down to a man. The bodies of the 600 dead French soldiers were all mutilated and Captain Riviere's head was mounted on a pole.

Black Flag troops prepare to launch an ambush on French forces. Most of
the Black Flag troops had been Taiping Rebellion refuges from China.

The news of the massacre caused the French parliament to vote for
more than 5 million francs to be appropriated for a full scale expedition to impose a protectorate on all of Indochina. On September 27,
1883, a force of 6,000 French Foreign Legionnaires set sail from Algiers
for the Far East. Morale was high among the legionnaires for anything
seemed better than the god forsaken deserts of North Africa. Most of

the legionnaires had no idea of what they were up against, nor did they understand that their heavy coats, ninety pound packs, and 10 pound Gras rifles would prove quite cumbersome in the humid, tropical weather of Southeast Asia.

Earlier in July of 1883, Emperor Tu Duc died "with curses of the invader on his lips," as a court communiqué put it. His death caused a multiple sided civil war that pitted 6 different mandarins against each other since Tu Duc had no son to ascend the throne. Within a year, three emperors had been enthroned and deposed.

For all practical purposes the real leader of Vietnam was a warlord named Liu Young-fu, also known as Liu Vinh-Phoc. He was the leader of the Black Flags, who had virtual control of most of Vietnam. The Vietnamese emperors had to pay "protection money" to him and get his approval and aide for anything that they chose to do. Liu was born to an extremely poor family in 1837, in Kwantung province, China, near the Vietnamese frontier. His parents died when he was 16 and he joined a Chinese bandit gang of over 200 young men called the Black Flags who had no future to look to other than a life of crime. Within a few years, he worked his way into the top leadership position of the gang. In 1865, Liu and his gang had taken in several thousand defeated insurgents from the Taiping Rebellion and decided to base the Black Flags in northern Vietnam to get away from Chinese government forces in southern China. Tu Duc offered a large sum of money to Lui if he would put down a rebellion by Montagnard tribesmen in northern Vietnam and in Laos. The Black Flags fought a number of inconclusive battles with the Montagnards, but mostly concentrated on building a formidable army from the thousands of Taiping refuges crossing into Vietnam seeking sanctuary. Eventually, he commanded an outlaw army so strong that the Vietnamese emperor feared and respected him.

In August of 1883, a French fleet appeared at the mouth of the Perfume River not far away from the Vietnamese capital of Hue.

A message was sent to Emperor Hiep Hoa demanding the unconditional surrender of Vietnam within 48 hours or "the words Annam, and Cochinchina would be erased from history." Before the Vietnamese could respond, the French warships had bombarded Hue causing heavy casualties among military and civilian personnel alike. Emperor Hiep Hoa signed a treaty granting France a protectorate over all of Indochina. Unfortunately, for the French, they had asked the wrong people for the treaty. The Black Flags were vigorously preparing for a major war with France.

The French Foreign Legionnaires were disembarked at Haiphong and allowed to enjoy prostitutes, rice wine, and the beautiful scenery of this area from August to November of 1883. The men felt that the war was over and all they had to do was garrison duty and to enjoy the delights of Vietnam. On November 18, the 6,000 legionnaires were sent up the Red River and were landed to occupy Hanoi. Everything seemed calm and fine to the French who didn't realize the threat that the Black Flags presented. It was decided to send the legionnaires 30 miles through the jungle to destroy the main Black Flag stronghold at Sontay. The French did not know that there was a black Flag garrison there of 25,000 men who had experience in war.

Day after day, the Legion toiled in their heavy backpacks through the swamps and rice paddies, at times waist deep in stinking mud and water, and at times hacking their way through the oppressively humid, mosquito and leech infested jungle. All along the way the Legion had lost men to wounds from the sharpened bamboo pits that impaled feet. Other legionnaires cursed as they had to carry these wounded men and all of their gear through the hot jungles. The artillerymen cursed the most as they dragged their heavy artillery pieces through the jungles and swamps. At night, legionnaires on guard duty or stragglers were disappearing. In the mornings, the heads of these men would be found in the camp. After the Legion troops had covered over 20 miles of impenetrable jungle, the Black Flags started daily and nightly ambushes that would kill several legionnaires at a time. At one point, the legionnaires came upon a grisly site – the heads of Captain Riviere and all of his ill fated men stacked in jars pickled in brine. Now this new country did not seem so alluring after all to the unnerved legionnaires who began to think that they were better off in North Africa.

On December 16, 1883, the legionnaires reached Sontay and faced a mighty fortress built in Chinese military fashion. The fortress had a strong citadel in the center with 16 foot high walls on the outside, surrounded by a dry deep moat filled with sharpened spikes. On the outside of the moat was a bamboo hedgehog obstacle with thousands more of the dung covered bamboo spikes. Outside the bamboo hedge was 400 yards of open rice paddies with thousands more of sharpened bamboo spikes concealed in the shallow rice paddy water.

The French assault at Sontay in 1883.

The French artillery began pounding the fort with little success. The legionnaires fixed bayonets and started wadding across the rice paddies. Screams could be heard all across the rice paddies as men discovered that they had bamboo spikes piercing their feet. Yet, the legionnaires kept on. All the while, Black Flag artillery and muskets were blazing away. Many more legionnaires cut themselves up climbing over the bamboo hedgehogs only to fall into the unseen moat to impale themselves on the bamboo spikes below before climbing, bleeding and cursing their way up to the walls. After this journey from hell to reach the walls, the legionnaires discovered that the French artillery had not made a breach in the walls. A runner was sent to tell the artillery to open a breach in the wall as the legionnaires huddled as best as they could in the moat as they suffered casualties from Black Flag grenades and from friendly artillery fire. A French artillery shell finally struck a pile of Black Flag canon balls and sacks of gunpowder on the fortress wall which blasted a 20 meter breach. All the legionnaires that could still walk charged into Sontay with yells of "Vive la Legion! Vive la France!" Once inside, the legionnaires skewered hundreds of Black flag troops on their 19 inch bayonets in retribution for their sufferings. By nightfall, the Black Flag garrison had melted away after suffering 2,000 dead while the legionnaires suffered close to 600 casualties. Most of the legion wounded had suffered crippling wounds from the dung covered bamboo stakes which caused gangrene infection that led to many amputations and deaths over the days and weeks to come.

The legionnaires settled down for a short period of garrison duty at Sontay. In addition to losing many wounded, many more men were dying from tropical diseases. In February of 1884, 1,000 more legionnaires arrived from Algeria, but they only replaced those who had died thus far in the campaign. In March, the legionnaires were ordered to march east to Bac Ninh where a garrison of 15,000 Black Flag and Chinese regulars that had been sent from orders from Beijing to help stop the French threat.

On March 12, the French column reached Bac Ninh and began slashing and burning the surrounding villages and fortified outposts in an effort to isolate the main fortification. French artillery had blasted open the front gate of the main fortification followed by a Legion bayonet charge by 600 men. Once the legionnaires had gotten inside the front gate they found that they were caught in a killing zone and blocked by a second gate which was common in Chinese fortifications. The legionnaires retreated to just outside of the front gate and sent 20 sappers who ran in and set up explosives against the second gate. Only 5 sappers made it back to the front gate before the second gate was blown open. Bloody hand to hand fighting took place before the Black Flag and Chinese troops faded before the larger legionnaires and their vicious bayonet work.

During the next few months, the Black Flags were driven from town after town, and French garrisons were left in each one. As a result, the French were spread thin across the Tonkin and northern Vietnam. Heat exhaustion, malaria, dysentery, cholera, and typhoid Fever were taking a toll and killed hundreds of Legion troops. In the meantime, Liu Yin fu was gathering together his scattered Black Flag forces in the north of Tonkin and in southern China as he awaited for Chinese reinforcements to go on the offensive to retake the thinly garrisoned towns that he had lost to the French. In November of 1884, several thousand Chinese troops arrived with modern rifles instead of the muskets that the Black Flag forces had been using, Nordenfeldt type (Gatling) guns, and Krupp field artillery. In January of 1885, Liu moved south with an army of 20,000 men along the Claire River to Tuyen Quang which was about 100 miles north of Hanoi.

The French garrison at Tuyen Quang consisted of 390 legionnaires and 200 Vietnamese colonial troops. The legionnaires garrisoned a captured Chinese fort that was made of bamboo stockade walls that desperately needed repairs from the damage they had done to it when they had captured it. The first sign that something was wrong was when the Vietnamese in and around the town began evacuating in panic. Then Black Flag scouts began appearing. The legionnaires who realized that an attack was eminent began digging communication trenches between the various points within the fort and to a blockhouse they had built outside of the fort.

On January 26, the Black Flag and Chinese forces launched 2 massive attacks on the outer blockhouse which would have been overrun had it not been for French artillery support from batteries in the fort. Nevertheless, the blockhouse garrison of 18 men barely held off the attacks with only 9 men surviving. After the second attack, the surviving legionnaires retreated along the communication trench back to the fort after blowing up the blockhouse with explosives.

Chinese sappers dug tunnels toward the fort, with the idea of mining the walls to breach them for an assault. Early in the morning of February 14, a mine was exploded, causing a corner section of the bamboo wall and tower to collapse killing 15 legionnaires. Immediately, an assault column of Black Flag and Chinese troops rushed the breach with trumpets blowing, gongs beating and black flags waving. Most of the attackers were cut down by rifle and artillery fire and from a mitrailleuse (a French type Gatling gun). Those few who made it to the breach were impaled on French bayonets.

Over the next few days, more mines were exploded which divided the wall in 2 places. Wave after wave of screaming Black flag and Chinese attackers took staggering casualties from French lead, but still by sheer numbers forced their way into the breaches in the fort. Groups of reserve legionnaires counter-attacked and drove off the Black Flag and Chinese attackers in desperate hand to hand fighting. Day after day, more mines were exploded until there was little of the fort left standing. The French kept all of their troops in the interior of the fort in order to meet the attackers on top of the debris mounds caused by the explosions to repulse the attacks despite taking heavy casualties. The ground in front of and on top of the fort ruins was strewn with thousands of bloated stinking Black Flag and Chinese bodies. The losses didn't seem to discourage the attackers that felt that they were willing to take huge casualties in order to destroy the French garrison. The Black Flags and Chinese decided to try a surprise night attack. Quietly moving out from their trenches under the moonlight they overwhelmed the sentries and poured into the fort ruins. The weary legionnaires and colonial troops were roused from deep sleep to clamor to battle. A bitter hand to hand, no quarter battle was fought in the moonlight of bayonets and rifle butts against swords and pikes until the last of the attackers were killed or had fled from the fort.

On February 26, the Chinese detonated 6 mines that blasted what little was left of the walls and creating new lanes through the debris into the fort interior. Dazed legionnaires groped through the smoke, dust, and debris as hordes of attackers climbed over the ruble from all sides and seemed on the verge of overrunning the garrison when Sgt. Major Edmund Hasband yelled out from the center of the fort, "A moi la Legion! A moi la Legion!"(To me the Legion!). All the legionnaires and colonial troops ran, walked, hobbled, or were carried to the center of the fort and formed a square of bayonets. The attackers recoiled from the wall of blade points, but continued to climb over their own dead to attack the French square which couldn't be broken. At last, after 2 hours of desperate fighting and the grim determination of the legionnaires and their colonial troops won out as the Black Flags and Chinese fell back. The Black Flags and Chinese attacked a few more times, but the defenders determination to survive won out during the 36 day siege. The stench of decomposing bodies of both sides was overwhelming. Finally, on March 3, a French relief column received the salute of over 187 exhausted legionnaires and colonial troops (they had taken 403 casualties). The Black Flags and Chinese lost over 4,000 men in the siege.

After this, the dejected Black flag and Chinese forces retreated back to Long Son near the Chinese border. A French column attacked and scattered this force after only token resistance. Lui Yung-fu took the remainder of his forces and retreated back to China where the bandit warlord and his forces were treated like heroes for daring to defy France. France then began bombarding Chinese ports in what became an undeclared war with China. On April 4, 1885, the Chinese imperial government and France signed the Treaty of Tientsin which recognized a French protectorate over Laos, Cambodia, and the Vietnamese provinces of Tonkin, Annam, and Cochinchina. The region was to be known as French Indochina. The 13 year old Vietnamese emperor, Ham Nghi, went into hiding for the remainder of his life as 1,000 French legionnaires sacked Hue in an orgy of looting and killing. In 1887, Laos, Cambodia, and Vietnam officially became colonies of France. The French Foreign Legion lost another 2,000 soldiers fighting Vietnamese resistance guerrillas until 1910. To the Vietnamese this was just another long war for nationalism. It was a war that wouldn't truly be resolved for another 88 years after the French and United States phases of the Vietnam Wars. It was Ho Chi Minh who best described the situation that the French and then the Americans got themselves into. He said, "We will be like the elephant and the tiger. When the elephant is strong and rested and near his base we will retreat. If the tiger ever pauses, the elephant will impale him on his mighty tusks. But the tiger will not pause and the elephant will die of exhaustion and loss of blood."

BIBLIOGRAPHY

Buttinger, Joseph. *The Smaller Dragon: A Political History of Vietnam*. New York, Praeger, 1958.

Cady, John. *The Roots of French Imperialism in Asia*. Ithaca, Cornell University Press, 1954.

Karnow, Stanely. *Vietnam: A History*. Hammondworth: Penguin Books, 1991.

McAleary, Henry. *Black Flags in Vietnam*. Ithaca: Cornell University Press, 1955.

McLeave, Hugh. *The Damned Die Hard: The Story of the French Foreign Legion*. Saxon House, 1974.

Osborn, Milton. *The French Presence in Cochinchina and Cambodia 1859 - 1910*. Ithaca, Cornell University Press, 1969.

Porch, Douglas. *The French Foreign Legion*. Perennial, 1991.

Sheldon, Walter. *Tigers in the Rice*. London, Crowell-Collier Press, 1969.

Thompson, Virginia. *French Indo-China*. New York, Octagon Books, 1968.

CHAPTER 18

The Russo-Japanese War 1904 – 1905: The First Modern War

The Japanese arrived in the harbor completely unnoticed and had achieved the element of surprise as they watched their torpedoes slam into 2 battleships and a cruiser. The first wave of attackers had done well and another 2 waves were on their way toward the harbor. This first torpedo attack was not on Dec. 7, 1941, on the U.S. fleet at Pearl Harbor, Hawaii, but it was on February 8, 1904, on the Russian fleet at Port Arthur in Manchuria, China. The attack on Port Arthur was made by three waves of Japanese torpedo boats and destroyers to preemptively win the still undeclared war against Russia at a stroke. The 2nd and 3rd Japanese attacks on Port Arthur had lost the element of surprise and didn't strike anymore Russian ships, but the damage had been done and the Russian Far East fleet was unnerved and psychologically crippled after war had been declared. Historians have called this attack a dress rehearsal for the Pearl Harbor attack that would take place close to 36 years later.

The origins of the Russo-Japanese War from 1904-1905 came from both Russia and Japan seeking spheres of influence in Manchuria and

Korea to exploit new markets and political leverage in East Asia. Japan became a political threat after defeating China in the Sino-Japanese War from 1894 to 1895. Japan destroyed the antiquated Chinese army and navy and demanded Korea, Formosa, and Port Arthur in Manchuria as the spoils of war. Czar Nicholas II did not like this because it gave Japan a more powerful influence in China that Russia coveted. Russia persuaded Germany and France to put diplomatic pressure on Japan to pull out of Port Arthur. Bitterly, Emperor Mikado of Japan relinquished control of Port Arthur only to see Russia to come in and occupy the strategic port. For Japan, this was unacceptable and made Russia a very real threat to Japanese interests in Korea and Manchuria. Japan began a series of fruitless talks with Russia in an effort to try to get them to also agree to evacuate Port Arthur.

Japan crushed the Chinese army in 1894 which made China irrelevant in a war between Russia and Japan which was fought entirely in China.

The Boxer Rebellion created a rivalry between Japan and Russia for mastery of Manchuria and the warm water port of Port Arthur, China. The Boxers were Chinese martial arts students and experts whose spears and swords were no match for the multinational force's modern bolt action rifles, Gatling guns, machine guns and artillery.

In 1900, the Chinese Boxer Rebellion broke out to rid China of all foreign influences from British opium being brought in from Burma to the European and American Christian missionary presence. Great Britain, France, Germany, Italy, Russia, the United States, and Japan joined together to put down the rebellion and to rescue their embassy personnel who were being besieged in Peking. Out of a force of 20,000 that was sent to relieve the besieged foreign legation in Peking, 10,000 were Japanese and 4,000 were Russians. From the onset the Japanese and the Russians tried to race each other to be the first ones to break the siege. In the meantime, other Russian forces occupied all of Manchuria using the Boxer Rebellion as a pretext for their own interests. Russia would do this again in 1945 as the Soviet Union during World War II. The foreign legations were rescued, but Japan demanded that Russian troops withdraw from Manchuria. Czar Nicholas II made an agreement to withdraw all Russian forces from China on October 8, 1903, but that date came and went with no withdrawal. Japan began making secret preparations for war.

The Japanese had come a long way since 1868 when Japan had decided to modernize from a medieval, feudal society dominated by samurai warriors and their warlords called Daimyo to a modern society during the Meiji Restoration. Japan had seen the necessity of modernization after seeing China and its outdated army being dominated by the modern armies and navies of Britain and France. Within 20 years, Japan had the most modern army and navy in Asia, but was still considered inferior by the European powers who believed that Europeans would always be superior to Asians in military and trading affairs. Japan had purchased several of their battleships from Great Britain and had purchased rifles and Krupp artillery pieces from Germany along with bringing in Prussian advisors to train the Japanese army with German training and fighting methods. Though there were no longer samurai warriors in Japan, Japanese soldiers were indoctrinated in the Samurai Code which stressed obedience, sacrifice and a suicidal fanaticism for an honorable death in battle as the greatest achievement for Japan's soldiers. The greatest secret in 1904 was just how formidable Japan's army and navy really were and how much of a major world power they would become.

The Russian army of 1904 was considered to be one of the greatest in the world by virtually all of the European powers of the day. The Russian army was equipped with the newest innovations in artillery and heavy machine guns. The Russian army knew how to build trenches and underground fortifications fronted by barbed wire entanglements and mines and naphtha cylinder containers that could be blown up by electrically wired control boxes from the trenches and fortifications. The Russian navy also had a reputation as being second only to the British navy in modern battleships and cruisers. A little nation like Japan was given little chance of beating Russia by world opinion.

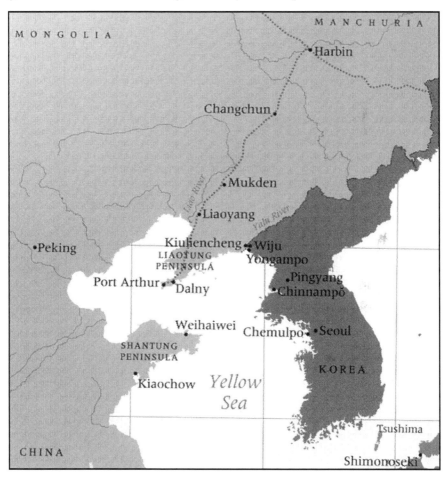

Area of operations during the Russo-Japanese War.

The next day after the February 8, 1904 attack on Port Arthur, Japanese torpedo boats sank 2 more Russian ships that were anchored at Chemulpo, Korea. Then a minelayer named the *Yenisei* was laying mines on a particularly choppy day outside of Port Arthur when a wave threw the ship into a mine that it had just laid which took the ship and all aboard to a dark watery grave. The Russian cruiser called the *Boyarin* rushed out to aide the *Yenisei* in the false belief that the ship was under attack only to strike another mine which sunk that ship as well. The Japanese then sacrificed 21 older ships and their crews in an attempt to block the entrance to Port Arthur with sunken ships. On 3 occasions the Japanese ships tried to scuttle their ships to bottle up the Russian fleet. Only 2 of these Japanese ships were able to partially block the entrance to the port, but the Russian fleet still had enough room to come out in single file.

On March 12, the Japanese fleet baited the Russian fleet to come out and chase them into a minefield that they had laid as a trap outside of Port Arthur. The battleship *Petropavlovsk* led the Russian fleet out of the port to try to force a battle when the ship struck a mine that ignited a forward magazine and took one of Russia's best battleships down to the bottom of the sea in just a few minutes with over 900 sailors onboard. Worst of all for Russia was that Admiral Markarov who was considered the best and the most aggressive Russian admiral who also commanded the defenses at Port Arthur went down with the ship leaving a major leadership void in the Russian command structure. Another commander of Markarov's ability and popularity was not to be found by the Russians for the rest of the war. This setback caused morale to be low among the defenders at Port Arthur from the onset of the war.

At the end of April, the Japanese had landed their army in Korea and had advanced to the Yalu River between Manchuria, China and Korea virtually unmolested except for a few minor Cossack cavalry raids. The Russians had 25,000 infantry entrenched across the Yalu and Ali Ho Rivers with machine gun and artillery emplacements with barbed wire entanglements that fronted the trenches. The Japanese forces secretly crossed the Yalu River with 42,000 men on the night of May 1 to get in position to make a massed bayonet attack across the Ali Ho River the next morning.

The Japanese heavy Krupp howitzers opened up a devastating barrage that knocked out most of the Russian artillery pieces and collapsed trenches which caused over 1,500 Russian casualties. Then the Japanese advanced with bayonets gleaming in the sun in tight formations that their Prussian advisors had taught them to use prior to the war. The Russian lines opened up a devastating fire from rifles and machine guns at 1200 yards with the Japanese struggling to cross the Ali Ho River. Over 1,000 Japanese troops were cut down trying to cross the river or drowned in the strong currents of the Ali Ho. Once the surviving Japanese troops reached the far bank of the river they reformed their tight infantry formations and advanced into the Russian fire once again. Russian machine guns cut down whole formations of Japanese soldiers as they grimly advanced into the barbed wire entanglements. Japanese soldiers then threw themselves onto the barbed wire to make paths with their bodies through the wire to the Russian trenches for the others to cross over on. Japanese bayonets clashed with Russian bayonets in the trenches in vicious hand to hand fighting. The Russian forces then broke and retreated before they would be completely overwhelmed and outflanked by greater Japanese numbers. A Siberian unit fought a desperate holding action to the last man at a mountain pass so that the other Russian forces could retreat to safety to fight another day. The Japanese suffered 2,200 casualties to the Russian losses of over 2,700 men in the first land battle of the war.

Japanese infantry prepare to attack Russian trenches for control of a key
Russian supply train depot. The Japanese bravely took massive casualties from
human wave assaults against Russian trenches throughout the war.

The defeat at the Yalu River put the scattered Russian forces that
guarded the Trans-Siberian railway from Port Arthur to Mukden in
Manchuria in a vulnerable position to have their rail lines cut and their
forces to be split in two. The Japanese moved 35,000 troops with 215
artillery pieces to attack 4,000 Siberian troops with 10 machine guns
and 114 artillery pieces at Nanshan which sat on the rail line between
Russian positions at Port Arthur in the south and Mukden in the north.
The Siberian positions at Nanshan were located in trenches reinforced
with sand bags and fronted by barbed wire and mines. On May 25,
thousands of Japanese in column formations rushed toward the Russian

trenches screaming in a reckless charge. Russian machine guns mowed down wave after wave of Japanese attackers who came on despite the terrible losses. To get through the mines, Japanese soldiers purposely ran in to blow themselves up so that the men behind them could get through to throw themselves onto the barbed wire only for the followers to be mowed down by machine gun fire. Nine Japanese human wave assaults failed to break into the Russian trenches. It was at this point something peculiar happened when the Russian co-commander, General Fock, became rattled by an attempt by the Japanese to outflank the line that he ordered the western half of the Russian line to withdraw despite the fact that a well placed machine gun had the flank covered and had produced piles of Japanese corpses up to this point in the battle.

General Tretyakov, who commanded the eastern half of the line rode up to plead with General Fock to maintain his positions when a shrapnel shell dismembered his body and sprayed his blood and guts all over the nice white uniforms of Fock and the other Russian officers in the area. At this sight, the Russian forces began melting away in panic. The Japanese took advantage of the chaos that was created and began overrunning the Russian trenches. One company of Siberians obeyed Tretyakov's last command and fought to the death. The Russians had lost close to 400 men defending their trenches, but lost another 1,200 men in the retreat. The Japanese had lost close to 5,000 casualties in their human wave assaults on the Russian trenches. This battle showed that Russian soldiers would fight and die to defend their trenches, but that many of their senior officers were easily unnerved by the aggressive tactics of the Japanese and their fanatical, suicidal determination to win at any cost. The battle had turned a great victory into a disaster for the Russians who now had their forces split between Port Arthur and Liaotung.

Russian troops bravely defended their trenches followed by
demoralizing orders to retreat by their incompetent generals.

Part of the Japanese army under General Nogi Maresuke began
digging trenches outside of Port Arthur to begin a siege of the city as
the remainder of the Japanese army dug trenches and laid barbed wire
facing north toward the Russian trenches at Liaotung. Russian forces
under General Alexei Kuropatkin were ordered to assault and take the
Japanese trench system facing them at Liaotung. The Russian infantry
attacked the Japanese trenches with great élan, but were mowed down
by the thousands by Japanese machine guns and artillery. These failed
attacks on the Japanese trenches were as close as the Russians would
come to relieving Port Arthur. Western correspondents and military
attaches were appalled at the carnage that they were witnessing in a
mini version of what the Western Front would be like over ten years
later in World War I.

On August 26, 1904, 120,000 Japanese troops began a counter offensive against the 147,000 Russian troops at Liaotung. The Japanese launched suicidal attack after attack that never reached the Russian trenches because they were cut down by the thousands by machine gun fire and dismembered by mines and artillery shells. The Japanese were able to reach some Russian trenches on the flanks when they approached through some 10 foot tall kao-ling millet and then rushed through 30 yards of barbed wire by running over the backs of those that had sacrificed themselves by throwing themselves onto the wire to fight hand to hand with bayonets, rifle butts, and shovels in the trenches. The Russians were finally able to repulse the Japanese after piles of corpses had filled the trenches with the dead and wounded of both sides. On the morning of August 27, the Japanese were amazed to see that the Russians had evacuated their front line trenches. General Kuropatkin was unnerved by the attempted Japanese attacks on the Russian flanks and decided to pull back to a secondary line of trenches called the "main position." Kuropatkin was starting a pattern of retreating farther away from Port Arthur rather than closer to relieve the besieged city.

Sporadic fighting broke out until August 30 when the battle erupted all across the Russian secondary line of trenches with massive artillery bombardments by both sides that collapsed trenches and buried men alive. The Russians took huge casualties from the Japanese bombardments because they did not build bomb shelters under their trenches nor moved men back to secondary lines until the bombardments let up. The Japanese then hurled their infantry in fanatical massed columns to assault the Russian trenches. Over 45,000 Japanese were sent to overwhelm a Siberian corps of 15,000 men to try to turn the Russian left flank. The Japanese kept coming against the Siberian trenches until a wall of dead bodies blocked their way so that they would have to climb over or go around the piles of dead corpses. The Russian machine guns, rifles, mines, and artillery couldn't miss killing the thousands of Japanese as they grimly kept coming. The piles of dead Japanese corpses got closer and closer through the barbed wire as they advanced with suicidal determination to the Siberian trenches until they finally reached the Siberians who fought desperately to survive with bayonets, and hand shovels that were used to cleave a man's head or arm off. The Japanese fell back in despair at the great sacrifice of their men with little to show for it.

One last assault was planned that night. The exhausted Japanese troops scrambled out of their trenches under the moonlight and formed their assault columns in an eerie silence. The Japanese quietly climbed over their dead from that day's fighting and found that the Russian trenches had been abandoned. General Kuropatkin had again been unnerved by the fanatical Japanese attacks and fell back to another line of trenches again in fear that his flank might be turned.

The Japanese attacked the 3rd line of Russian trenches until September 3, 1904, when Kuropatkin ordered a retreat back to the rail center at Mukden. The Japanese lost 23,000 men to the Russian losses of 19,000 at the Battle of Liaotung. Most of the Russian casualties had come from the crushing barrages from the Japanese Krupp artillery. Russian morale was very low from fighting desperately and causing frightening casualties on the Japanese to defend their trenches only to then be ordered to withdrawal without having actually been defeated. Though the Japanese were winning battles there was fear among the high command that they could not sustain the huge casualties that they were taking in their fanatical human wave assaults. This new kind of twentieth century warfare put a new kind of strain on ordinary soldiers and on nations to be able to keep feeding men into a meat grinder that required huge losses to make small gains.

As the fighting was raging in battles along Russia's cut rail lines in Manchuria, the Japanese were also tightening their siege lines around Port Arthur. General Fock who had abandoned Nanshan also abandoned two outer defense lines after they had been successfully defended by Russian troops in fear they might not hold or would be flanked. Now General Fock had no where to retreat to, for his forces had the sea to their backs. Nevertheless, Port Arthur's defenses were formidable. It was surrounded by forts, trenches, and redoubts on top of hills that overlooked the surrounding area. In front of the fortifications were extensive wire entanglements with deep pits in front that contained spikes as well as thousands of electrically detonated mines and canisters of naphtha that burned attackers in an inferno of flames. Port Arthur was defended by 40,000 Russian soldiers that were tired of retreating and were motivated to fight.

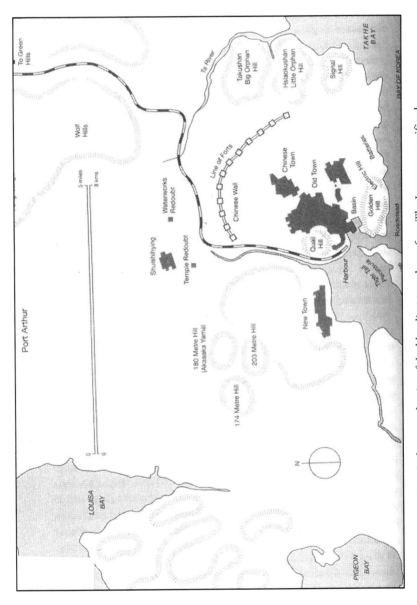

Port Arthur was the site of the bloodiest trench warfare. The Japanese sacrificed more than 10,000 men to capture Hill 203 where the siege was decided.

Once the Japanese began digging their siege trenches around Port Arthur, the Japanese began blindly shelling the Russian fleet which was bottled up in the port with their Krupp siege artillery. The fleet tried to make a run for Vladivostok, but returned after a Japanese shell from a cruiser struck the lead battleship which killed the commanding Russian admiral. The unnerved second in command of the Russian fleet ordered a retreat back to Port Arthur. A few of the Russian ships became separated and had to go to foreign ports where they were interned for the rest of the war. Most of the 17,000 sailors in the bottled up Russian fleet had to be pressed into the trenches to replace the huge losses from the infantry and to serve as reserve units to counter attack lost positions as the siege progressed.

In mid-August, 1904, the Japanese launched a massive assault on the eastern defenses of Port Arthur. This sector was first shelled by heavy Krupp siege guns for 2 days which collapsed trenches and bunkers that buried and suffocated hundreds of soldiers and destroyed much of the Russian artillery. Surprisingly, the Japanese neglected to bombard the Russian minefields and bared wire. The Japanese attackers then came in fanatical waves against the Russian fortifications and trenches. The first waves of Japanese were engulfed in explosions and flames as the minefields and naphtha canisters were electrically detonated. The first waves of attackers began screaming in agony almost in unison as men were incinerated alive from the naphtha canisters and dismembered with legs, arms, and heads flying in all directions from the mines being detonated. The second waves of suicidal Japanese attackers ran through the charred remains of the first waves and threw themselves into the pits of iron spikes and onto the barbed wire for those that followed to run over their bodies as Russian machine guns and rifles cut down thousands. The attacks continued like this for several days until the Japanese had sacrificed 20,000 men who lay stinking and rotting in front of the Russian trenches and redoubts. General Nogi, whose own son had been sacrificed in an earlier suicidal attack, realized that Port Arthur would have to be taken in a slow arduous siege.

The Japanese began sapping and mining tunnels and trenches toward the Russian positions. The Japanese moved their trenches under heavy fire to within 50 or 60 yards of several Russian redoubt and fortress positions when they detonated mines that had been tunneled under these fortifications. The Russian redoubts or fortresses were then blown followed by a dash by Japanese infantry to take the positions. Russian reserve units of sailors counter attacked and fought viciously over the wreckage of these blown fortifications before having to abandon the positions with great losses on both sides.

In September, the Japanese brought in special Krupp siege guns that fired 550 lb. artillery shells. These shells destroyed underground bunkers and fortifications and drove men mad because of the constant bombardments. There was no real safe place for the Russian soldiers to hide where the threat of death wasn't looming. This was a new kind of war that caused many men who had not been physically wounded to suffer psychologically from shell shock due to the intensive strain that this new kind of war put men through.

The Japanese received intelligence that the Russian Baltic fleet was on its' way to the relief of Port Arthur. The Japanese high command felt a new sense of urgency to take Port Arthur before the arrival of the Baltic fleet. To do this, the Japanese needed 203 Meter Hill which commanded Port Arthur and its harbor. Over 500 Russians defended the trenches below 203 Meter Hill with another 300 infantry and a reserve of 120 sailors that defended the redoubt at the top of the hill.

On November 27, the Japanese began their suicidal assaults on the trenches at the base of the hill. The Japanese sent wave after wave of soldiers through minefields and barbed wire in an assault that lasted all night under huge Russian search lights from the top of the hill. Finally, the Japanese had captured the Russian trenches at the foot of

203 Meter Hill just before dawn on the 28th in desperate hand to hand fighting. The Russians then rolled 18 lb. guncotton mines that exploded in the trenches with such force that they collapsed the trenches onto the wounded and exhausted Japanese soldiers that occupied them. The mines made a gigantic flame which caused the Japanese to run around in torment like human torches.

The Japanese then sent wave after wave of attackers in relentless attacks that lasted day and night for 9 more days against the redoubt on 203 Meter Hill. Russian machine guns fired until they ran out of ammunition. The Japanese would then overrun the Russian positions in desperate hand to hand fighting only to be killed by counter attacks from the bayonet charges from the sailors from the fleet. The Japanese blew the redoubt up with mines and by the suicidal charges of sappers armed with explosives that often blew themselves up after they had jumped into a Russian trench or dugout. The Russian sailors each time retook the ruins of the redoubt in desperate counter attacks. Finally, on December 5, after an entire night of desperate hand to hand fighting was followed by an eerie silence. In the quiet morning sunlight, a Japanese company managed to enter the remains of the redoubt to find only a handful of wounded Russians there surrounded by piles of corpses from both sides. Over 400 Russians and over 10,000 Japanese died for possession of the redoubt on 203 Meter Hill. The stench could be smelled for miles around from the rotting bodies compressed into only a hundred yard area.

General Nogi ordered the bodies to be pulled off of 203 Meter Hill and burned and for the heavy Krupp artillery to be pulled up and placed in newly built fortifications on the hill. In less than 2 days, the Russian fleet in the harbor was sunk. The Japanese then began bombarding the town of Port Arthur and began destroying the remaining Russian fortifications. The Russians had taken 30,000 casualties mostly from the Japanese artillery that smashed trenches, dugouts, redoubts, and the supposedly impregnable underground fortifications from shells from the Krupp howitzers. The Russian troops that were not casualties were demoralized and in no condition to fight much longer. Finally, on January 4, 1905, the Russians under General Fock formally surrendered Port Arthur to the Japanese. The Japanese had lost over 60,000 men mostly from their suicidal human wave assaults against Russian machine guns and trenches. The Siege of Port Arthur was a microcosm of what the Battle of Verdun would be like 12 years later in World War I and showed just how deadly that modern war could and would be.

Russian and world public opinion was in shock that Russia was losing the war to a perceived insignificant Asian nation. Unrest, protests, and talk of revolution against Czar Nicholas II became rife in Russia. Vladimir Lenin wrote that the capitulation of Port Arthur was the prologue to the end of Czardom and the beginning of a communist revolution. On January 22, 1905, over 300,000 peasants marched on the Winter Palace in St. Petersburg to demand an end to the Russo-Japanese War and for better working and living conditions. Czar Nicholas II ordered that the palace guard was to disperse the crowd or to fire on it. Over 4,000 peasants were shot down in what would be known as Bloody Sunday and was considered the first event toward what would later become the Russian Revolution in 1917.

While the Siege of Port Arthur was going on between October 4 and October 16, 1904, the Russian forces under General Kuropatkin launched an offensive in an effort to break through to relieve the beleaguered city. This time bayonet wielding Russians made suicidal human wave assaults against the Japanese trenches. Russian artillery destroyed Japanese trenches and bunkers in a great loss of life before the Russian infantry advanced shoulder to shoulder in mass toward the Japanese trenches. The surviving Japanese came out of their bomb proofs and from the secondary trenches and set up their machine guns and with artillery support just mowed down wave after wave of the Russian attackers. The Russians captured sections of the Japanese front trenches in vicious hand to hand fighting, but then were forced back by well timed counter attacks. The Battle of the Sha Ho River cost the Russians 41,000 casualties to the Japanese casualties of 16,000. The Russian forces fell back and planned on waiting until the spring to launch anymore offensives.

In January, Czar Nicholas II pressured General Kuropatkin to go on the offensive and to not just sit the winter out. On January 28, General Kuropatkin issued orders for an attack with instructions that were so lengthy and complicated that one observer commented that the battle was arranged as if it were a ballet. The Russian assault completely surprised the Japanese because it took place in a snowstorm in gale force winds and in temperatures of 28 degrees below 0. The Battle of Sandeup was a bloody hand to hand encounter in a blinding snowstorm. Units and smaller groups of men from both sides got lost in the blizzards and froze to death from exposure. Nearly all of the wounded from both sides froze to death because they couldn't be located or heard through the roaring winter wind. Kuropatkin ordered a withdrawal back toward Mukden as the Japanese retook the ground that they had lost. The Russians lost 14,000 men and the Japanese lost 10,000 casualties in the most confusing battle of the war.

THE FALL OF MUKDEN

Tiehling

Original Russian Dispositions

A   Kaulbars's Second Manchurian Army
B   Bildering's Third Manchurian Army
C   Linievich's First Manchurian Army
D   Rennenkampf

The Battle of Mukden involved 700,000 troops from both sides and sealed Russia's defeat.

The last major land battle of the war started on February 24, 1905, on a front that spread from 75 to 100 miles long involving more than 380,000 Russians and 320,000 Japanese with the addition of general Nogi's army from Port Arthur in the largest battle in modern history up to this point. The Japanese began by using a pinning force of 100,000 troops to attack the Russian trenches in the center of the line as General Nogi's forces tried to outflank the Russian eastern flank. The Japanese attacked and the Russians counter attacked each other's trenches in mass formations of men that were cut down by machine gun, rifle and artillery fire in the center of the battlefield. The artillery of both sides blew apart the front trenches as the area between the trenches became a dark, macabre moonscape of piles of stinking rotting corpses. Fighting was also very bitter and bloody in the mountains and hills on the Russian eastern flank with some of the bloodiest fighting being fought over some contested bridges which the Japanese eventually took.

LA BATAILLE DE WAFANGHOU. — Une mêlée sous l'orage et la tempête

LA GUERRE RUSSO-JAPONAISE

(Voir l'article : Nos gravures)

A large cavalry battle was fought between Russian Cossacks and the Japanese cavalry that helped the Japanese forces to outflank the Russian army at the Battle of Mukden.

Les Japonais à l'assaut des retranchements de Kin-Tcheou

Siberian troops who fought with their distinctive fur hats face
one of many suicidal Japanese human wave assaults.

On February 27, a cavalry battle took place farther east on the Russian's left flank. The Japanese cavalry fought more as mobile infantry with ponies that dismounted and fought on foot in tight lines for maximum fire power. The Cossack cavalry charged with lances and swords more than 10 times only to be cut down by massed Japanese rifle fire. Over 12,000 Russian infantry on the flank were cut off and captured after the defeat of the Cossack cavalry. With his flank turned, Kuropatkin ordered a retreat which was covered by a brave rear action battle by a corps of Siberian troops. The Russians lost 156,000 casualties to the Japanese losses of 70,000 casualties in the Battle of Mukden. The Japanese did not attempt anymore offensive actions after this because they had depleted their reserves in Japan and had taken close to 250,000 casualties in dead, wounded, and sick and could not sustain anymore bloody assaults against Russian trenches. The Japanese high command feared that one or two more Russian offensives would cause them to lose all that they had gained given that they could no longer replace manpower losses in battle.

Czar Nicholas II replaced General Kuropatkin with General Linievich in frustration after the Battle of Mukden. The Russian army didn't attempt anymore offensive actions against the Japanese either, not knowing of the Japanese predicament of not having any more reserves. Linievich didn't want to attempt anymore offensives because Russian ground forces were in a traumatized and demoralized state having lost more than 217,000 dead and wounded with another 70,000 troops that had been captured in the war.

Kuropatkin would regain face in Russian public opinion from his memoirs that were published in 1909 where he defended his actions in the war. Kuropatkin was called out of retirement in October of 1915 to lead a Russian army against the Germans in World War I. He was relieved of command by Czar Nicholas II in July of 1916 for his failed offensives and for his continual retreats that lost so much Russian territory to the Germans. Kuropatkin would die in virtual anonymity in 1925.

Russia's last hope in gaining some leverage for a respectable peace was its Baltic fleet that left the Baltic in the summer of 1904 and took an arduous 9 months to reach East Asia. The fleet consisted of 11 battleships and 8 cruisers along with 9 destroyers. The Russian Baltic fleet entered the Tsushima straits on May 27, 1905, between Korea and Japan in 2 columns in an effort to get to Vladivostok to re-supply and to refit their ships as well as to add a few extra warships to the fleet for the battle to come. The Japanese knew what the Russian intentions were and intended to force a battle in the Tsushima straits.

The Japanese battle fleet of 4 battleships, 27 cruisers, and 58 destroyers and torpedo boats crossed in front of the Russian fleet's path and opened fire. The inexperienced Russian gunners (mostly old men and reservists) opened fire in return with little effect and soon were in a state of chaos as the Japanese shells struck the hulls of the Russian ships with great effect. The *Oslylabia* was the first Russian battleship hit with huge wholes in its hull from a torpedo and several artillery shells at the waterline which caused the ship to capsize with most of its sailors going down with the ship. One of the few survivors who had been moved before the battle from an engine stoker to a topside gunner described the hell down below in the engine and stokehold rooms. He said, "So the stokers and mechanics without exception remained below: 250 men stayed there bolted in that iron coffin. The torture these men went through must have been unimaginable. When the ship turned over with its heel in the air they would have flung down head first and after them, killing and maiming would have dropped all those iron fittings which were not firmly fixed. There would be banging, crashing, and roaring. The electric lights would have failed at once, so it would have been completely dark. Into these sealed compartments water would have entered slowly, so those who had not been killed would have lived for some time in great fear and agony before drowning."

The Russian Navy was horrifically destroyed at the Battle of Tsushima.

The battleship, *Suvorov,* was knocked out of the battle after its conning tower was blown apart which killed and wounded most of the crew. Later that night, the *Suvorov* sank with hundreds of wounded still onboard the ship. Next, the battleships *Alexander III,* and the *Borodino* were blown apart and capsized. Of the 900 man crew of the *Borodino,* only one man survived. Later, the *Navarin* was sunk as well. The rest of the Russian fleet scattered with several ships scuttling on the Korean coast. The Russian fleet had 21 ships that were sunk including 7 battleships and another 7 ships captured with 4,380 dead and 5,917 sailors that were captured in the Battle of Tsushima. The Japanese lost only 700 casualties and had 3 torpedo boats sunk in the lopsided battle.

After Tsushima, President Theodore Roosevelt from the United States mediated the Treaty of Portsmouth on August 23, 1905. Russia acknowledged Korea and central and southern Manchuria as Japan's sphere of influence. The Japanese also were allowed to annex the southern part of Sakhalin Island. Russia also ceded the rights it had recently acquired in Port Arthur to Japan. Russia retained northern Manchuria with its' railway as it's' sphere of influence. Conspicuously absent from the treaty was China whose land had been fought over between Japan and Russia despite the fact that over 50,688 Chinese died in the war as forced laborers who had to dig trenches and fortifications as well as to carry supplies to the front for both sides. Both sides purposely fired their artillery at the Chinese laborers to stop them from carrying ammunition and food to the front. The Japanese made it a policy to massacre any Chinese laborers captured that had supplied the Russians and had worked on their fortifications despite the fact that all of these Chinese had been forced to provide labor to the Russians against their will.

The impotence that China showed during the Russo-Japanese War led to the downfall of the Qing (Manchu) Dynasty in 1911 and the beginning of 37 years of internal civil wars before the communists under Mao Tse Tung emerged to rule a new and stronger China in 1949. The Russo-Japanese War showed the world just how deadly modern war could and would be. Many German, French, Italian, Austrian, and British attaches observed and criticized both sides for needlessly losing tens of thousands of men in pointless massed trench assaults. Despite these criticisms, none of these nations learned anything from the war and in fact had repeated all of the same mistakes on a much larger scale during World War I from 1914-1918.

BIBLIOGRAPHY

Asakawa, K. *The Russo-Japanese Conflict: Its Causes and Issues* , New York, Houghton and Mifflin Company, 1905.

Connaughton, Richard. *The War of the Rising Sun and Tumbling Bear: A Military History of the Russo-Japanese War 1904-1905.* Routledge Press, 1992.

Kuropatkin, Alexei. *The Russian Army and the Japanese War.* (Volumes I and II) New York: E.P. Sutton and Company, 1909. Translated by Captain A.B. Lindsay.

Sedgwick, F.R. *The Russo-Japanese War.* London: Swan Sonnenschein & Company, 1909.

Westwood, J.N. *The Illustrated History of the Russo-Japanese War.* London: Sedgwick & Jackson, 1973.

Westwood, J.N. *Witness to Tsushima.* Diplomatic Press, 1970 – 1st Printing was in 1907. Tsushima Quotation came from this book which was suppressed after the 1907 publication by Czar Nicholas II.

CHAPTER 19

The War of Gog and Magog, Armageddon and World War III: The War that more than Half of the World is Expecting in the Near Future

Many of the world's over 2.5 billion Christians (33%), the over 1.5 billion Muslims (22%), and many of the over 18 million Jews the world over are expecting in the near future a time of war that will dwarf any of the other wars that have taken place in all of history up to this point. Christians, Muslims, and Jews all have similar detailed end time's war prophecies that many believe from their scriptures will take place in the times we now live in. All three religions believe in a similar Armageddon battle and campaigns or wars centered in the Middle East that the world may later refer to as World War III.

The books of Ezekiel, Daniel, Zechariah, and Revelation as well as Mathew 24 and Luke 21 state that these events will occur in the end times at a time when "knowledge and travel are greatly increased and men would go to and fro across the Earth (Daniel 12)." The most important sign to Christians and Jews that this time is near is the re-emergence of the nation of Israel as a nation which occurred in 1948 after ceasing to exist for almost 2,500 years. Ezekiel 37 states that Israel would re-emerge as a nation in the later days from a longtime of not existing as a nation. Ezekiel 37 goes on to state that Israel would be brought back as a nation after a great persecution represented by a multitude of dry bones which most Jewish and Christian scholars interpret to be the Holocaust of World War II that killed 6 million Jews. How many nations have reemerged after 2,500 years of non-existence? Another sign includes a worldwide financial crisis that causes world leaders to feel perplexed in how to solve it. An increase in geothermal and natural disasters that affect the seas and oceans of the world is considered another sign. Unlike the Mayan prophecies that said that Dec. 21, 2012, was supposed to be the end of the last age, Jesus Christ said that no man would know the day or the hour of the end, but would like the change of seasons know when the end times were upon the world when people could see these things happening on the Earth.

Iran's Ayatollah Khamenei (not the Ayatollah Khomeini from the 1979 US hostage crises), the dominant Islamic Brotherhood of North Africa, as well as a many of both Shia and Sunni Muslims in the Middle East are convinced that the "End of Days" are upon us even though these groups oppose each other on other issues. On several occasions since 2012, the Ayatollah Khamenei has announced to the Muslim world that the time for the final battle for Jerusalem had come and the coming of the Mahdi and with him an Islamic Jesus and a one world Islamic government was here. Former Iranian President Ahmadinejad stated on numerous speeches given between 2009 and 2013 that the Mahdi was at hand and would reveal himself to "give an answer to Israel on Jerusalem and to the United States about nuclear weapons."

Iranian President Hassan Rohani who won the election on June 15, 2013, was touted as a moderate by Iranian and Western media. Rohani stated publically that he thanked the "12th Imam Mahdi and the last

Mahdi in these last days" for his victory. Hassan Rohani headed Iran's Revolutionary Guards and oversaw tribunals against those accused of not upholding Islamic laws. Rohani is believed to be connected to Jihadist bombings in Argentina in 1994 and in Saudi Arabia in 1996. He is also believed to be behind terrorist activities conducted by the Revolutionary Guards posing as foreign Jihadists in Iraq, Afghanistan, and in Syria over the last several years including in 2012.

The Ayatollah Khamenei has often stated in his Friday sermons that the time of the Mahdi's coming was at hand with great conviction as August 22 came closer each of the last six years. August 22 is believed by Muslims as the day in the 630's A.D. that Mohammed ascended to Heaven from Jerusalem on a donkey (some Muslim texts say a stallion) to receive messages from God and it would likely be on that day that the Mahdi would reveal himself to set up a one world Islamic government.

Since 2011, the Iranian government has released videos that have been shown across much of the Islamic world that state that Iran would soon usher in the coming of the Mahdi known as the "Twelfth Imam." The Twelfth Imam who with a returned Muslim Jesus are believed to one day to establish a worldwide Islamic government under sharia law after the destruction of the "Great Satan" (the United States) and the "Little Satan" (Israel). Official Iranian as well as numerous Muslim Brotherhood and Hezbollah websites from across the Islamic world has stated that "the Zionist Regime of Israel faces a dead-end and will under God's grace be wiped off the map." Imams all over the world have increasingly stated in weekly Friday sermons that the Mahdi cannot come until Israel is wiped off the map.

The Mahdi or "Twelfth Imam" was believed by Shiite Muslims to have disappeared at age 5 in the year 941 (some say the year 868) and has never died, but influences events in the Islamic world to this day. Muslims believe that Jesus was the 2nd greatest prophet after Mohammed and will return to Jerusalem to set up a one world

396 | Unknown Wars of Asia, Africa and The America's That Changed History

Islamic kingdom with the Mahdi after an Armageddon like battle that will give Muslims a one world government. The official Iranian and Muslim Brotherhood websites feature a video stating that the coming of the Mahdi and the second coming of an Islamic Jesus whom the Muslims call Isa cannot take place until some Islamic entity has conquered Jerusalem in the name of Islam. Muslims for centuries have fought to control Jerusalem because they believe that the Mahdi and the Islamic Jesus cannot come back if Jerusalem is not under Islamic control politically. This is what the Crusades, the Arab-Israeli Wars and the conflicts between Israel and the Palestinians have really been about from the Islamic perspective.

The signs given from Muslim scholars and scriptures that the imminent coming of the Mahdi and the "End of Days" was to come would be that right before the coming of the Mahdi the nations of Syria, Egypt, Libya and Iraq would go through a period of great turmoil followed by new governments with a more fundamentalist Islamic ideology. The US state department had originally stated that it saw the Arab Spring revolts of 2011 and 2012 as a victory for democracy in the Middle East. The group that led the Arab revolts in Tunisia, Libya, Egypt, Mali, and Syria was the Muslim Brotherhood which has a very fundamentalist Islamic ideology that supports worldwide sharia law and believes as Iran's leadership that they are to usher in the rule of the Mahdi and the Islamic Jesus in Jerusalem. The Egyptian parliament that was dominated by the Muslim Brotherhood expelled Israel's ambassador and issued a proclamation that said, "Revolutionary Egypt will never be a friend, partner, or ally of the Zionist entity of Israel, which we consider to be the number one enemy of Egypt and the soon to be unified Arab nation." These are all seen as signs to many Muslims that the period known as the "End of Days" is here. Both Sunni and Shia Muslim extremists, who have often been at odds with each other since 674 AD agree on their eschatology beliefs about the coming of an end time's one world Islamic government.

Islamic prophetic scriptures also teach that in the end of days there would be the "red death" and the "white death" that would destroy 2/3rds of the world's population. The "red death" is violence, terrorism, war and geothermal destruction which Muslims believe will kill 1/3rd of the world's population. The "white death" is believed to be plague and disease that is resistant to all medicines that will also kill another 1/3rd of the Earth's population.

The Ayatollah Khamenei has claimed to have spoken with the Mahdi or the "Twelfth Imam" in July of 2010 and has stated that he was told that the time for Iran to usher in the end time's one world Islamic government has come. Khamenei claims that the "Twelfth Imam" could not return until Iran or some Islamic entity had captured Jerusalem as a prerequisite to prepare the way for the one world Islamic government to come. Khamenei who is the true power holder in Iran and has stated that Islamic nations need nuclear weapons to destroy the Great and Little Satan of the United States and Israel in a great destructive battle so that Jerusalem can be prepared for the coming of the Mahdi and the Islamic Jesus. Part of this preparation would be a new holocaust to kill off the entire Jewish population of Israel which has been promoted as the only answer to deal with the "Zionist problem." These messages have been proclaimed by many fundamentalist Islamic Imams, and by Iran's and other fundamentalist Islamists on a weekly basis through sermons throughout the Islamic world. Though the Iranian leadership has denied that the Holocaust during World War II even happened, they and many fundamentalist Islamists and groups venerate Adolf Hitler for his opposition to the Jews and to Zionism.

After the destruction of Israel, according to Islamic scriptures, the Mahdi and the Islamic Jesus would then destroy 80% of the remaining world's population including many Muslims that are not believed to be true Muslims (Sunni and Shiite Muslims each believe it will be the other denomination that will be destroyed). Khamenei has stated in Friday sermons that even if Iran would be destroyed in a nuclear holocaust in its efforts to destroy the great and little Satans that this would result in the martyrdom of the entire nation and automatic admittance into Paradise for all Iranians killed in a war to come with the United States and Israel. A number of Pakistani Islamists and Imams have made the same kind of statements in weekly sermons in reference to their own nuclear capabilities being used to further the cause of Islam. The ongoing turmoil in the Middle East and North Africa along with the rise of fundamentalist Islam are seen by many Islamists as signs of the coming of the Mahdi, the "End of Days" and the final prophetic wars.

According to Jewish and Christian scriptures, there are three wars that will bookend a difficult seven year period (from Daniel and Revelations) that Christians call the seven year tribulation. The first war is from Psalm 83 where Egypt (referred to as the Hagrites by the Hebrews), the Palestinians of the Westbank (the tents of Edom), the Palestinians of Gaza (Philistia in ancient times), Lebanon (Hezbollah), Syria, and possibly Iraq (both being Assyria) would attack Israel "so that the name of Israel may be remembered no more." Israel defeats this coalition of nations "as the fire burns the woods, and as the flame sets the mountains on fire." The coalition is made desolate in a very lop-sided Israeli victory. It seems possible that the Israeli air force will cause the Islamic coalition of nations on the mountains north of Israel to be destroyed in such a way that the mountains appear to be on fire. One thing that is made clear is that the coalition of Psalm 83 does not appear in either of the next two prophetic wars. Egypt, Syria, Iraq, Lebanon and the Palestinians are not mentioned again in the prophetic scriptures as part of the next two prophetic wars.

In Isaiah 17 and Jeremiah 49, there is a prophecy that states that Damascus which is mentioned by name will be completely destroyed in a prophetic war and left uninhabited afterwards. This event could be part of the Psalm 83 war or possibly could be a separate event from the next prophetic war or an accident from the infighting from the Syrian Civil War. Israel made a strike on what is believed to be a chemical weapons facility and a weapons convoy meant for Hezbollah supplied by Iran and Russia outside of Damascus in early 2013. Isaiah 17:1 says, "An oracle concerning Damascus: See Damascus will no longer be a city, but will be a heap of ruins." The prophecy goes on to say that the city and area around Damascus will be deserted ruins. A nuclear or biological weapon event would cause a populated area to become deserted and unlivable. In 1986, the nuclear plant at Chernobyl, Russia had a core meltdown in its nuclear reactor. The radiation for more than 20 miles around Chernobyl is so bad still more than close to 40 years after the core meltdown that no living person or animal can live there today. So if a major nuclear or biological event ever takes place in or near Damascus, this would explain why one of the world's oldest cities would be left deserted and in ruins. Damascus has never been destroyed or abandoned in its' 4,000 year old history which makes this an event that could only happen in the future. Jeremiah 49: 27 also states that Damascus will be consumed as a "wall of fire" and that its' palaces and government buildings will be consumed with fire as well. The Bible which includes the Jewish Torah and Tanakh (Old Testament) contains over 2,500 prophecies of which more than 2,000 have been fulfilled in history.

Another war that is prophesied to take place from the Bible will most likely take place not long before or after the Psalm 83 war. This second prophetic war is from Ezekiel 38 and 39 is another attempted invasion of Israel by a new coalition of Russia, Iran, Turkey, and the Islamists from northern Africa in the last days which is called the War of Gog and Magog. This event according to the Bible will be toward the beginning of this difficult seven year period. Neither of these wars or campaigns is the Battle of Armageddon which will be at the end of the seven year tribulation, because it is a completely different group of nations that participate in each of the three prophetic wars. The Bible states as does the Muslim Koran that 1/3rd of all of mankind (more than 2.5 billion people) would eventually die in these end time's wars.

Ezekiel 38:2-6 uses the ancient names for the countries that participate in the war of Gog and Magog. Iran (Persia) and Russia lead the coalition against Israel. Russia is referred to as Gog, Magog, and the Prince of Rosh (it also states the nations of "the far north" from Israel) being the lands north of the Caucus Mountains. Tubal and Meshech are in the Russian Caucus region. Togarmah is the ancient name for Turkey. The nations of Put (Libya, Algeria, Tunisia, and Mali), and Cush (Sudan and Somalia) also send troops or possibly terrorists to join the coalition. The African nations mentioned in Ezekiel are now dominated by a fundamentalist Islamic ideology as well. Russian leadership has in recent years expressed a desire to return as the dominant world power. Leading the Islamic coalition will give Russia such an opportunity. Russia will see a chance to dominate the Middle East and thus the world which is so dependent on its oil.

Map of the future War of Gog and Magog.

Ezekiel says that a "hook in the jaw" will pull Russia into this war. This "hook" will be an opportunity for Russia to re-emerge as the world's greatest and richest power. The "hook" could be the Syrian Civil War that has seen both Russia and Iran already providing military aide for the Assad administration. Both nations have protested the United States support for the rebel forces in Syria. Russia is also providing military assistance to Iran and is building a nuclear reactor for them as well. The United States has cautioned Israel about the potential fallout of bombing the Russian built reactor with the possibility of killing Russian workers that could serve as Ezekiel's hook in the jaw also.

In Ezekiel 38:8-9, God speaks to the coalition and says, "After many days 'you' (Russia, Iran and the Islamic coalition) will be called to arms. In the later years, you will invade a land (Israel) that has recovered from a terrible war (the Holocaust of World War II), whose people were gathered from many nations to the mountains of Israel which had long been desolate…You and all your troops and the many nations with you will go, advancing like a storm; you will be like a cloud covering the land (possibly an airborne assault)."

There is a possible mention of NATO, Great Britain, and the United States in Ezekiel 38:13 stating that Sheba (Saudi Arabia), and the "merchants of Tarshish (NATO, and Western Europe) and the young lions thereof (Britain and the United States)" say, "Have you come to plunder?" in protest. Tarshish was in the B.C. period a city in southern Spain where all the merchants of Western Europe including from the isles of Britain gathered to trade with the Phoenicians, Carthaginians, and the Romans who then traded European goods throughout the Mediterranean Sea region. The trade was so lucrative with the merchants of Tarshish that Rome and Carthage spent a good deal of the 1st and 2nd Punic Wars fighting for control of southern Spain and control of the trade out of that city. Great Britain is symbolized as a lion and the young lions thereof are thought to be the United States and the other former British colonies that came from Britain. Ezekiel was describing nations that would not exist for almost 2,600 years into the future. It is not clear from Ezekiel 38 if Britain, the United States, and NATO just protest or actually get involved militarily in this war.

The Russian, Iranian, and Islamic coalition forces "descend like a cloud" (Ezekiel38:15) into the mountains north of Israel and all hell breaks out with a description of fires in the sky and with mountains that are destroyed by fire. Something will go very badly for the Russian,

Iranian, and Islamic coalition forces because 80% of these troops die in the mountains north of Israel in one of the worst military disasters that will ever take place in history.

Perhaps, a Russian or Iranian nuclear weapon is mishandled and they blow themselves up. Jeremiah 49 speaks of a time when Elam (Western Iran) is devastated so completely that no inhabitants can live there for years after the destruction. Elam is the part of Iran today where their massive underground nuclear facility is located. So the specific mentioning of this area to have gone through such devastation is intriguing given that much of Iran's nuclear program is located there. In fact, the entire area of operations for the coalition north of Israel undergoes a terrible accident that depopulates this area or nuclear weapons are exchanged. Perhaps, the Israeli, U.S., and British air forces quickly gain air superiority and then just bomb the Russian and Iranian ground forces into submission north of Israel.

In Ezekiel 38:18 - 23, God addresses the Iranian and Russian led coalition when He says, "When Gog attacks the land of Israel, my hot anger will be aroused declares the sovereign Lord....all the people on the face of the Earth will tremble at my presence...mountains will be overturned...I will summon a sword against Gog on all of the mountains. I will execute judgment upon him with plague and bloodshed... torrents of rain, hailstones, and burning sulfur will fall from the sky on him...then they will know I am the Lord."

Ezekiel 39:4-14 goes on to say, "On the mountains of Israel you will fall, you (Gog and Magog) and all your troops and the nations with you....it is coming! It will surely take place declares the sovereign Lord... On that day I will give Gog a burial place in Israel...It will block the way of travelers because Gog and all his hordes will be buried there... for seven months the house of Israel will be burying them in order to cleanse the land." Israel will have suffered very little during this war and will go through a revival of faith because of the great victory. As said before, the War of Gog and Magog is a completely different event and involve different nations than the Battle of Armageddon that will take place from three and a half years to seven years later.

After the War of Gog and Magog, there aren't anymore possible references to the United States, Russia, Britain, nor Iran as having anymore role in the end time's prophetic chronology of events. Possibly, the United States' financial problems become so bad that the U.S. has to withdraw from being the world's policeman or maybe the Russians exchanged nuclear strikes with the U.S. in the War of Gog and Magog despite the fact that Israel was spared. It seems that Khamenei will get their wish that the whole nation of Iran would be martyred in this war because Persia is not mentioned again in Bible prophecy. Many Evangelical Christians believe a taking up of believers in an event called the Rapture could also be a reason that the U.S. would cease to be important because possibly 40 - 60% of the American population would disappear if such an event occurred.

The Bible is clear that the events of this war will make the world to tremble at the destruction that takes place. This much is known, a man will emerge after the War of Gog and Magog who will seem to have all the answers for the world's financial mess with debt that is getting close to $200 trillion dollars worldwide. In fact, the current world financial crisis is believed by many to be the catalyst that brings the man known as the antichrist in the Book of Revelation and in Islamic scriptures onto the world stage. Everyone at first will think this man will be the savior of mankind, but then like Hitler would become the world's nightmare.

This man whom both Christians and Muslims refers to as the antichrist (Islamic scriptures say he has only one good eye) will force everyone in order to buy or sell or to get paid from their jobs to get a mark like a computer chip or a tiny barcode placed under the skin in their hand or forehead. The Book of Revelation warns not to take the mark that is called the "mark of the beast" and has some association with the number 666. Most people who at first refuse to take the mark or computer chip will seal their doom by eventually signing on to the antichrist system because they won't be able to have jobs or to eat without participation. Nations that sign on to the system will have their debt forgiven, but nations that refuse to sign on will be required under military threat to pay their debts and they will be shut out of the global market. Most nations and individuals will see no other choice, but to sign onto the one world economic system. Many Bible scholars believe from scriptures that this man that will be the antichrist will be a suave European while "the beast" that accompanies him could actually be the financial computer system that will control the world market and tracks everyone through the mark of the beast.

While this is going on, China will emerge as the great world power and does not appear to be part of the antichrist's one world economic system. One of China's motivations in launching this war of conquest will be that there doesn't seem to be a nation such as the United States to prevent the Chinese from expanding west. The Book of Revelation mentions that this nation from the East as being able to field over 200 million troops for a massive campaign of conquest toward the Middle East. Mao Tse Tung boasted in the early 1970's that China could field 200 million troops at that time. Today, China is still realistically the only nation in the world that could pull off fielding this many men into an army.

There also will be massive geothermal disasters and strange celestial events in the sun, moon, and stars as well as a meteor or asteroid that Revelation calls "Wormwood" that will poison 1/3rd of the world's water and will cause massive tsunamis and flooding. A very close call that woke the world up as to the possibility of danger from a comet or asteroid was the asteroid that blew up over Russia in February of 2013. The very foundations of the Earth will shake according to numerous scriptures. The Bible refers to these tumultuous events as the "time of trouble."

The final event of the "End of Days" according to the books of Revelation, Zechariah and Daniel will be the Battle of Armageddon when the forces of the Antichrist from Europe and his world confederacy will meet to fight against the 200 million man Chinese/Asian army as it converges on the Middle East and Jerusalem for a final huge bloody battle where it is said that the piles of dismembered and bloody bodies would reach a horses bridal (neck) for over a 200 or 300 square mile area. The battle would be fought throughout the Jezreel Valley and over a large area surrounding it. The Book of Zechariah seems to indicate that there will be nuclear weapons in use because it says that multitudes will have their eyes and tongues to melt from the intense heat and power of the weapons used at Armageddon. Perhaps, Iran getting a hold of nuclear weapons will open the way for the free use of these weapons. The Bible makes it clear that unless the Lord intervenes in those days that no flesh would be left alive upon the Earth. It is at this time where the book of Revelation states that Jesus Christ will return with the armies of Heaven to set up a 1,000 year period of peace on the Earth (there has never been even a year of peace in human history to this point). Only between 2 and 3 billion people will survive the ordeal from the entire planet. Many Jews believe that the end time wars will be the catalyst that will cause the messiah to be revealed.

These are the events that many of the world's Jews, Christians, and Muslims are expecting to begin sometime in the near future. The three wars mentioned from various prophecies could actually be three campaigns of what will be World War III in which, if true, would be the worst war in history that would dwarf World War II in casualties and destruction. Sometimes believing and having expectations that something is supposed to happen so strongly can cause people to actually put forth the actions that make those events to happen.

Humans throughout history have proved very good at bringing about self-fulfilling prophecies.

THE MAHDI (THE TWELFTH IMAM), THE ISLAMIC JESUS, AND STRANGE APPARITIONS

The Twelfth Imam (the Mahdi), who was also known as Muhammad Ibn Ali was born in Samarra, Iraq in either the 9th or 10th centuries A.D. and was a direct descendant from Mohammad. He was believed to have had supernatural powers from an early age. At age 5, in either 868 or 941, Muhammad Ibn Ali fell into a well or was hidden in the well (his story has a couple of different versions) by his mother to prevent him from being captured and killed by the current ruler who felt threatened by him (similar to the King Herod and baby Jesus story). The boy never re-emerged from the well and was believed to be invisible and very much alive on the Earth. It is believed that the Mahdi or Twelfth Imam was immortal and was involved in affairs in the Muslim world until he would lead a one world government from Jerusalem and Mecca after winning an Armageddon like battle in the "End of Days."

Over twelve men in history have claimed to be the Mahdi mostly in the Shia Islamic areas of Iraq and Iran, but also in Morocco and the Sudan. Most of these men claiming to be the Mahdi had lead revolts against other Muslim rulers and then died or disappeared not long after their appearance. The most famous man to westerners who claimed to be the Mahdi was Muhammad Ahmad from Sudan who defeated an Egyptian force and captured Khartoum in 1885 followed shortly by his death. His army was then defeated by the British at the Battle of Omdurman in 1898. The Mahdi is believed to be behind the Muslim Brotherhood and the Arab Spring Revolts in 2011 and 2012 according to Iran's and Egypt's leadership. He is believed to be waiting on an Islamic move to take Jerusalem to finally reveal himself and to usher in the return and rule of an Islamic Jesus.

Jesus is actually mentioned more in the Koran than even the prophet Mohammad and has a huge role in Islamic end time's teachings. The Koran teaches that Jesus came from a virgin birth through Mary, but was the 2nd greatest prophet after Mohammad and was not believed to be the son of God. Muslims believe that Jesus did great miracles and cast out demons, but they believe that Jesus was taken to Heaven before the crucifixion and deny that the crucifixion and resurrection ever happened (the most important part for Christians). Muslims believe the same as Christians in a second coming of Jesus, but Muslims believe that he will set up a one world Islamic kingdom rather than his own Christian kingdom. Most Muslims believe that the Mahdi and the Islamic Jesus will then kill 80% of all the people left on the Earth after the final apocalyptic war for refusing to convert to a sharia form of Islam (including many incorrect or moderate thinking Muslims).

A Youtube video of this apparition of whom the Iranians say is the Imam Mahdhi
has caused many Muslims to believe that the Islamic endtimes are at hand.

The Iranian government has been showing on TV since October of
2009 a video that surfaced of an apparition of the Mahdi doing a Shiite
war dance with a sword among a group of Muslims that seem unaware
of his presence (the video can be seen on YouTube under "Imam Mahdi
apparition"). The Iranian government has made claims on TV that
the Mahdi is among them and the time for his revealing of himself is
very soon and to prepare for the Great and Little Satans (the U.S. and
Israel) destruction that must come. The Iranian government has set up
a hotline for Iranians to call to hear about how recent events are setting
the stage for the Islamic end of days, but a number of Iranians have

been calling the hotline claiming to have seen the Mahdi briefly since the airing of the video. Christians have been hunted down and jailed across Iran and North Africa after a Christian pastor claimed on TV to a reporter that was unaware that he wasn't a Muslim that the New Testament says that even Satan comes as an angel of light to deceive many in reference to the apparition video. The Iranian government is deadly serious in promoting the idea that the Islamic End of Days and the Mahdi are at hand.

Apparition of Jesus or Mary seen on October 17, 2009 over a Christian Coptic Church just prior to the turmoil in Egypt began was seen as a sign or omen of dangerous times coming to this nation.

Another apparition of what onlookers say was Jesus with the Trinity and
Mary also seen in December 10, 2009 in Egypt over a church.

There have also been a number of sightings of apparitions of Jesus
and the Virgin Mary prior to the Arab Spring Revolts from October
to December of 2009 at Catholic and Coptic churches throughout the
Muslim world including a sighting in Cairo, Egypt where 100,000
Egyptians witnessed the apparition (the videos can be seen on YouTube
under "Apparitions of Mary"). Mary has been reported to be giving
warnings to Muslims and Christians of a time of difficult endtimes
events that are about to take place. Because Muslims venerate Mary also,
they have not viewed the apparitions as endorsements for Christianity,
but have seen them as confirmation that the "End of Days" are here.

THE ARMAGEDDON BATTLEFIELD:
THE MOST FOUGHT OVER PLACE IN HISTORY

There have been over 35 battles fought at Megiddo and the Jezreel Valley for close to 4,000 years in northern Israel which is mentioned in the book of Revelation as ground zero for the future Battle of Armageddon. Megiddo and the Jezreel Valley have been the most fought over place on Earth. The very first and the last recorded battles in history are believed to be at Megiddo. The Egyptians, Hittites, Canaanites, Israelites, Philistines, Assyrians, Babylonians, Persians, Greeks, Romans, Byzantines, the early Islamic armies, the Mongols, the Mamlukes, the Crusaders, the Ottoman Turks, the French under Napoleon, the British Empire, the Arabs, the Germans, and the revived nation of Israel have all fought desperate and bloody battles for control of Megiddo and the Jezreel Valley. The Jezreel Valley has been a strategic location for invading the land of Israel which is the crossroads to three continents and the home of the most sacred and fought over city in history which is Jerusalem. Here are some of the most significant of the many battles fought at Megiddo and in the Jezreel Valley:

- In 1476 B.C., Egyptian Pharaoh Thutmosis III with 10,000 soldiers defeated the King of Kadesh with an equal number of troops in a confusing swirling chariot battle that gave Egypt control of the lands from Palestine to Syria.

- In 1016 B.C., King Saul, his son Jonathan, and 20,000 Israelites were massacred after they were flanked by a Philistine army and chariot force that numbered more than 30,000 men at the Battle of Mount Gilboa. The Israelite defeat was according to the Bible a punishment from God because King Saul had made the pre-battle sacrificial offerings himself rather than to wait for the Prophet Nathan or a Levite priest to do it.

- In 609 B.C., the army of Judah and King Josiah were massacred at Megiddo by an Egyptian army under King Necho II after they had asked for and had been refused permission to cross through Israel on their way to join Assyria in an attack on Babylon.

- In 218 B.C., Antiochus III and his Seleucid army ambushed a force of Ptolemy IV's Egyptian army at the Battle of Mount Tabor after feigning retreat.

- In 67 A.D., Vespasian's Roman army massacred close to 10,000 Jewish rebels as they attempted to escape from Mount Tabor to seek refuge in Jerusalem during the Jewish War from 66 to 73 A.D. Only 1,000 Israelites made it to Jerusalem.

- In 1182, 1183, and 1185, Saladin and his Muslim armies fought with Crusader forces in the Jezreel Valley prior to retaking Jerusalem in 1187.

- In 1260, a force of 20,000 Mamluke cavalry defeated and wiped out a force of 20,000 Mongol horse archers in the Battle of Ayn Jalut. The Mongols were forced to accept the outskirts of Syria as the southwestern boundary for the Mongol Empire.

- In 1799, Napoleon with just 1,500 French troops followed later by another 2,500 reinforcements audaciously attacked and routed an Ottoman army of 25,000 Turks at the Battle of Mount Tabor. The Turks lost 6,500 casualties to the loss of only 62 French soldiers. Disease eventually forced Napoleon's army back to Egypt.

– In 1918, the British XXI Corps blasted breaches in the Turkish trench lines in the Jezreel Valley followed by massive cavalry charges by British, Australian, and Arab cavalry forces that penetrated into the Turkish rear areas which caused a route of all the Ottoman forces. RAF strafing and the relentless pressure by the British, Australian, and Arab cavalry forces destroyed the remains of three Turkish armies and led to the capture of Damascus 350 miles away. General Allenby was quite aware that he was fighting on the site for the Battle of Armageddon. The victory gave Britain control of the Middle East who then remapped the region to create the nations that exists there to this day. The victory also paved the way for the formation of the nation of Israel in 1948.

– In May and June of 1941, an Allied force of 34,000 British, Australians, Indians, and free French defeated 45,000 Vichy French and Germans in an offensive that started in the Jezreel Valley and swept through Syria. Over 9,000 Vichy French and Germans as well as 4,000 Allies became casualties in the campaign. The campaign was the first Allied victory over Axis forces which foiled Hitler's plan to use Syria as a jumping off point to invade British occupied Palestine and to destroy the Jewish communities that had sprung up there since 1918 and any hopes of a new Israeli nation.

- In 1948, 1967, and 1973, Israeli forces defeated Syrian and Arab forces around Megiddo and the Ramat David Airfield ('67,'73).

- In the future, during the War of Gog and Magog, a coalition of Islamic nations led by Russia, and Iran will have 80% of their army destroyed in the mountains north of Israel and in the Jezreel Valley when they go to attack the nation of Israel.

- In the future, the Battle of Armageddon will be the largest battle in history and will involve a Chinese army of 200 million men who will oppose the massive forces of a worldwide confederacy under a man the Bible refers to as the Antichrist. The piles of bloody bodies will pile up to the height of a horse's neck (bridle) and will cover hundreds of miles in and around the Jezreel Valley. Jesus Christ and the armies of Heaven will intervene and put an end to the Antichrist and the gathered armies and create a 1,000 year period of peace on the Earth.

BIBLIOGRAPHY

www.allaboutpopularissues.org- "12th-Imam."

Brennan, David. *The Israel Omen II,* Teknon Publishing, 2011.

www.babylonforsaken.com – "Iran, the Mahdi, and the Anti-Christ."

cbn.com - CBN News – Iranian Video Says Mahdi is 'Near.' By Erick Stakelbeck.

Cline, Eric H. *The Battles of Armageddon: Megiddo and the Jezreel Valley from the Bronze Age to the Nuclear Age.* University of Michigan Press, 2000.

Fox News – "Why Iran's Leaders Believe That the End of Days Has Come. "By Joel C. Rosenberg, 11/07/2011.

"Mahdi"an article by *Encyclopedia Britannica* Online.

Salas, Bill. *Psalm 83.* Prophecy Depot Ministries. La Quinta, Ca, 2013.

Syaikh Hisyam Kabbani. *The Approach of Armageddon. (Islamic Supreme Council of America, 2002).* ISBN 1930409206.

Walvoord, John F. *Every Prophecy of the Bible.* Chariot Victor Publishing, Colorado Springs, 1999.

www.trackingbibleprophecy.org

Youtube – "Imam Mahdi Aparition" and "Mary Apparitions in Egypt"

Index

Made in the USA
San Bernardino, CA
11 December 2015